OLD
TESTAMENT
HISTORY

THE SERIES

Volume I
The Pentateuch

Volume II
Old Testament History

Volume III
Wisdom Literature and Poetry

Volume IV
The Major Prophets

Volume V
The Minor Prophets and the Apocrypha

Volume VI
The Gospels

Volume VII
Acts and Paul's Letters

Volume VIII
Revelation and the General Epistles

INTERPRETER'S CONCISE COMMENTARY

OLD TESTAMENT HISTORY

A COMMENTARY ON
JOSHUA, JUDGES, RUTH, I & II SAMUEL, I & II KINGS,
I & II CHRONICLES, EZRA, NEHEMIAH, ESTHER

By
Robert Houston Smith
Herbert G. May
John William Wevers
Charles T. Fritsch
H. Neil Richardson

Edited by Charles M. Laymon

Abingdon Press
Nashville

THE INTERPRETER'S CONCISE COMMENTARY
VOLUME II: OLD TESTAMENT HISTORY

Revised and Concise Edition

Copyright © 1971 and 1983 by Abingdon Press

Third Printing 1984

Library of Congress Cataloging in Publication Data

Main entry under title:
Old Testament history.
(The Interpreter's concise commentary; v. 2)
Previously published as part of the Interpreter's one-volume
commentary on the Bible.
Bibliography: p.
1. Bible. O.T. Historical Books—Commentaries.
I. Smith, Robert Houston. II. Laymon, Charles M. III. Series.
BS491.2.I57   vol. 2   220.7s [222'.07]   83-4617
[BS1286.5]

ISBN 0-687-19233-1

(Previously published by Abingdon Press in cloth as part of
The Interpreter's One-Volume Commentary on the Bible, regular ed.
ISBN 0-687-19299-4, thumb-indexed ed. ISBN 0-687-19300-1.)

Scripture quotations unless otherwise noted are from the Revised
Standard Common Bible, copyright © 1973 by the Division of Christian
Education, National Council of Churches, and are used by permission.

MANUFACTURED BY THE PARTHENON PRESS AT
NASHVILLE, TENNESSEE, UNITED STATES OF AMERICA

EDITOR'S PREFACE

to the original edition

A significant commentary on the Bible is both timely and timeless. It is timely in that it takes into consideration newly discovered data from many sources that are pertinent in interpreting the Scriptures, new approaches and perspectives in discerning the meaning of biblical passages, and new insights into the relevancy of the Bible for the times in which we live. It is timeless since it deals with the eternal truths of God's revelation, truths of yesterday, today, and of all the tomorrows that shall be.

This commentary has been written within this perspective. Its authors were selected because of their scholarship, their religious insight, and their ability to communicate with others. Technical discussions do not protrude, yet the most valid and sensitive use of contemporary knowledge underlies the interpretations of the several writings. It has been written for ministers, lay and nonprofessional persons engaged in studying or teaching in the church school, college students and those who are unequipped to follow the more specialized discussions of biblical matters, but who desire a thoroughly valid and perceptive guide in interpreting the Bible.

The authorship of this volume is varied in that scholars were chosen from many groups to contribute to the task. In this sense it is an ecumenical writing. Protestants from numerous denominations, Jews, and also Roman Catholics are represented in the book. Truth cannot be categorized according to its ecclesiastical sources. It is above and beyond such distinctions.

It will be noted that the books of the Apocrypha have been included and interpreted in the same manner as the canonical writings. The value of a knowledge of this body of literature for understanding the historical background and character of the Judaic-Christian tradition has been widely recognized in our time, but commentary treatments of it have not been readily accessible. In addition, the existence of the Revised Standard Version and the New English Bible translations of these documents makes such a commentary upon them as is included here both necessary and significant.

The commentary as a whole avoids taking dogmatic positions or representing any one particular point of view. Its authors were chosen throughout the English-speaking field of informed and recognized biblical scholars. Each author was urged to present freely his own interpretation and, on questions where there was sometimes a diversity of conclusions, each was also asked to define objectively the viewpoints of others while he was offering and defending his own.

Many persons have contributed to the writing and production of this volume. One of the most rewarding of my personal experiences as editor was corresponding with the authors. On every hand there was enthusiasm for the project and warmth of spirit. The authors' commitment to the task and their scholarly sensitivity were evident in all of my relationships with them. The considerate judgments of the manuscript consultants, Morton S. Enslin, Dwight M. Beck, W. F. Stinespring, Virgil M. Rogers, and William L. Reed, were invaluable in the making of the character of the commentary. The copy editors who have worked under the careful and responsible guidance of Mr. Gordon Duncan of Abingdon Press have contributed greatly to the accuracy and readability of the commentary.

—Charles M. Laymon, Editor

PUBLISHER'S PREFACE

The intent of the *Interpreter's Concise Commentary* is to make available to a wider audience the commentary section of *The Interpreter's One-Volume Commentary on the Bible*. In order to do this, the Publisher is presenting the commentary section of the original hardback in this eight-volume paperback set. At the same time, and in conjunction with our wish to make *The Interpreter's One-Volume Commentary* more useful, we have edited the hardback text for the general reader: we have defined most of the technical terms used in the original hardback text; we have tried to divide some of the longer sentences and paragraphs into shorter ones; we have tried to make the sexually stereotyped language used in the original commentary inclusive where it referred to God or to both sexes; and we have explained abbreviations, all in an attempt to make the text more easily read.

The intention behind this paperback arrangement is to provide a handy and compact commentary on those individual sections of the Bible that are of interest to readers. In this paperback format we have not altered the substance of any of the text of the original hardback, which is still available. Rather, our intention is to smooth out some of the scholarly language in order to make the text easier to read. We hope this arrangement will make this widely accepted commentary on the Bible even more profitable for all students of God's Word.

WRITERS

Robert Houston Smith
Professor, The Department of Religion, The College of Wooster, Wooster, Ohio

Herbert G. May
Professor Emeritus of Old Testament Language and Literature, Oberlin College, Oberlin, Ohio, and Vanderbilt Divinity School, Nashville, Tennessee

John William Wevers
Professor of Near Eastern Studies, University College, University of Toronto, Toronto, Canada

Charles T. Fritsch
Professor of Hebrew and Old Testament Literature, Princeton Theological Seminary, Princeton, New Jersey

H. Neil Richardson
Professor of Old Testament, Boston University School of Theology, Boston, Massachusetts

CONTENTS

THE BOOK OF JOSHUA

Robert Houston Smith

INTRODUCTION

A story of conquest, a testimony to faith, a statistical record, a geography—Joshua is all of these. Beginning where Deuteronomy ends it tells how, under the leadership of Joshua and the protection of Yahweh ("the LORD"), Israel entered Canaan and there carved out a place for itself. The early chapters deal mainly with military aspects of the conquest. The later ones concern the apportionment of the land of Canaan to the tribes of Israel. There are also episodes revolving aroung Joshua's impending death.

Literary History

Although its overall arrangement is simple, Joshua is a complex document. It did not spring into existence full blown—whether from the hand of Joshua himself or of any other single author. Rather it grew by a process which spanned many centuries. The earliest traditions of the conquest were apparently songs which celebrated the victories of Israel under Yahweh. Only fragments of these songs have survived—notably Joshua's famous speech at the battle for Gibeon (10:12c-13a). By studying other bits of early poetry in the Old Testament—for example, Judges 5; Exodus 15:1-18; and Psalm 68—we see that such songs arose in the cultic worship of Israel's God (see comment of Judges 5). By a process familiar to students of the history of literature these songs were replaced during the early centuries of the Hebrew occupation of Palestine by prose accounts of the same events.

Like the poetic traditions these prose narratives seem to have originated not so much around the campfire as in the sanctuary. Of great importance in the early traditions in Joshua are the shrines at Shiloh, Gilgal, and Shechem. Perhaps this connection with the cult accounts for the emphasis on religious ceremonies in the work, especially in chapters 3–5 and 24. Some of these stories may seek to explain the origin of certain religious practices or to justify the importance of the traditional places of worship. Occasionally the stories show an interest in explaining the existence of certain places or place names, but that interest seems to be relatively minor. Such traditions form the basis of chapters 2–11 and parts of the remainder of Joshua.

Much of the first four books of the Old Testament are based on two separate sources:

(1) J—standing for Yahwist. This source used the name Yahweh (translated "the LORD") for God.

(2) E—meaning Elohist. In this source God is called Elohim (translated as "God").

For many decades scholars supposed that the stories in Joshua came from the J and E sources. There are indeed many similarities, but the evidences of relationship are much less clear than in the earlier books. Recently, therefore, a number of scholars have come to doubt that the J and E categories of Genesis-Numbers can be appropriately applied to Joshua. The final word on the early sources of this book has not yet been said—and perhaps never will be—but we can no longer use the terms J and E quite so confidently as did former generations of scholars.

The J and E sources are generally believed to date respectively from the tenth and eighth centuries. It is thought that they were combined to form JE after the fall of the northern kingdom, probably early in the seventh century. The supposed

JE portions of Joshua may have been part of this process. If not, their content suggests that they should be attributed to an author who lived in the later years of the northern kingdom—that is, in the eighth century, or possibly earlier. He brought together a number of the stories about the conquest and settlement of Palestine and wove them into a single account. This work may have included also the nucleus of Judges, since a verse found at the end of the Greek translation of Joshua but now missing from the Hebrew text (see below on 24:32-33) is a transitional sentence which leads directly into Judges 3:15.

The sanctuaries of Israel were the repositories not only of old narratives but also of statistical records of various sorts. Some of these records, mainly descriptions of tribal boundaries and lists of cities within these tribal areas, appear in chapters 13–21. Detailed study of these lists has shown that they date from different periods, all much later than the time of the conquest, perhaps from the early monarchy to the end of the seventh century.

The editor-author responsible for shaping the major part of Joshua essentially in the form in which it has come down to us probably lived in the last quarter of the seventh century or the first half of the sixth century. He had close connections with both the religious traditions of northern Israel and the temple in Jerusalem. Some scholars find three editions of Joshua by this editor or his colleagues, but in any case the style remains remarkably uniform throughout.

This editor was working at a time when there was a resurgence of interest in the northern Palestinian traditions, to which much of the content of Joshua belongs. He was a man of consuming religious passion, whose concern was not to preserve old traditions in an academic manner but to present the conquest in such a way that it would have clear theological significance for his readers. To this end he added introductions, transitions, summaries, conclusions, and blocks of theology in the form of speeches. His theology can be seen most clearly in chapters 1 and 23. Here, in speeches attributed to Yahweh and to Joshua, he expresses the concept that Yahweh has unfailingly carried out all the promises to the chosen people. It is this conviction which led the editor to portray the conquest of Palestine under Joshua as more extensive than the older traditions indicate. His message also carries the warning that Yahweh's kindness will continue only so long as people obey.

Because these convictions are expressed in a much fuller way in Deuteronomy, those who share them are known as Deuteronomists or the Deuteronomic ("D") school. It may well be that the editor-author of Joshua was the originator of these ideas. He may have compiled the laws of Deuteronomy, composed the framework for them, and then proceeded to demonstrate historically the necessity of obedience to them.

The commoner view is that it was the publication of the core of Deuteronomy in 622 (II Kings 22–23) which inspired another person or persons to compile Joshua and also Judges, I and II Samuel, and I and II Kings. Since the last event recorded in II Kings occurred during the exile, in 561, opinions differ on whether the compilation involved two or more editions or was prepared only after this last event (see Introduction to I Kings). In any case recent study seems to make clear that the bulk of the entire series Joshua-Kings was the work of a single compiler, or possibly a small group working together. He intended that it should be joined to Deuteronomy to form a history of Israel from Moses to his own time. Joshua shows as much affinity with the other books of this D history as with the first four books of the Old Testament.

There are inconsistencies and other signs that the tribal boundary and city lists of chapters 13–21 were added to the original D edition of Joshua. It was long assumed that these came from the P source, the material written by priestly authors after the Babylonian exile. However, recent study has shown that these are genuine preexilic records, and it therefore seems probable that they were added by another D editor early in the exile. Several scattered sentences with P characteristics are apparently individual insertions by later editors rather than signs of a substantial P contribution to the book.

Historical Reconstruction

At the time of the Israelite conquest the dominant people in Palestine were the Canaanites. They were a Semitic people who lived mainly in the valleys and coastal regions where water was relatively plentiful and farming was fairly easy. The lives of the Canaanites revolved around sturdy walled cities scattered throughout the lowlands. There was no central government. Each city was virtually a little kingdom with its own ruler, aristocrats, military establishment, commercial enterprises, religious institutions, and serfs. This feudal culture had been in existence for more than six centuries. At its height it had been technologically advanced and artistically refined, but by the fourteenth century it had lost much of its vigor and creativeness.

The hill country, which runs like a backbone down the middle of Palestine, was only sparsely settled. Water was scarcer and farming more difficult on the stony hillsides. The Canaanites could not exercise strong military control there, and merchants did not wish to take their caravans into the hills if they could go by way of the coast and valleys. As a result, the mountains became a refuge for dispossessed people of various sorts—for example, the Jebusites, Hivites, and Perizzites, of whom we know little but their names. These people seem generally to have lived a more rural life than their neighbors in the plains. In Transjordan semi–nomadism was a long-established pattern of life.

It was against this background that the Israelite conquest took place. Joshua presupposes that all of the Israelites who settled in Palestine came in from Transjordan in one surge. But there are indications both in this book and in other Old Testament materials that the number of Israelites who entered Palestine in this manner was not large. Rather it appears that the great majority of those who called themselves Israelites did not take part in the descent into Egypt and in the exodus but continued living in Palestine.

These people, like those who participated in the exodus, were descendants of wandering traders called "Habiru." These people had come into the country early in the second millenium and eventually settled down. The Habiru were apparently not an ethnic group as such, though they perhaps consisted largely of related Semitic tribes. As they had settled down in Palestine they had learned the ways of the Canaanites and adopted their language, which became the parent of the Hebrew language. But the Canaanites seem to have never allowed these landless people to forget that they were outsiders, and treated them as a lower class. They continued to call them Habiru, or Hebrew, which became a scornful term like "serf" or even "slave"—a connotation which some Old Testament passages still recall (e.g. Genesis 39:14; 43:32; I Samuel 4:9).

Aware that their situation was hopeless in the closed society of the Canaanites, these Habiru or Hebrews began to wander off to the sparsely settled hill country, where they were largely free of Canaanite oppression. Already by the early fourteenth century, documents show they were disrupting some of the city-states by living as brigands. In some cases they maneuvered to force the grudging cooperation of certain hill-country cities. The majority of Hebrews probably settled down, however, to building villages and tilling the soil. In each locality conditions were different, and there were many local Hebrew leaders.

The number of villages and cities taken by outright battle was probably small, for the Hebrews lacked the strength to take the populous and relatively well-defended lowland cities of Canaan. It is true that many Canaanite cities show destruction during the period 1400-1200. However, much of this can reasonably be regarded as the result of warfare among the cities—not to mention destructive invasions by Egyptian armies from time to time.

This picture of how the Hebrew nation began is strongly supported by archaeology. The remains of early Hebrew settlements show no sudden and significant cultural changes but only a normal development from late Canaanite culture. Far, then, from being a nomadic people encountering civilization for the first time, most of the Hebrews were people who left the urbanized Canaanite environment for a more rural life in the hills.

The Hebrew conquest of Palestine seems to have gone on for at least two centuries—about 1400–1200. The earliest traditions in Joshua may come from the later part of that time, when the Israelite immigrants from Egypt joined their relatives who were already in Palestine. This later phase perhaps fell around 1250-1200, the period to which most scholars now date the conquest, rather than the traditional 1450-1400.

It may be, as the biblical accounts indicate, that these incoming Israelites brought with them the faith in Yahweh. It is unlikely, however, that the name of this God was entirely unknown to the Hebrews who had stayed in Palestine. In any case the memories of the two groups of Hebrews were remarkably similar. Both had originally had the same background as traders and free people. Both had settled in foreign lands and eventually become serfs. Both had at last broken free and fled to the hill country of Palestine seeking land and freedom.

These dissidents were united in these experiences and in their belief in Yahweh, and shared a common distrust of oppressive human rule of all sorts. They lived in a loose confederation cemented by treaties, welcoming all who wished to join their ranks. These relationships were later to be systematized by Israelite thinkers into the picture of twelve tribes which has come down to us in the Old Testament.

Joshua the Man

The role of Joshua in this process of Israelite settlement is difficult to assess, so extensive is the legend which has grown up around him. To judge from the earliest traditions, Joshua's raids seem to have been chiefly on enemies in the territory traditionally occupied by the tribe of Benjamin, below the southern border of his own tribe of Ephraim. These may have been blows inflicted on the Benjaminites themselves (cf. Judges 19–20) or strikes against independent strongholds which threatened Ephraim (cf. Judges 1:22-26).

Joshua may have carried out raids farther south, in the territory of Judah (cf. chapter 10). But there is no indication that he was attempting to expand Ephraim's frontiers. The tradition of his military activity in the north (chapter 11) may reflect raids carried out to protect the northern border of Ephraim's sister tribe, Manasseh. Thus Joshua's military activities can be seen as deeds defending the territories of the closely related tribes of Ephraim, Manasseh, and Benjamin.

Some scholars have suggested that Joshua was not involved in the Israelite entry into Palestine from Transjordan. They believe that the stories of his leading the Jordan crossing are early editorial harmonizing of the Joshua traditions with those about Moses—traditions which otherwise are separate.

The traditions have little to say about Joshua as a person. In Exodus, Numbers, and Deuteronomy he appears as Moses' military assistant, but the allusions do not seem to have been a part of the earliest Mosaic stories. The picture of him is highly stylized. Later editors, influenced by their knowledge of Hebrew kinship, have tended to portray him as a king in all but the title. In only one scene, where Joshua joins his soldiers in a dangerous ruse outside the walls of Ai (chapter 8), does one get a personal glimpse of the man. Here he seems to be a daring, clever warrior. He is not unlike some of the judges, Jonathan, and the young David.

Religious Outlook

The question of the religious values in Joshua merits careful attention. Clearly the book hammers out an impressive statement of the conviction that God is active in history. Modern readers, however, are apt to be disturbed by the way Yahweh is depicted as callously indifferent to non-Israelites. It may be pointed out, though it is perhaps small comfort, that throughout history devout persons have often scorned other races and cultures. They have assumed they were serving God rightly when they suppressed all viewpoints contrary to their own. With regard specifically to Joshua one may recognize that the concept of God and morality presented in the work is part and parcel of its time.

We can see just how true this is by comparing an inscription which King Mesha of Moab ordered cut on a commemorative slab in the mid-ninth century. The name Mesha comes from the same root, "save," as the name Joshua ("Yahweh saves"). Mesha uses language similar to that in Joshua when he tells how, in the process of extending Moab's boundaries and settling new areas, he defeated his enemies—in this case Israel. He utterly destroyed their towns as an act of devotion to his god Chemosh, to whose help he attributes his victories. In viewing the times in which Joshua originated one becomes less demanding that its theological outlook conform to later standards.

Historical events are sometimes greater than those who pass on the record of them recognize. In some ways the actual circumstances of the conquest of Canaan, as reconstructed above, offer religious insights which may be more meaningful to the modern reader than the interpretations of it which the biblical editors give. The Hebrews who settled in the hill country of Canaan were a free association of serfs fleeing from the stifling environment of the Canaanite city-states. United in their rejection of the ancient system of human overlords, they insisted that no one is inherently better than any other. Thus they came remarkably near a concept of a democracy under God. Far from building their nation on the extermination of all those outside their group, they welcomed into their confederation any people who shared this longing for a new society. Thus their society was inclusive, not exclusive. The worship of their God was likewise inclusive. These early Hebrew views stand in sharp contrast to those later ones which saw Israel as an ethnic group, which believed that loyalty to God could be measured by conformity to cultic requirements, which assumed that some could be made serfs, and which asserted that God was revealed only to selected leaders.

I. ISRAEL'S CONQUEST OF PALESTINE (1:1–12:24)

A. JOSHUA'S ACCESSION TO LEADERSHIP (1:1-18)

1:1-9. *Yahweh's Commission to Joshua.* The story of the conquest of Palestine begins where Deuteronomy 34 ends.

Israel is encamped at the foot of the Moabite hills at the southeastern end of the Jordan Valley. **Moses** has just died. In verses 2-9 Yahweh commissions **Joshua**, Moses' former lieutenant, and instructs him to cross the **Jordan** and enter Palestine. This speech presupposes a scene very much like that of an ancient oriental coronation. There are also implications of a covenanting ceremony similar to those in Genesis 15 and elsewhere. Yahweh promises to give Israel **the land,** described idealistically in verse 4, and other benefits in return for Israel's obedience. The passage is reminiscent of the commissioning of Joshua in Deuteronomy 31, but bears marks of the hand of the D editor, especially in its stress on the keeping of the Torah, or divine **law.**

The editor thus makes clear at the outset that this book is not to be a matter-of-fact record but a religious document. Furthermore, he intends that these ancient happenings shall have relevance in his own day. He stresses that Yahweh will continue to be beneficent to those who follow Joshua's example in obeying the divine commandments (verse 8).

1:10-18. *Joshua's First Council.* In ancient Near Eastern coronation ceremonies the private encounter between the new ruler and the deity was followed by acclamation by the people. Sometimes these were represented by members of the nobility or royal council. The D editor maintains this convention. In a scene which is virtually one of covenanting the **officers of the people** pledge their loyalty to Joshua. Verses 10-11 are basically from a pre-D source; the rest is the composition of the D editor.

1:12-17. The tribes of Reuben, Gad, and Manasseh have already settled in Transjordan (cf. 13:7-8; Numbers 32; Deuteronomy 3:12-17). From these Joshua demands troops who will aid the rest of Israel in conquering Palestine. The leaders agree to this, cautioning only that if Joshua is to be their leader the LORD must remain with him. By stressing the participation of the Transjordanian tribes the editor presents the conquest of Palestine as the unified undertaking of Israel. This is a matter of theological importance to him. The emphasis on their willingness may be an attempt to counteract a common opinion that these tribes were reluctant to fight on behalf of the rest of Israel (cf. Judges 5:15b-17a).

1:18. The threat of **death** to rebels may have originated under the influence of the story of Achan's disobedience (chapter 7). Possibly it only expresses the traditional demand of loyalty which, on penalty of death, oriental rulers placed upon their subjects.

B. THE RECONNAISSANCE OF JERICHO (2:1-24)

This story is one of several extended narratives in Joshua which have come from early traditions. Two or more accounts have been interwoven, as certain differences of detail reveal. Many scholars identify these sources as J and E, but the complex history of the early traditions is difficult to unravel. Judges 1:22-25 preserves a brief narrative which shows some broad similarities to this story. This has led some interpreters to suspect that the two traditions may be related. The place name **Shittim** has previously appeared in Numbers 25:1—a reminder that the intervening material in Numbers 25–36, Deuteronomy, and Joshua 1 is largely an expansion by D and P writers.

While the people prepare for the crossing of the Jordan, Joshua acts as a good tactician by sending spies to survey his first object of attack (cf. the spies sent to Canaan in Numbers 13). **Jericho** was the only important city in the arid region at the southern end of the Jordan Valley, where a number of powerful Canaanite cities were in the central and northern part. If one may judge from the reference to **stalks of flax** laid on the **roof**, presumably to dry, the season was spring, the usual time for military campaigns.

The motif of the story, which appears also in the account of the fall of Sodom (Genesis 18–19), is a familiar one in folk tradition. Divine agents come incognito to a hostile region and find hospitality in the home of the humblest persons in the community. They promise salvation to these righteous people and prepare for the destruction of the rest.

11

A modern reader, inclined to want a tightly constructed plot, will perhaps wonder how the spies got into Jericho, why their speech failed to betray them, how the king came to know of their presence, etc. But the ancient storytellers focused on dramatic effect. They knew that their audience would delight in the vivid sequence of images—the rush of the bumbling Jericho police in the wrong direction, the escape of the spies down the wall.

The story gives glimpses into the life of an ancient Palestinian city, details which archaeological discoveries largely confirm. Jericho was an independent city-state with its own king, just as most other pre-Israelite cities of Palestine were. Houses at Jericho were crowded right up to the city wall, even as they are today in Damascus. The city's **gate** was closed at dusk. The roofs of the houses were flat and were used for such practical matters as drying and storing produce. Prostitution was a tolerated practice, possibly in connection with the local religion. The **scarlet cord** which Rahab ties in her **window** hints at a magical practice intended to keep evil from the house (cf. the blood on Israelite houses on the night of the slaughter of the firstborn in Egypt, Exodus 12:7, 13, 22-23).

Rahab is portrayed not simply as a brave and clever woman but as an apostate from her native religion. Thus the storyteller made possible her later veneration not only by Hebrews but also by Christians (cf. Hebrews 11:31 and James 2:25). Rahab's words in verses 10-11*a* are a D addition. Her description of Israel's God as **he who is God in heaven above and on earth beneath** also has a D ring. However, recently discovered Canaanite texts sometimes use similar expressions for the god El—evidence either that the D language has ancient roots or that Rahab's words are not so anachronistic as previously assumed.

C. THE CROSSING OF THE JORDAN (3:1–5:1)

This episode seems to be set in April, during the spring harvest (cf. 3:15; 4:18), a time consistent with that of the preceding story. Two or more old traditions lie behind this lengthy account with its occasionally confusing details. The story is often assumed to be from J and E, which have been compiled in one narrative.

The crossing is described as a religious rite involving purification, a solemn procession, a sermon, and the erection of memorial stones. Because these rites take place at or near **Gilgal** on the western side of the Jordan, some interpreters have felt that the story reflects a rite at Gilgal in which the crossing was reenacted from time to time. If some rite was performed, it was possibly at the passover festival in the spring (cf. 5:10).

Israel's passing through parted waters is reminiscent of the exodus tradition (Exodus 12–15). The ritualistic passing between the cleft waters is also reminiscent of the practice of passing between the cleft halves of an animal in a covenanting ceremony (cf. Genesis 15:7-17) since not long afterward Joshua does institute a covenant (8:30-35). These motifs combine to make the story a subtle but compelling statement of the important Old Testament themes of God's covenanted relationship with Israel and the deliverance of the people from danger.

The D editor is concerned as always with the contemporary significance of the events in Israel's past. Therefore he has added to the old tradition several short indications of what he feels to be the religious values of the story. In 3:7 he says that the miraculous crossing takes place so that Joshua will be remembered even as Moses was remembered for his part in the crossing of the Red Sea. In 4:4-7, 21-24 he explains the importance of the stones set up in memorial. In 4:24 he concludes that the overall significance of the stopping of the Jordan's flow is that all the peoples of the earth may know that the hand of the LORD is mighty; that you may fear the LORD your God forever.

3:1-17. *The Preparation and the Crossing.* A large number of people crossing the Jordan at one time would naturally present a problem. In biblical times there were no bridges and few fords. The later storytellers undoubtedly presupposed a vast populace (cf. 4:13; Exodus 12:37; Numbers 1:46; etc.), but most modern commentators estimate that not more than a few thousand persons could have been involved. Similar exaggeration of numbers appears in Canaanite and other ancient Near Eastern literature.

The **ark** plays an important role in the story, though its existence in the earliest traditions has been questioned. The storytellers assume that from it emanates power, somewhat like—one might say—an electric current or a laser beam. Only authorized priests and Levites are immune to this power. The layperson must stay a respectful distance away—**two thousand cubits** (around a thousand yards) according to a later editorial insertion in verse 4—or risk being harmed (cf. II Samuel 6:6-7). The power residing within the ark is apparently that which holds back the waters of the Jordan.

Many interpreters have accepted the idea that the stopping of the Jordan was a natural phenomenon—for example, a temporary damming of the river by a landslide. But this explanation leaves unanswered the question of why such a rare occurrence happened so opportunely. Many readers may wish to conclude that a miracle did occur. Others will prefer to see the account as the Israelite thinkers' way of expressing, in a day when both philosophical and scientific language did not yet exist, their deep faith in their God as the Lord of nature and as one who saves his people from peril. The use of the image of water to represent all that threatens a person is a very ancient one. It often finds expression in the Old Testament, as does the concept of Yahweh as the one who pushes back the waters to make dry land and a place of safety.

4:1-24. *The Memorial of Stones.* Joshua orders **twelve stones** set up—according to one tradition, on the bank of the Jordan (verse 8); according to another, in the Jordan itself (verse 9). These have long fascinated readers. The fact that the name of the camp, **Gilgal,** may mean "[sacred] circle"—rather than **rolled away** as 5:9 declares—suggests that the episode may be based on the tradition of a shrine at Gilgal containing a group of sacred stones. Perhaps these stones were set up in pre-Israelite times

but were taken over by the Israelites and linked with their
religious traditions. The earliest sources in chapter 4 offer no
explanation for the stones. The D editor, who is probably
responsible for verses 5-7, understands them to be a memorial of
the crossing of the Jordan. Gilgal has not been definitely
located, but it must have been within a few miles of Jericho.

5:1. *An Editor's Conclusion.* In an appended note the D
editor describes the reaction which the Israelite crossing
produced among the rulers of Palestine (cf. Rahab's words in
2:10-11). That the Israelites disturbed rulers of the city-states is
likely (see Introduction). But subsequent battles in Canaan
show that not all **spirit** deserted the inhabitants of the land. The
editor himself recognizes this in 9:1-2.

D. THE INAUGURATION OF A NEW ERA (5:2-12)

5:2-9. *Circumcision of Israel.* In preparation for the coming
passover (verses 10-12) Joshua circumcises the Israelites. Here,
as elsewhere in the book, Joshua is shown as the chief officiant in
religious rites. Near Eastern rulers were often the titular heads
of the religious institutions of their lands. The Old Testament is
not entirely clear about the origins of circumcision. The P
tradition attributes this rite to Abraham (Genesis 17:9-27). The J
source first speaks of it in connection with Moses (Exodus
4:24-26). The tradition here, which some scholars link with the
E source, shows Joshua as instituting the rite (omitting **again the
second time** in verse 2 as a later addition). Verses 4-7 are an
editor's attempt to reconcile the differing traditions by
explaining that circumcision had not been instituted as a
perpetual rite but only ordered for the generation of Israelites
who left Egypt. Several ancient Near Eastern peoples practiced
circumcision, sometimes in mass ceremonies at irregular
intervals in a way similar to that suggested in this passage. On
the explanation of the name **Gilgal** see above on 4:1-24.

5:10-12. *Celebration of the Passover.* This passage is the work
of an author with P interests. It links the passover with the entry

into Canaan—as well it might, in view of the similarity of motif between the exodus from Egypt and the crossing of the Jordan (see above on 3:1–5:1). The celebration of the passover is presented as marking the end of one era in Israelite history and the beginning of another—as does also the cessation of manna. The connection of the passover with Gilgal may be very ancient. If, as some scholars have suggested, the Hebrew word for "passover" originally came from the verb "limp," it may originally have alluded to a dance performed in the passover rites (cf. I Kings 18:21, 26). In any case it is possible that the passover was a pre-Israelite agricultural festival.

E. THE CONQUEST OF JERICHO (5:13–6:27)

5:13-15. *The Divine Manifestation to Joshua.* This is one of several bits of old tradition in the Old Testament which allude to manifestations by heavenly military leaders (cf. Genesis 32:1-2 and II Samuel 24:15-17). The scene is reminiscent of the burning bush in Exodus 3:2-5. The story may have been preserved because it shows Joshua as a new Moses. But as it stands, it serves as a prologue to the story of the taking of Jericho. The episode ends without narrating the divine instructions. Perhaps it is a fragment of a longer tradition, or the compiler may intend 6:2-5 to continue the scene.

6:1-27. *The Siege and Fall of Jericho.* Two somewhat differing traditions, usually said to come from J and E, have been interwoven here. This is seen in the repetition and variance of some details. **Jericho** lay at the intersection of important trade routes in the Jordan Valley and had been a commercial center thousands of years before Joshua came on the scene. Small by modern standards, the city could not have been more than a few acres in size nor have contained more than a few thousand inhabitants.

6:1-14. For an unspecified time the Israelites have been besieging Jericho. The final siege begins as Joshua's army marches **around the city** each day for a week. Many details of

Joshua's siege seem to be based on reasonable military strategy—devices for insuring complete blockade of supplies to the city, ways of unnerving the enemy while keeping up the morale and physical condition of Israel's army, signals to indicate the maneuvers to be executed, etc. But the marching, ark carrying, horn blowing, and shouting also seem to have overtones of religious ritual. Such acts might perhaps be performed as sympathetic magic before a siege in hope of influencing the battle, or perhaps be enacted at a shrine in the repeated commemoration of a great victory.

6:15-20. In light of the above military and cultic considerations the question of whether or not the wall of Jericho actually **fell down flat** seems almost beside the point. To explain its collapse as due to an earthquake is to stretch probability. Possibly this is only a bit of dramatic exaggeration—especially if the story was first told in song—of what was actually a victory by ordinary military procedures.

It is also possible that the story means to hint that **Rahab** played traitor to her people and opened the gates to Israel when she heard the **great shout** outside. Still another possibility is that in an earlier stage the tradition assumed that some of Israel's spies remained in Jericho and at the signal opened the gates of the city. An Egyptian text from the fifteenth century tells how Egyptians took Joppa by bringing in soldiers hidden in baskets, who later opened the city's gates.

Conclusions about how Jericho fell are made more difficult because archaeology has revealed little trace of habitation of the city at the time of the Israelite conquest. What excavators of 1930-36 thought to be the wall that fell down was shown in excavations of 1952-57 to be of much earlier date. There is no trace of the walls of Joshua's day—possibly because of erosion in that part of the ruins.

6:21-27. The Israelites completely destroy Jericho and its inhabitants except for Rahab's household. To destroy everything in a captured city, exept perhaps the precious metals, was regarded as an act of high devotion to Yahweh. The Israelites were not alone in practicing this king of piety. In a later century

King Mesha of Moab declares on his commemorative stele that he slew all the Israelite inhabitants of Nebo because he had dedicated their city to his god Ashtar-Chemosh (see Introduction).

In verse 26a Joshua lays a curse on anyone who **rebuilds** Jericho. To this curse an editor has added a bit of poetry (verse 26b) which seems rather unrelated to the story, since it concerns the Canaanite practice of offering a child as a sacrifice to the gods when erecting a building (cf. I Kings 16:34). This appears to be a fragment from some longer poem, possibly not originally connected with Jericho.

F. The Conquest of Ai (7:1–8:29)

Next the Hebrews attack the city of **Ai,** generally identified as the modern et-Tell, a mound about fifteen miles west and a little north of Jericho. But archaeologists have discovered no evidence that a city existed there in Joshua's time. To explain this puzzling fact some scholars, taking "Ai" to mean "ruin" (cf. 8:28), have suggested that the story of the conquest of Ai grew up to explain the presence of ruins which the early Hebrews saw. Others, however, have more recently noted that in the Old Testament "Ai" is the name of inhabited places, not ruins. The word can better be translated "heap" or "pile of stones." If Ai was a thriving city at the time of the Israelite conquest, it should perhaps be sought elsewhere than at et-Tell. As to the ancient name of et-Tell, it has been suggested that it was Beth-aven, mentioned in 7:2. There are so many uncertain factors that the question must be regarded as unresolved.

7:1-26. *Achan's Disobedience.* As in the previous narratives, at least two underlying traditions can be detected, often identified as from J and E.

7:2-9. Joshua sends spies to Ai. On their return they predict an easy conquest and suggest that the entire army need not make the steep climb to the city (which must have been some three thousand feet higher in altitude than Gilgal). Joshua sends

out a detachment of **three thousand men.** In the disastrous
battle which follows, the Israelites lose **thirty-six men**—a figure
which suggests that the attacking force was perhaps in the low
hundreds rather than in the thousands. News of the disaster
prompts Joshua to conclude that Yahweh is in some way
displeased. He tears his garments, throws dust on his head, falls
to the earth and prays—all traditional gestures of sorrow and
humility intended to evoke the compassion of the deity.

7:10-26. Yahweh tells Joshua that someone has **stolen** part of
the forbidden loot from Jericho (cf. 6:18-19). Joshua devises a
test by the casting of lots to discover the wrongdoer. The
selection narrows to Achan, who confesses his guilt and then is
put to death by stoning or, according to the other source,
burning. The story ends with an explanation of the place name
Valley of Achor.

Though this account is fairly straightforward as it stands, there
may be more behind it than first appears. When Hittites
suffered military defeat they assumed that the gods were
displeased and performed a human sacrifice to appease them.
Other peoples—the early Greeks, for example—sometimes
performed human sacrifice before a major battle in hope that
this supreme sacrifice would bring victory (cf. Agamemnon's
sacrifice of his daughter Iphigenia). The story of Jephthah's
daughter in Judges 11:29-40 shows that on occasion Israelites
followed such a practice. Achan's execution may thus be
primarily a sacrifice to try to insure victory in the coming battle
for Ai; as a confessed criminal (verses 20-21) he is the most
expendable person.

The modern reader may well feel that Achan's death could not
really please God and that in any case his fate was not
commensurate with his crime, especially since his household
perished with him. The concept of the family as so unitary that
all had to perish for the offense of one member was eventually
rejected by the Israelites themselves. They eventually came to
the idea that each person should be judged as an individual—
though the older idea reappeared from time to time (cf. John
11:50).

The belief that Yahweh demanded human sacrifice was also rejected in time—as the story of Abraham's attempt to sacrifice his son Isaac (Genesis 22) seems to indicate. But the belief that religious leaders had the right to determine capital punishment for the violation of religious regulations persisted for a much longer time (cf. the stoning of Stephen in Acts 7 and perhaps even the story of Ananias and Sapphira in Acts 5:1-11).

8:1-29. *The Successful Attack on Ai.* The way is now clear for the conquest of Ai. Unlike the first attack, which did not proceed by instruction from Yahweh, the fresh assault is divinely commanded. Verse 2 is a D addition. The number of soldiers in verse 3 seems to be exaggerated. Some of the details of the attack are not clear because of the editorial linking of the two sources. The general plan is that Joshua lures the defenders of Ai outside with a small body of soldiers as a decoy, enabling the main body of the Israelite soldiers to enter the city and take it.

In telling of his role in the ruse the storyteller gives a few personal glimpses of Joshua as a daring hero not unlike some of Israel's later great warriors. The public execution of the **king of Ai** and the display of his body follow the standard Near Eastern practice of disconcerting the conquered people and emphatically indicating the end of the old regime.

G. JOSHUA'S ALTAR (8:30–9:2)

8:30-35. *A Ceremony at Shechem.* Here we find Joshua at **Mount Ebal** and **Mount Gerizim,** the twin mountains flanking Shechem in central Palestine, over twenty miles north of Ai. The story is unexpected, since Joshua has not yet attempted the conquest of this region. Clearly an editorial addition, the passage is D throughout, showing Joshua's fulfillment of Moses' instruction (Deuteronomy 11:29-30; 27). The scene is one of covenanting. It has affinities with the account of Joshua's covenant at Shechem in chapter 24 (see comment), which some interpreters suspect once stood at this point and was later replaced by this passage.

In stressing Joshua's writing of the **law of Moses** on stones the D author shows, as elsewhere, his assumption that Joshua's experiences often parallel those of Moses. These **stones** are apparently freestanding rather than part of the **altar** (cf. Deuteronomy 27:2-7). They may be compared with the stones set up at Gilgal (chapter 4).

9:1-2. *An Editorial Conclusion.* The D editor summarizes the effect of Joshua's victory over Ai on the peoples of Palestine. As elsewhere (2:9-11; 5:1), he pictures consternation among them. Here, however, he reports, not despondency, but willingness to withstand Israel. The statement serves as a foil to the story which follows. **Beyond the Jordan** here refers to Palestine, not Transjordan as the expression usually does.

H. ISRAEL'S COVENANT WITH GIBEON (9:3-27)

Gibeon was an important town six miles northwest of Jerusalem. Its inhabitants in Joshua's time were apparently not Canaanites. Verse 7 speaks of them as **Hivites.** Another source calls them Amorites (II Samuel 21:2)—but contrast the story of an Amorite attack on them in 10:1-27. Excavations at the site have revealed evidence of Late Bronze Age occupation not long before the time of the Hebrew conquest of Canaan.

The story of how the Gibeonites save themselves by deceiving the leaders of Israel into making a treaty with them comes from two major accounts, usually identified as J and E, which have been woven together. The episode originally followed the conquest of Ai (8:29). There is a bit of D embellishment in verses 24-25 and an addition in verses 17-21 which many interpreters assume to be from a P source.

9:6-15. The **covenant** which the Gibeonites seek is of the suzerainty type—that is, they agree to accept political subservience to Israel in return for protection of their peace. The covenant may have been accompanied by a solemn feast (cf. Genesis 26:30). But the food which the Gibeonites bring (cf.

verses 4-5) is probably not to be understood as provisions for such a meal, since it was customarily offered by the dominant party—in this case Israel. The food must therefore be part of the deception.

9:16-27. The Gibeonites' deception is successful. They accept the role of **hewers of wood and drawers of water** which the covenant imposes on them. This terminology appears in the Canaanite Keret text of the fourteenth century as a description of the work of women. In this context it seems to imply that the Gibeonites are to disband their army and rely on Israel for their defense.

Hebrew storytellers were unwilling to concede that the Gibeonites went unpunished for their deception. They modified the tradition so that the role appears to be some sort of disgrace which Joshua imposes on the Gibeonites after he learns of the deception. Indeed they speak of the Gibeonites as becoming **slaves** and having to serve in the **congregation** (the temple in Jerusalem) as servants of an especially low class (verse 27). Such modifications largely reflect conditions of later centuries. The Gibeonites seem eventually to have merged with the Israelite population. Part of the reason for the preservation of this story was that it served as background for the following episode and for II Samuel 21:1-14.

I. The Conquest of Southern Palestine (10:1-43)

10:1-27. *Defeat of a Coalition of Southern Kings.* For the first time since the conquest began the Canaanite rulers attempt to take offensive action. However, this is directed, not toward Israel, but toward Israel's new vassal, **Gibeon.** The tendency of kings to band together for warfare was natural, since each city-state was too small to exert strong military power alone. Most of the cooperating cities had been yokefellows under Egypt's rule in previous centuries and had known the threat of the Habiru, or Hebrews. The name of the leader of the coalition,

Adoni-zedek, resembles that of Adoni-bezek in Judges 1:5-7. It is possible that the two stories are in some way related.

10:6-11. When Gibeon is threatened, Joshua fulfills his responsibility as the protector of the vassal city (cf. the covenant in 9:15) and comes to the rescue. Following a practice successfully employed at Ai (8:3) he directs a forced nighttime march from his base at Gilgal. Surprising the enemy, he not only wins a victory but drives deep into southern Palestine. More than one source can be detected in this narrative. It bears some resemblance to the story of the coalition of five kings against four kings in Genesis 14. Perhaps both traditions are based on a common old motif.

10:12-15. Like perhaps other parts of chapters 2-11 (see Introduction) this story may originally have been in the form of a poem. The four lines of verses 12*c*-13*b* may be a fragment from that poem as it once existed in the now-lost **Book of Jashar.** The standing still of **Sun** and **Moon** has long fascinated readers, who have often attributed to it far more significance than the original storyteller probably intended. Possibly there is nothing more complicated here than a wish to defeat the enemy before nightfall. The prose writer of verse 13*cd* takes the poem literally, explaining that the sun stopped its movement until the battle was won.

Assuming that some unusual but natural phenomenon occurred during the battle, modern interpreters have often sought to explain that event as an eclipse, a hailstorm, the presence of sun and moon in the sky together at dawn, a clouding of the sky, etc. But these interpretations seem strained. The poet is probably speaking metaphorically, like the author of the Song of Deborah when he speaks of the stars fighting against Sisera (Judges 5:20).

Behind the metaphor may lie interesting concepts of cosmology (cf. Habakkuk 3:11) and perhaps even astrology. Indeed it is possible, as some interpreters have suggested, that Joshua was uttering an incantation to the sun and moon to help him defeat his enemies. Verse 13*a* (which may, however, be an early addition) and the prose explanation imply that the command to sun and moon occurred before the battle. On the other hand the fact that the song is placed after rather than before the battle suggests that it was originally a song of victory. It may have been related to a religious celebration and possibly to the establishment of a special commemorative ceremony. But to what extent these cultic associations belong with the original tradition cannot be determined.

10:16-27. This relatively lengthy description is somewhat separate from the preceding episode. It tells of the pursuit and execution of the **five kings** who fought against Israel. Again two sources have been interwoven, resulting in some confusion in detail. One suspects that originally there was a good deal of significance to this story which can no longer be discovered.

The scenes show considerable stylization. The idea that defeated kings hid in caves is widespread, not only in Hebrew tradition (cf. I Samuel 22:1) but in Egyptian as well. Joshua's command to his associates to place their **feet upon the necks of these kings** as a symbol of their utter defeat follows ancient oriental custom. It is interesting to note that Joshua shares the heady moment of triumph with his lieutenants. As in 8:29, he orders the bodies of the kings displayed publicly.

10:28-43. *Further Conquests in Southern Palestine.* This section, which builds directly on the preceding narrative comes from D. Apparently the earlier tradition said nothing of any conquests of Joshua, other than possibly raids, in southern Palestine. But the D editor, looking back from a vantage point many centuries later, knew that Israel had come to occupy southern Palestine. Perhaps drawing on certain older traditions available to him, he here attributes to Joshua the conquest of a number of southern cities. In every case he shows them as suffering utter destruction. Accurately enough, he does not say the Joshua actually took **Gezer** (verse 33).

10:40-43. This is the D editor's summary of the southern campaign. The **Negeb** is the dry region south of Beer-sheba. The **country of Goshen** here is not in Egypt. It is the southern

hill country surrounding the town of Goshen. Many scholars
have doubted that Joshua conquered any of southern Palestine.
The traditions in Judges 1:1-20 suggest that this region was
conquered by various groups, probably over an extended
period.

J. The Conquest of Northern Palestine (11:1-15)

Verses 1, 4-5, 7, and 8*b* are generally recognized as coming
from an old tradition, often identified as J or JE. They tell briefly
of Joshua's defeat of **Jabin king of Hazor** and his three
confederates at the **waters of Merom,** a place northwest of the
Sea of Galilee. The remaining verses are a D expansion of the
story which shows Joshua as conquering virtually all of Galilee.

11:1-5. On **Jabin** see comment on Judges 4:1-24. The **Arabah**
is the deep valley of the Sea of Galilee, Jordan River, and Dead
Sea. **Chinneroth** (or Chinnereth, New Testament Gennesaret)
may mean either the town on the northwestern shore of the Sea
of Galilee or the lake itself.

11:6-9. Joshua defeats the kings and pursues them apparently to
the northern border of Palestine. **Great Sidon** is generally taken to
mean the boundary of Sidonian territory. The **valley of Mizpeh** is
probably the same as the **land of Mizpah** at the foot of Mt.
Hermon (verse 3).

11:10-15. That **Hazor** was a chief Canaanite city is confirmed
by references in Egyptian and Mesopotamian records. Excavation has revealed that it was destroyed and rebuilt a number of
times, one destruction possibly occurring in the thirteenth
century. This is a D section and contains some old material. For
example, it tells us that Joshua destroyed **none of the cities that
stood on mounds**—that is, none of the powerful old Canaanite
walled cities of the lowlands. Behind this statement lies the
recollection that the Israelites, settling in the rural hill country,
did not have the strength or technological knowledge to defeat
the chariot armies of the Canaanite cities. That Israel carried out

so extensive a program as the D author describes in verses 12 and 14 is unlikely. The statements may have come from his zeal in showing the success of Israel under Yahweh.

K. SUMMARY OF JOSHUA'S CONQUESTS (11:16–12:24)

11:16-23. *An Editorial Summary.* This passage is largely, and perhaps entirely, D. Eager to show that Yahweh fulfilled the promise that Israel would make its home in Canaan, the author declares that **Joshua took all that land,** from **Lebanon** to **Mount Halak** in the **Negeb** (see above on 10:40-43). He probably represents the conquest as far bloodier than it was, and he devotes only passing attention to the fact that some regions remained outside Israelite control (verse 22). The **Anakim** were a tribe then living in Palestine, traditionally described as gigantic in size (cf. Numbers 13:32-33). The concluding sentence serves as a transition to the second half of Joshua, which begins in chapter 13.

12:1-24. *A Statistical Summary.* This chapter seems largely to be an independent record compiled by an unknown archivist. The D editor made it a part of Joshua.

12:1-6. This is a summary of the Transjordanian kings and kingdoms said to have been defeated by the Israelites under Moses (cf. Numbers 21:21-35 and Deuteronomy 2:24–3:11). It also tells of Moses' allotment of these territories to Gad, Reuben, and Manasseh. On **Sea of Chinneroth** see above on 11:1-5. **The sea of the Arabah, the Salt Sea** is the Dead Sea.

12:7-24. The kings and peoples defeated by the Israelites under Joshua in Palestine proper are listed. The fact that many of these names have not previously been mentioned indicates that this section is not simply a summary of the preceding stories. The cities of verses 10-16*a* are in southern Palestine. Some of the places of verses 16*b*-24 are in the territories of Ephraim and Manasseh in central Palestine, where no conquests have previously been described. Many scholars believe that the lack of traditions about Joshua's conquests in Ephraim and Manasseh indicates Hebrew settlement in that region well before his time.

II. THE APPORTIONMENT OF THE LAND (13:1–22:34)

The content of this large section differs considerably from that of chapters 2–11. Though it contains some D editorial materials, it consists mainly of statistical information about persons, places, and tribes which Israelite archivists gathered from various sources. Some of the data may have their roots in the conquest, but as they stand they seem to reflect conditions of later centuries. Such records must have been compiled for cultic or administrative use.

Some of these materials were undoubtedly first preserved in northern Palestinian sanctuaries. Sometime after the centralization of Yahwist religion in the temple they were transferred to Jerusalem. Not surprisingly, the sections dealing with southern Palestine, where Jerusalem was located, are more detailed than those concerning northern Palestine and Transjordan. The statistical records which have been preserved here probably represent only a small part of the total body of archives which once existed. Parts of these chapters have shorter parallels in Judges 1:1–2:5.

A. PREFACE TO THE ALLOTMENT (13:1–14:15)

13:1-7. *Summary of Unconquered Areas.* Except for verse 1 this passage is D. It is the fullest D statement in Joshua of those parts of Canaan which the Israelites were not able to conquer. The author idealistically includes not only the coastal lands of the **Philistines** and **Sidonians** (Phoenicians) but other territories to the south and north never occupied by Israel. The **Geshurites** of verse 2 are a southern people different from the Aramean Geshurites of verse 13. Yahweh instructs Joshua to allot to the tribes of Israel even those portions of the land which were not then under Israelite control.

13:8–14:5. *Review of Tribal Allotments Under Moses.* This section reviews the traditional allotment of Transjordan by Moses to the tribes of Gad, Reuben, and Manasseh (cf. 1:12-18; 12:1-6; 22:1-34; Numbers 32; Deuteronomy 3:12-17). Verses 8-12 and 14 are usually recognized as D. The remaining material is from one or more archivistic records. The D editor takes note of the fact that the **tribe of Levi,** who served as priests and presumably lived throughout the country, received no allotment. 14:1-2 prepares for the allotment of the land west of the Jordan described in 14:6–19:51. Some interpreters believe that 18:1 originally stood before 14:1 and therefore that the place of the allotment tradition was originally Shiloh. The reference to **Eleazar the** (chief) **priest** in 14:1, next to whom Joshua takes second place, seems to reflect P interests.

14:6-15. *Caleb's Inheritance at Hebron.* In view of Joshua's prominence, the place which Caleb occupies in the exodus and conquest traditions is remarkable. This story tells of Joshua's gift of land to Caleb, the only other Israelite of the exodus generation who has lived on into the conquest period (cf. Numbers 14:20-24). Variant traditions in 15:13-19 and Judges 1:11-15 (see comments) indicate that Caleb actually gained his territory by military conquest. The account here, apparently D, retains a hint of this tradition (verse 12), but portrays Joshua bestowing the land as if it had already been taken (on the **Anakim** see comment on 11:16-23). The time span of **forty-five years** is notable. It implies that the Israelites conquered all Canaan, including Transjordan, within seven years (cf. verse 7 and Deuteronomy 2:14). The author could compress and simplify events in this way because he was greatly removed from them in time.

B. THE ALLOTMENT TO JUDAH (15:1-63)

15:1-12. *The Boundaries of Judah.* This is the first and most complete of the boundary lists. It indicates that the compiler had fuller records for Judah and that gave this tribe preeminence. The limits of Judah are set at their greatest possible extent. They include desert and coastal regions which were not historically a part of the tribe's territory.

15:13-19. *An Interpolation on Caleb's Territory.* Since the portion given to Caleb and his family lay within Judah, the editor can now introduce an old tradition about Caleb's inheritance. Some interpreters identify this as coming from J. A parallel account is found in Judges 1:11-15. In both passages Caleb is shown as taking his territory by force. Contrast 14:6-15, composed in D circles (see comment).

15:20-63. *The Cities of Judah.* This list presents a number of difficulties both of geography and of dating. Many scholars would agree that it is based on a list of districts within Judah and was drawn up for governmental administrative purposes sometime after the time of David. It may have been based on records of pre-Davidic times. The list presupposes the existence of major cities, each surrounded by villages subservient to it. Among the later modifications of the list are the addition of Philistine cities in verses 45-47 and the omission of a block of cities between verses 59-60. Although these are missing in the Hebrew text, they are fortunately preserved in the Greek text.

15:63. This appended bit of ancient tradition is important for the history of **Jerusalem.** Though 12:10 says that Joshua vanquished the king of Jerusalem and Judges 1:8 tells of the capture of the city, these traditions seem to grow out of southern interests in monarchical times—indicated by the editorial phrase **to this day.** This passage supports the more likely tradition that Jerusalem remained a stronghold of the **Jebusites** until David captured it. The city was closely bounded by both Judah (verse 8) and Benjamin (18:16) and was apparently open to both tribes. This verse mentions men of **Judah** living in Jebusite Jerusalem, whereas a similar passage in Judges 1:21 speaks of Benjaminites. If one must choose between the traditions, that which speaks of Benjaminite connectons with Jerusalem perhaps has the stronger claim.

C. The Allotment to the Joseph Tribes (16:1–17:18)

The borders of the territories allotted to Joseph's **descendants** are not entirely clear. No lists of cities are given. It is evident that the compiler did not have the same kind of detailed resources for these tribes as he did for Judah.

16:1-4. *The Area Broadly Defined.* The tribes of **Manasseh and Ephraim,** traditionally linked as the sons of **Joseph,** are treated together in verses 1-3. These verses come from an old tradition of the JE kind. Interpreters are not agreed on whether this treatment of Joseph as a single tribe is older than the treatment of Ephraim and Manasseh separately (verse 4–17:13). Most assume that it is.

16:5-10. *The Allotment to Ephraim.* Tribal boundaries are confusingly delineated in this brief note. It ends with a fragment from an earlier tradition which explains why Canaanites continue to live among the Israelites (cf. Judges 1:29). Compare the story in chapter 9 which explains the presence of Gibeonites in Israel. In both instances the original population is said to be reduced to slavery.

17:1-18. *The Allotment to Manasseh.* This treatment is more extensive than the preceding section because it includes two segments of narrative (verses 3-6, 14-18). Other materials can also be detected in this section—for example, the list of Manasseh's descendants in verse 2. Concerning boundaries, however, the details are sketchy.

17:3-6. This story of the **daughters** of **Zelophehad** and their claim to an **inheritance** may be based on Numbers 27:1-11, which is generally attributed to the postexilic P source.

17:11-13. This notice about the Canaanite cities which the Manassites were unable to take is informative (cf. Judges 1:27). The statement that they **put the Canaanites to forced labor** probably reflects conditions of a later time.

17:14-18. Ephraim and Manasseh are here treated as one tribe, **Joseph,** as in 16:1-3. This passage consists of two versions of the same tradition—verses 14-15 and 16-18. Both traditions recall that the Joseph tribes could inhabit only the **hill country**

during the conquest. They were not sufficiently strong or mechanized to challenge the Canaanite cities, which were defended with **chariots of iron** (that is, having iron armor plates). Thus they had to be content to wrest a livelihood from the rugged, unfarmed hills.

The passage says nothing of their leaving their **too narrow** territory. Yet it may be derived from an earlier tradition which told of the migration of these tribes to Transjordan, where Ephraim later had certain connections and part of Manasseh is traditionally said to have lived. The early tradition would be modified in the face of that other tradition which showed the Joseph tribes coming first to Transjordan, before the conquest of western Canaan. On the lack of space for expansion compare the story of the migration of the tribe of Dan to the far north of Palestine (Judges 17–18).

D. THE ALLOTMENTS TO THE OTHER TRIBES
(18:1–19:51)

18:1-10. *The Allotment Ceremony at Shiloh.* The D compiler has dealt with the major tribes of Judah, Ephraim, and Manasseh, which together occupied a large part of the hill country possessed by Israel. He now turns to the remaining **seven tribes**—omitting Gad and Reuben, who are assumed to be settled in Transjordan, and Levi, who is not given a territorial allotment (verse 7). He describes these allotments as being determined at a single gathering of Israel at **Shiloh,** one of the important shrines where Israelites worshiped. Some interpreters, however, have argued that verse 1 originally stood before 14:1 and that the original site of the present episode was Gilgal (reading "Gilgal" for "Shiloh" in verses 8-10; cf. 14:6).

In preparation for the ceremony Joshua orders representatives of the tribes to survey the remaining land and divide it into **seven portions.** He then proceeds to **cast lots . . . before the LORD** (cf. 7:14-18; 15:1; 16:1) in order to allot one portion to each tribe. That these tribes actually received their traditional territories in such a manner is unlikely. The process was probably a more complex one of historical settlement which took place at various times.

18:11–19:48. *The Individual Allotments to the Seven Tribes.* Joshua allots the remaining land—beginning with Benjamin and continuing with Simeon, Zebulun, Issachar, Asher, Naphtali and Dan. The descriptions, most of which consist of boundary delineations and lists of cities, are brief and frequently confusing. Behind them may lie various tribal records which the D editor, perhaps not entirely understanding them, has modified. The tribal boundaries of **Simeon** are lacking (19:1-9), probably because the tribe long had lived within the territory of Judah. The boundaries of **Dan** are likewise missing (19:40-48), perhaps because the tribe had only a few towns squeezed in among the surrounding tribes. In 19:47 the editor has added a brief note derived from an old tradition of the Danites' subsequent loss of their land and migration to the north of Palestine.

19:49-51. *Joshua's Inheritance; Conclusion.* The D editor appends a note drawn from a separate tradition often identified as from E. It says that Israel gave Joshua the city of **Timnath-serah** (called Timnath-heres in Judges 2:9) in **Ephraim** at his request. That Joshua, an Ephraimite (cf. Numbers 13:8), would choose to settle in his tribe's territory is not surprising. The gift is apparently not arranged by lot, as were the lands for the tribes, but, given instead as a reward for services well performed (cf. Caleb's portion, 14:13). The reference to **Eleazar the priest** in verse 51 is a P embellishment which reflects cultic interests.

E. The Cities of Refuge (20:1-9)

A Semitic common law held that one **who kills any person,** even unintentionally, is guilty of bloodshed and may be immediately executed by the family of the slain person. This passage provides that certain **cities of refuge** are to be "off limits" to vengeful relatives, thereby giving time for tempers to cool and a sober inquiry to be made. The P tradition of Numbers 35:9-15 attributes the establishment of such cities to instructions of Moses. Three of these were west of the Jordan and three were east. It is likely, however, that at least some of the cities set aside had functioned as havens in Canaanite times. There is no need to assume, as scholars often have, that the provision for these cities should be traced to Bedouin practice. D writers were also interested in the cities of refuge, as Deuteronomy 19:1-13 shows. Compare also the earlier tradition in Exodus 21:13.

F. The Allotment of Cities to Levites and Aaronic Priests (21:1-42)

This passage shows P interests more clearly than perhaps any other in Joshua. But it is not necessarily to be taken to be a postexilic creation. It attempts to show priests and Levites sharing in the divine promise of the inheritance of Canaan by receiving certain **cities** within the territories of the other tribes (cf. I Chronicles 6:54-81). The D view, as expressed in 13:14 and 18:7, seems to be that the Levites have no territorial allotment at all. This episode again is set at **Shiloh** and is described as apportionment by lot (see above on 18:1-10). The Levitic groups mentioned in verses 4-7 and elsewhere were traditionally said to be descended from Kohath, Gershon, and Merari—sons of the patriarch Levi.

21:9-42. This is a more extensive version of the allotment. Most attention is given to the Levites. Verses 13-19 list **thirteen cities** assigned to **the descendants of Aaron,** who himself is presented as a descendant of Kohath (verse 4). The scheme is highly idealistic. It is unlikely that Levites ever effectively controlled many of these cities, though they may have served in the religious establishments in many cities. All of the Levitic cities are in northern Palestine and Transjordan, while all of the

Aaronic cities are in southern Palestine and the vicinity of Jerusalem. The cities of refuge (cf. chapter 20) are listed among the thirty-five Levitical cities.

G. The Completion of the Apportionment of the Land (21:43–22:34)

21:43-45. *Summary of the Apportionment.* In this concise, idealized summary the D editor ends apportionment of Canaan. This graceful statement shows his firm conviction that Yahweh has faithfully fulfilled all that was promised to Israel.

22:1-9. *Dismissal of the Transjordanian Tribes.* This continuation of the D editorial addition begun in 21:43 seems to draw on earlier materials. Joshua's words in verse 8 are reminiscent of those in the D passage at the beginning of the conquest (1:12-15). On this note the Transjordanian tribes depart to their allotted territories. Verse 9, from a non-D source, serves as a transition to the story which follows.

22:10-34. *The Altar at the Jordan.* This is a lengthy appendix to the narrative of the division of the land. It tells how the Transjordanian tribes, as they are returning home, build an altar of great size on the west side of the Jordan. The other tribes take this act to be contrary to proper religious practices and send a delegation which criticizes the three eastern tribes. They are assured, however, that the altar was erected, not for sacrifices, but solely as a memorial of faithfulness to Yahweh.

Behind this tradition apparently lies the memory of a conflict of religious practices, though not necessarily one which occurred at the time to which it is attributed. Note that Joshua does not appear in the account and that the chief **priest** is **Phinehas,** rather than **Eleazar,** who has appeared several times previously. Commentators often assume that this story attempts to show the importance of the one central shrine at Jerusalem for Israelite worship. However, the story seems to attempt to justify the continued veneration of an old local shrine—which would otherwise have been forbidden following the centralization.

III. THE LAST ACTS OF JOSHUA (23:1–24:33)

23:1-16. *Joshua's Farewell Speech.* Compare this speech with the farewell addresses attributed to Jacob (Genesis 49:1-27) and to Moses (Deuteronomy 31–33). It is entirely D. In an earlier edition of Joshua it may have been the conclusion of the book, chapter 24 perhaps having been added later. In the speech Joshua, now an old man, assures the assembled Israelites that although the land is not yet entirely conquered (verse 4). Yahweh will ultimately give total possession of it to Israel if the people remain steadfast in keeping the law. Joshua ignores as insignificant the fact that the conquest was only partial. He emphasizes that not one of Yahweh's good promises has failed (cf. 21:45).

The D author wrote, of course, with knowledge of the events which had occurred during the centuries after Joshua's time. Anticipating the period of the judges, he has Joshua say that evil things will come upon Israel through failure to live by Yahweh's commandments. As elsewhere, he shows concern for contemporary problems and values. Notable is his warning to the Israelites not to marry among the other inhabitants of the land—a topic which was especially lively in the postexilic period. Like many other D speeches, this passage is gracefully written. But it shows a narrow concept of the proper worship of Yahweh and a highly particularistic view of Yahweh's actions with Israel. For the author other peoples have little or no significance.

24:1-28. *The Covenant at Shechem.* Joshua's speech in chapter 23 forms an appropriate conclusion to the original D edition of the book. Chapter 24 seems to be an appendix, perhaps added by a later editor of the D circle. The core of the story is older material which many interpreters identify as belonging to the E source. The review of Israelite history in verses 2-11a,c (verses 11b and 12-13 are largely D embellishment) concludes with a reference to the fall of Jericho. This suggests that the episode may once have stood approximately where the D story of covenanting at Ebal-Gerizim (near **Shechem**) now stands in 8:30-35.

The account first tells how Joshua summons the leaders of Israel to Shechem. This city was obviously not hostile to the Israelites (cf. Genesis 34). However, it is not necessary to assume that it was controlled by Israel at this time or that its religion was Israelite. Judges 8:33 and 9:4, 46 suggest that the cult at Shechem was that of Elberith (i.e. "El-covenant"), the Canaanite god of covenanting. The Israelites were able to gather here because of the covenant peace which gave them protection. Shechem is listed as a city of refuge in chapter 20.

Here, flanked by the mountains of Gerizim and Ebal, and using solemn language, Joshua acts as hierophant—an interpreter of sacred history—in a ceremony of covenanting. Customarily we would expect a covenant among the tribes themselves with Yahweh as a witness, however, Joshua's covenant is between Yahweh as the dominant part and Israel as the subservient one.

Little information is given about the ceremony itself. But by comparing older covenants described in the Old Testament, as well as various covenants now known in ancient Near Eastern literature, we may deduce the kind of rite lying back of the account. At some early point, in keeping with Near Eastern covenant forms, Joshua reviewed the historical relationship between Yahweh and Israel (verses 2-13). This may be seen as a "history of salvation," or very nearly a creedal affirmation (cf. Deuteronomy 26:5-11). Then followed a proclamation of the stipulations of the covenant, here given very briefly (verses 14-15). This was a general demand for loyalty to Yahweh and rejection of other gods—an interest possibly reflecting later concerns more than those of Joshua's day. To these the people responded (verses 16-18). Joshua then tested Israel's resolve by pointing out risks which this servitude involved (verses 19-20), and the people again responded (verse 21). A final series of declarations and responses solemnly ratified the covenant (22-24).

It is possible that there was a place for ceremonial blessings and curses such as appear in the covenanting scene in 8:30-35 (cf. Deuteronomy 27:11–28:19). The Israelites may also have performed the ritual of cutting sacrificial animals in two and passing between them (cf. Genesis 15:9-17), though standing between Gerizim and Ebal may have served the same function. They may also have eaten a sacred meal (cf. Genesis 26:30) and participated in a symbolic transfer of gifts (cf. Genesis 21:27-30). The reference to the **stone** erected **under the oak** implies that a public record of the covenant was set up. It is interesting to note that there is no mention of the ark, which was traditionally associated with Shiloh rather than Shechem.

There has been much debate about whether such a covenant including all the tribes of Israel was actually made in Joshua's time. But there can be little doubt that early tribal relationships were often cemented with treaties. With its great stress on Joshua's speech and the omission of all but a few descriptive details of the ceremony itself, the account clearly reveals that a long development lies behind the tradition. This development, as well as the very preservation of the tradition, may have occurred within the context of a ceremony of covenant renewal enacted at intervals among the tribes of Israel.

24:29-31. *Joshua's Death.* His work finished, Joshua dies and is **buried** at **Timnath-serah,** the Ephraimite town which the Israelites gave him for his services (19:49-50). There is a parallel tradition in Judges 2:7-9. Like the patriarchs before him, he is said to have lived an exceptionally long time. The D editor adds a sentence which may be intended as a transition to the period of the judges which is to follow (verse 31).

24:32-33. *Appended Notes.* Later editors have added brief notes, from earlier traditions, concerning the reburial of the remains of **Joseph** (cf. Genesis 50:26; Exodus 13:19) at **Shechem** (cf. Genesis 33:19) and the death of **Eleazar,** the chief priest. Both burials, we may assume, were in family tombs, cut into the bedrock, as was the practice throughout most of the Israelite times in Palestine.

The Greek version of Joshua adds that the Israelites took the ark about with them with **Phinehas** as priest. It also states that Israel began to worship foreign gods, so that the Lord gave them into the hands of Eglon, king of Moab, who dominated them for eighteen years. This latter statement leads directly into Judges 3:15 and may be a survival of a pre-D edition in which Joshua and a portion of Judges formed a single account (see Introduction).

THE BOOK OF JUDGES

Robert Houston Smith

Introduction

The history of Israel between the death of Joshua and the rise of the prophet Samuel is the subject of the book of Judges. The story is told in a series of episodes which revolve around a half dozen heroes, or "judges." Attached to this core are traditions dealing with the conquest of Palestine, six minor judges, the attempt of a leader named Abimelech to become king of Shechem, the migration of the tribe of Dan to the north, and a war between Benjamin and the other tribes.

Literary History

The stories of Israel's judges were early told in the form of songs. Some songs were apparently ballads, sung by minstrels who had a keen sense of what would delight an audience of simple people. Traces of these are preserved in several poetic utterances in the stories of Samson. More serious in tone were didactic poems. Jotham's fable in chapter 9 originally may have been such a poem. Most majestic of all were the cult poems, such as the Song of Deborah. Its formal content, ancient rhythm, and archaic language reveal that it was composed by one or more professional musicians in the service of a sanctuary. It is not implausible to trace poetic elements in Judges back to as early as the twelfth century, though their very nature rules out close dating.

Concurrent with the rise of songs was the appearance of prose accounts which dealt with the same, or similar, subjects. Like the songs, these prose accounts probably often had their origin in Israelite cults. In some cases they served to present a historical, or seemingly historical, basis for existing ideas and practices—as do the story of Jephthah's sacrifice of his daughter and perhaps the stories of Gideon's rites. Better than poetry for handling matter-of-fact details, these stories became increasingly popular as Israel's interest in historical records developed. Eventually they became the nucleus of Judges.

There were probably many more stories in circulation than have come down to us. Several versions of some stories came into being, as we can see in the tales of Gideon, Abimelech, and others. As the old accounts in Judges will show, these stories concerned heroes of individual tribes rather than of all Israel. It is therefore reasonable to suppose that these traditions—and for that matter the poems too—were best known within the tribes of the judges with which they were concerned. If there were accounts concerning the southern tribes of Judah and Simeon, no clear trace of them has survived. All the old stories in Judges concern the northern tribes.

Editors in northern Palestine began making collections of stories of the judges no later than the ninth century and may have continued through the eighth century. The relationship of these collections to other sources in the Old Testament is not entirely clear. Many scholars find behind the present accounts two major collections of stories, which some identify with the J and E sources in Genesis-Numbers. Others find the evidence for specific collections unconvincing and prefer simply to recognize that old sources underlie the nucleus of Judges.

This nucleus reached its essential form about the eighth century. It consists of most of 3:15–16:31 and may also have included chapters 17–18. The compiler added various brief summaries and transitions, among which were probably the number of years of each judge and each period of oppression, the total of which is 410 years. He may also have been responsible for the addition of six minor judges (3:31; 10:1-5; 12:8-15). Where the compiler got his information about these minor persons is not known. Possibly he summarized fuller traditions which he knew but felt had only limited usefulness. It is perhaps more likely, however, that he constructed these minor judges out of names he found in old lists.

The compiler's concern with the minor judges may have arisen from a desire to show that each of the ten northern tribes had one great deliverer. One might say that this was an early form of the idea that the judges delivered all Israel. In their present form the stories still show a considerable distribution among the tribes. Later alterations, however, have largely obscured any pattern which may once have existed.

The compiler seems also to have wished to show a different enemy—the Moabites, the Canaanites, the Midianites, the Ammonites, and the Philistines—in each of the stories of the major judges. The completed work seems to have followed directly after Joshua and to have led directly into the stories about Samuel, the last judge.

In the latter part of the seventh century or the first half of the sixth century the Deuteronomic school, affiliated in some way with the Jerusalem cult but well informed about the religious traditions of northern Palestine, took over this core of stories as a part of its extended history of Israel from Deuteronomy through II Kings (see the Introduction to Joshua). Leaving the older material unaltered except for a few transitions and summaries (notably 3:12-14; 4:1-3; 6:1; and 13:1) the D editor—or editors—prefaced it with a long introductory section (2:6–3:6) and with an opening story (3:7-11). Possibly he omitted chapters 9 and 17–18. This editor saw the judges as deliverers of all Israel and assumed that people from all Israel joined in battling the enemy.

In the postexilic period one or more editors associated with the priestly school expanded Judges by prefacing the D text with the block of material found in 1:1–2:5. This was taken from an old source which surveyed the conquest of Palestine. This P editor also reintroduced chapters 9 and 17–18—if indeed these chapters had been omitted from the D edition. He added chapters 19–21. To the same editor may also perhaps be attributed the separation of Judges from Joshua and I Samuel.

After these final additions the text of Judges began a trend toward abridgment and minor modification. This process seems to have continued down to the time when the present Hebrew text was standardized by Jewish rabbis around A.D. 100. These late alterations have done little except to obscure the text. Interpreters are sometimes able to discover an earlier and clearer form of a passage by consulting the Septuagint version of Judges, which is unique among Old Testament books in that the two oldest manuscripts differ greatly in wording. Also helpful are fragments of a slightly different Hebrew text found among the Dead Sea Scrolls.

Israelite History

This analysis of the process by which Judges came into its present form has direct relevance for the understanding of Israelite history during the period of the judges. The interpreter is freed from having to suppose that each judge delivered all Israel, that the judges followed one another in orderly sequence, and that the total length of the period was 410 years. One is able to reconstruct the history in broad outline and place it within the larger framework of Hebrew and ancient Near Eastern history.

The time of the judges, most scholars now agree, was around 1200–1050. By the beginning of this period the Egyptian, Hittite, and Mesopotamian powers had faded into insignificance in Palestine and Transjordan. The small nations of the region were free to pursue policies of expansion. From the north and west came a seafaring people known as the Philistines, who settled the southern coast of Palestine. The Israelite tribes were already established in the hill country and perhaps in parts of northern Transjordan. By this time they were occasionally having to fight off hostile forces of Midianites, Ammonites, Moabites, and others who wished to press west across the

Jordan. The Canaanites continued to occupy many of their old lowland city-states and a few isolated cities such as Shechem and Jerusalem in the hill country.

During this period Israel was mainly concerned with consolidating settlements peviously made—a process which involved defending the tribal territories from aggression by adjoining peoples. The tribes largely went their separate ways, though they shared a sense of common heritage and were bound by various treaties, or covenants, with one another. Life centered around tribal relationships rather than cities. Judges mentions Israelite cities, but these must have been small and rural by comparison with the great Canaanite and Philistine cities. Borders remained fluid and the people were relatively mobile. Marriages among the tribes were frequent, and intermarriage with Canaanites and Philistines was tolerated to a considerable degree. Most Israelites were farmers, cultivating such plants as wheat, olives, grapes, and figs.

Tribal leaders were apparently selected by the leading men of the clans. In principle they were chosen on the basis of leadership qualities, but in practice sometimes on the basis of familial status. These leaders came and went. They sometimes engaged in feuds and power struggles as they pursued their careers. Whether they were called "judges" in their own time is uncertain. The D editor so designates collectively the heroes of the book (2:16-19), and sometimes says that so-and-so "judged Israel." But no individual hero is actually called a judge, or is portrayed as rendering a courtroom verdict.

Yet the judge in ancient Canaanite and Israelite usage was not so much a legal expert as one who upheld the customs of the people. Consequently the judge became a deliverer of wronged persons who were not strong enough to obtain justice for themselves—widows, orphans, and victims of military aggression. Indeed the D editor several times refers to one or another of the heroes as a "deliverer." Clearly the tribal leaders did not conform to any one narrow role. Jephthah, for example, was a military commander and Deborah, a prophetess. Some of them may have had ties with certain sanctuaries. For example, Samuel was considered by the D editor the last of the judges.

The Israelite tribes resisted the Canaanite kind of kingship, of which they continued to have a deep distrust born of long and unhappy experience (see Introduction to Jushua). Nevertheless the process of consolidating tribal areas and defense against organized enemies gradually pushed them toward a more centralized government. The large and powerful tribes of Ephraim and Manasseh seem especially to have moved in this direction, as the attempt by Abimelech to extend his authority to the old Canaanite city of Shechem suggests.

Development in this direction was at first slow. The Israelites lacked the technological knowledge to enable any one leader to have the military force necessary for a strong central government. This lack is clearly reflected in the stories of victories in Judges. These stress, not formal battlefield tactics, but raids by small bands of brave men, individual acts of prowess, and assassination. The final phases in the development of a centralized government would come quickly only a short time later, under Saul, David, and Solomon.

Religious Outlook

The religious concepts and practices of the Israelites during the period of the judges were extremely diverse and frequently linked with the Canaanite religion. There is ample evidence of the survival of primitive concepts of reverence for trees, stones, wooden pillars, and idols. There were also crude prebattle rites involving magical ceremonies, the reading of signs, and human sacrifice. But this is only a relatively minor aspect of Israelite religion.

Canaanite religious texts of the fourteenth century found at Ras Shamra in northern Syria have shown that the Canaanite religion as it was practiced in major cultic centers was remarkably advanced at the time the Israelites settled in Palestine. Using a developed poetic style Canaanite thinkers set forth in their myths an elaborate attempt to understand the world which they knew. They were far from the heights of religious insight which would characterize Israelite religion in its classical form. Nevertheless they had reached a level that enabled them to make definite contributions to the religious quest of Israel.

Amid their cluster of ancient deities such as El, Anath, and Dagon these Canaanite thinkers were already stressing a god whom they called by the title of Baal, i.e. "Lord." They proclaimed Baal's dominance over his fellow gods and his beneficence to the earth as he gave fertilizing rain and acted as "king and judge" in the universe. Already they tended to identify the one diety Baal with a host of old local deities—for example, El-berith (i.e. "El-covenant"), the god of covenanting at Shechem (cf. 8:33; 9:4, 46).

It is not surprising that the Israelites could recognize in such a deity their own God, Yahweh—who for example was also a god of covenanting. Nor is it surprising that they could take names such as Jerubbaal without sensing any incongruity. The early traditions in judges thus do not bear out the D editor's idea that the worship of Baal and the worship of Yahweh were completely different things at this time.

Indeed, it was to be several centuries before the worship of Yahweh had become sufficiently unique that a total distinction between the two religions was possible. The extent of this process of differentiation by the end of the period of the judges can best be seen in the Song of Deborah. Though this is heavily Canaanite in some ways, it shows a theological sensitiveness unparalleled elsewhere in Judges.

This suggests the broader significance of Judges. The contemporary value of the book hardly lies in the moral example which the judges set. These heroes on occasion display such vices as lying, cruelty, murder, hatred, and sexual immorality. It is certainly not convincing to try to turn these vices into virtues—as interpreters have sometimes tried to do by praising Jael's bravery, Samson's vigor, and Jephthah's devotion to God.

The D editor attempts to find lasting value in the stories by depicting the sole issue as one of apostasy versus obedience to Yahweh. But his explanation does not do justice to the early traditions themselves. What Judges does show is the Israelites at an early stage of their search which was to continue throughout the whole of Old Testament times. It is to the lasting credit of the editors of Judges that they did not expunge or rewrite the stories of Israel's first uncertain steps in this process of religious discovery.

I. PROLOGUE (1:1–3:6)

A. SUMMARY OF THE CONQUEST (1:1–2:5)

This section is the survey of the Israelite conquest of Palestine with which a postexilic editor has prefaced the D edition of Judges (see Introduction). The material which the late editor used is quite old and resembles parts of Joshua. Actually it is a compilation of traditions from various early sources not identical with those in Joshua.

The passage agrees with Joshua in admitting that large areas of Palestine were not taken by Israel during this period, but it shows no acquaintance with the D idea that the conquest was accomplished by a united army of Israel. Rather, it stresses that the tribes settled individually in their respective areas. Because it offers this independent picture the passage has great value. It cannot, however, be uncritically accepted as necessarily the most accurate record of the conquest in every detail. Some portions of it seem to be less primitive than the corresponding materials in Joshua.

1:1-21. *Conquests by Judah.* The editor seems to assume that Israel is still camped at Gilgal in the Jordan Valley (cf. 2:1; Joshua 4:19; 10:43; 14:6) and that the territorial allotment has already been made (cf. Joshua 13–21). Of these matters the earlier traditions probably knew nothing. He also assumes that there was a second kind of allotment which determined the sequence in which the tribes would conquer their assigned regions. That Judah goes first shows the editor's presupposition that Judah was the preeminent tribe, as does the undue proportion of space given to the stories of Judah's conquests. The tendency of Hebrew storytellers to personify tribes as individual persons can be seen vividly in these stories connected with Judah.

1:5-7. This short account of the defeat of **Adonibezek** is reminiscent of the story of Adoni-zedek of Jerusalem in Joshua 10. Verse 7 hints that Adoni-bezek may have been king of **Jerusalem** rather than of **Bezek.** Many interpreters have concluded that "Adoni-bezek of Bezek" was originally "Adoni-zedek of Jerusalem" and that the two stories stem from a single event. Cutting off the **thumbs** and **great toes** was apparently intended to render the king unfit as a military leader, and perhaps as a religious leader as well (cf. Leviticus 21:16-23). More broadly it was an act of humiliation. Adoni-bezek's plaintive statement in verse 7 indicates that such barbarity was not uncommon, and that it reduced conquered kings to a life no better than that of dogs who ate **scraps** dropped from the king's table. **Seventy** is a round number, used especially often in connection with noblemen.

1:8-9. Verse 8, which tells of Judah's conquest of Jerusalem, appears to be a later addition to the account. It cannot easily be reconciled with verse 21 and 19:10-12 (see comment on Joshua 15:63). The **Negeb** is the arid region to the south of Palestine.

1:10-15. This account duplicates, with variations, Joshua 14:6-15 and 15:13-19 (see comments). It is concerned in part to explain the ownership of important sources of water in arid southern Palestine.

1:16-18. Here Hobab, **Moses' father-in-law** (cf. Numbers 10:29), is called a **Kenite** instead of a Midianite. **The city of palms** is usually taken to be Jericho (cf. 3:13). However, it was apparently a city in the south and may reflect a tradition that elements of Judah invaded Canaan from the south. Only one city, **Zephath,** is said to have been put under the sacred ban of total destruction (the meaning of **Hormah**). This is in contrast to the numerous cities which the D editor of Joshua supposes were so destroyed. Verse 18 is generally regarded as a late addition, inasmuch as the Philistine cities of **Gaza** . . . **Ashkelon** . . . **Ekron** remained

47

outside Israelite control throughout this period. The D editor realizes this (3:3; cf. Joshua 13:3). The Septuagint resolves this difficulty by reading "did not take" instead of **took**.

1:19-21. On verse 19 see comment on Joshua 17:14-18. On verse 20 see above on verses 10-15. On verse 21 see comment on Joshua 15:63.

1:22-36. *Conquests by Other Tribes.* The conquest of **Bethel** is by the **house of Joseph,** a term used in old traditions in Joshua 16:1-3 and 17:14-18. Usually the two Joseph tribes are treated separately as Ephraim and Manasseh. It is not certain which of the forms is the earlier. With its reference to **spies** the story is similar to that of the reconnaissance of Jericho in Joshua 2. The entrance into the city which the spies are looking for may have been a secret water tunnel from the city to the spring (cf. II Samuel 5:8). Verse 26 seems to allude to a fuller tradition which is now lost. No one knows where **Luz** was, but a south Syrian site is implied by the reference to the **land of the Hittites.** This story may be connected with the account of the capture of Ai (Joshua 7:1–8:29), especially since it is possible that Bethel was originally called Ai.

1:27-36. This unit deals almost entirely with those peoples whom the Israelites did not conquer. Its origin seems to differ from verses 22-26, since it treats **Manasseh** and **Ephraim** as separate tribes. The Transjordanian tribes of Reuben and Gad are not mentioned in the list, nor are Issachar, Benjamin, and Levi. As a tribe of priests, however, Levi was never thought to have a territory (but cf. Joshua 21). No battles are mentioned, a fact which implies a largely peaceful settlement in the areas named.

Only Dan gets special notice as unable to dominate a territory. The **Amorites** mentioned appear to be Canaanites. Eventually the Danites migrated to northern Palestine. Verse 36 concerns the region south of the Dead Sea and is not related to verses 34-35. That the Canaanites were put to **forced labor** for Israel, as verses 27-36 several times say, was probably not true until the time of David and Solomon.

2:1-5. *Significance of the Incomplete Conquest.* In verses 1a and 5*b* the editor borrows an old tradition which told of the transfer of the Israelite sanctuary from **Gilgal** to Bethel—here called **Bochim.** Here he explains the meaning of the survey of the conquest which he has given in chapter 1. Speaking through an angelic intermediary Yahweh declares that because the Israelites have allowed the Canaanites to live peacefully among them rather than exterminating them (cf. Exodus 23:31-33) Yahweh will not give Israel complete possession of the Promised Land. The editor links the name Bochim ("weepers") with the weeping of Israel over its plight.

B. The D Introduction (2:6–3:6)

2:6-10. *The Last Years and Death of Joshua.* This material comes from an old tradition which interpreters have often associated with E. It appears to have been used by the D editor as a transition from the narrative in Joshua to the editorial preface to the stories of the judges. The content is almost identical with Joshua 24:28-31. If the D edition of Joshua ended with Joshua 23, this passage dealing with the death of Joshua served to link it to the D edition of Judges.

2:11–3:6. *State of Affairs After Joshua's Death.* Drawing on earlier materials, the D editors offer three interpretations of Israel's troubles following Joshua's death. These are now interwoven into a single text. That Israel was beset with threats to its peace is assumed throughout. But the explanation of what the affliction was, why it occurred, and how Israel responded differ.

(1) The simplest explanation, probably taken from a very early source, suggests that Yahweh allowed Israel to be oppressed in order to teach the people the art of warfare (3:2).

(2) A more elaborate view sees Israel as falling into the worship of Canaanite gods (2:13) and Yahweh as consequently giving Israel **over to plunderers** (2:14*a*). But this produces no effect on the people, who refuse to respond to **judges** whom Yahweh raises up. Yahweh then declares that Israel's enemies

will not be driven out from the land (2:20-21) but will be left to **test Israel** (2:22).

(3) The most typically D view sees Israel turning to the **gods** of neighboring peoples (2:12) and Yahweh handing Israel over to these nations for punishment (2:14*b*-15). Israel then repents and obeys for a time **judges** whom Yahweh sends to rescue them (2:18), but they back into apostasy after each judge's death (2:19). This third view recurs several times in Judges (especially 3:7-11, 12-14; 4:1-3; 10:6-16). As in Joshua the D editor's attack on apostasy reflects his interest in showing the lasting relevance of the events in Israel's history.

II. ISRAEL'S DELIVERANCE BY THE JUDGES (3:7–16:31)

A. OTHNIEL (3:7-11)

In contrast to the accounts which follow, the first story of a judge is cast in D form. The D editor's reason for introducing this story is not clear. Some interpreters have suggested that he wished to show that the first judge was from Judah. If so, he was unable to find a strong figure. Othniel was from the Caleb clan (cf. 1:13), a group only loosely associated with Judah. Behind the highly stylized D wording of the story may lie the memory of an actual judge. The editor has preserved only his name and the name of his opponent, **Cushan-rishathaim king of Mesopotamia.** This king is an unknown figure, and there is little likelihood that any invasion of Palestine from Mesopotamia occurred at this time. The most plausible explanation for this difficulty is that Cushan was a desert tribe from the southeast which foraged into southern Palestine and was repulsed by the Caleb clan.

B. EHUD (3:12-30)

Verses 12-13 are a D introduction to the story of Ehud. **The city of palms** seems to be Jericho, the city west of the Jordan closest to **Moab.** Apparently the D editor believed that the city was taken by the Moabites, but there is no archaeological evidence that Jericho was inhabited at this time. Presumably the original setting was some other city in the lower Jordan Valley, probably east of the river, where the Moabites had established headquarters. That **Ammonites** and **Amalekites** joined Moab in oppressing Israel is not suggested in the older tradition which follows. Verse 14 is the work of the pre-D compiler of the stories of the judges (see comment on Joshua 24:32-33).

3:15-25. *The Assassination of Eglon.* This story has been drawn from two slightly differing acounts, but the tradition is essentially the same. **Eglon the king of Moab** is exacting tribute from Israel—or, probably more accurately, from the tribes of Reuben and Gad in Transjordan and Benjamin just across the Jordan from them. Already established by the thirteenth century, Moab had become a strong little nation which for the next several centuries was to live in tension with Israel. Israel was sometimes the oppressor of Moab very much as Moab is here shown as Israel's oppressor. Israel's **tribute** would consist largely of produce—oil, wine, hides, and wool—carried in by porters (verse 18).

Ehud, who is a **Benjaminite,** supervises the delivery of the tribute. Being **left-handed** (cf. 20:16; I Chronicles 12:2) he is able to hide a **sword** under his robe by fastening it to his **right thigh,** where a weapon would be unexpected. **Cubit** here translates *gomed,* a word not found elsewhere. Since the sword was probably shorter than a cubit, which was originally the distance from elbow to fingertips, a gomed may have been from elbow to knuckles, about thirteen and a half inches.

3:19-25. Ehud ostensibly sets out for home and reaches the **sculptured stones near Gilgal** (cf. Joshua 4). He returns on the pretext of having a divine message for Eglon—perhaps one allegedly received at the shrine at Gilgal—and slays the king with his concealed sword. This takes place on the **roof** of the house, where there is a room with a veranda. As he flees, Ehud pulls the latch string on the outside of the **doors of the roof**

chamber, thus drawing shut a wooden bolt on the inside. In order to enter, the king's **servants** have to use a **key** which pushes back the bolt.

3:26-30. *The Defeat of Moab.* Ehud hastens to gather an army **in the hill country of Ephraim.** This may be simply a geographical name for the central highlands where he rallies his own Benjaminite tribesmen. Or it may mean that he secures the help of the Ephraimites adjoining them on the north. Under Ehud's leadership they blockade the Jordan to cut off any retreat of the Moabite forces occupying Benjaminite territory and proceed to kill them all. The pre-D compiler's addition in verse 30 assumes that this victory freed all Israel from Moabite domination. There is no evidence that Ehud's leadership continued after the battle.

C. SHAMGAR (3:31)

This allusion is tantalizingly brief. Like Ehud, **Shamgar** is remembered for his unusual method of exterminating Israel's enemies. That the enemy are **Philistines** seems to place the episode relatively late in the period of the judges, when this people had become a major threat to Israel. This element may account for the fact that the Septuagint places this verse at the end of the Samson stories in 16:31. It will be noted that Samson also battles Philistines, and slays them with a similarly improvised weapon (15:15-17). On the other hand, since 5:6 places Shamgar before Deborah, the name **Philistines** may be a later addition or alteration.

If Shamgar was indeed a hero of Israel, a fuller story of his dramatic deed probably once existed. Some interpreters, however, have doubted that Shamgar was an Israelite. His name does not seem to be Semitic. Indeed it has been suggested that he was one of Israel's oppressors or a Canaanite warrior hero (cf. 5:6). The name of his father, **Anath,** is unusual in that it is the name of a Canaanite goddess mentioned often in the Ugaritic texts from Ras Shamra in northern Syria. Possibly the name was originally Shamgar of Beth-anath (cf. 1:33 and Joshua 19:38).

All in all, the passage seems rather contrived. Its lateness is indicated by the fact that the customary statement of the pre-D editor about the length of the judge's reign is lacking. The verse came into its present position after the major editions of Judges were completed; 4:1 shows no knowledge of it but builds directly on 3:30. No doubt it was placed just before the story of Deborah because of the reference to Shamgar in 5:6.

D. DEBORAH AND BARAK (4:1–5:31)

4:1-24. *The Prose Account.* Verses 1-3 are a D transition of the familiar sort (cf. 3:12-14). The account in this chapter appears to be a composite of two originally separate stories. One account may have dealt with Jabin, king of Hazor in the far north of Palestine. It involved Heber the Kenite, the city of Kedesh, and the tribes of Zebulun and Naphtali. The other perhaps concerned Sisera, king of Harosheth-ha-goiim in the valley of the Kishon. This involved Deborah, Barak, Jael, Mt. Tabor, and Issachar. The Jabin tradition, the less prominent of the two, appears to be related to the account of Jabin of Hazor in Joshua 11:1-15. Jabin was apparently so noted a foe that his name became legendary in Israel. In the process of conflation Jabin has become **king of Canaan** and Sisera has become his general.

In addition to this combination of traditions the story has also undergone expansion, especially in the role of Deborah. She was probably represented in the earliest tradition only as a prophetess whose favorable oracles aroused Barak to go into battle (cf. the role of Samuel). Deborah's tribal connections are obscure. Verse 5 associates her with the **palm of Deborah,** located in the territory of either **Ephraim** or Benjamin (see above on 3:26-30). Possibly she is confused with Rebekah's nurse Deborah, who was buried under an oak near **Bethel** (Genesis 35:8). 5:15 suggests that she was of the tribe of Issachar.

4:6-16. Because of the combination of the two stories the

53

details of the battle are not entirely clear. It seems that the Sisera tradition told of an encounter in the valley of the Kishon, not far from Sisera's city of Harosheth-ha-goiim. Since this region was still in Canaanite hands, it appears that Sisera was defending his territory from an Israelite attack.

Barak gathers his army on **Mount Tabor**—perhaps, it has been suggested, for prebattle religious rites. He then marches into the valley, where he is at a disadvantage since Sisera's **chariots** operate most effectively on the plain. The description of the battle in verse 15 is almost entirely lacking in detail but implies that Barak's soldiers win their victory by combat. The enemy flee to Harosheth-ha-goiim. The statement that Sisera **fled away on foot** may be a conventional way of indicating the king's utter defeat, for it occurs in other ancient Near Eastern texts. The Israelites do not attack the city itself.

4:17-22. The framework of the account of Sisera's flight **to the tent of . . . the wife of Heber the Kenite** and his assassination may come from the Jabin tradition, since it is set near Kedesh (verse 11), some forty miles northeast of the site of the battle. If so, this part of the tradition may originally have belonged at the end of the Jabin story in Joshua (Joshua 11:9-15). The details of Jael's slaughter (see below on 5:24-27) are presumably taken from the Sisera tradition. However, the material has been so interwoven with the Jabin tradition that the two stories cannot be entirely disentangled.

5:1-31. *The Song of Deborah.* This is the only deliverance story in Judges which is told in poetry. The poem is archaic in form and diction. Possibly this was intended even at the time of its composition in the eleventh or twelfth century. It is certainly one of the most magnificent works of art in the Old Testament. Its text, however, is full of obscurities, partly because of its archaic vocabulary and partly because of alterations which seem to have crept in as it was transmitted.

Virtually all interpreters regard the poem as a spontaneous, natural outburst by an eyewitness of the battle. Actually it is highly stylized and contains almost no specific information. Features of both the Jabin and the Sisera traditions can be seen in it (see above on 4:1-24). These appear in a manner which suggests that the traditions were combined before the composition of the poem, which thus may date from two or three generations after the battle. It was probably composed by professional musicians in the service of one of the major Israelite sanctuaries in northern Palestine. Their craft had been evolving for centuries—perhaps originally under the influence of Egyptian musicians in the courts of Canaanite kings.

The song is built around a complex standard pattern. This consists of the interwoven theological motifs of the glory of Yahweh, the Sinai experience, the conquest of Canaan, and the worship of Yahweh. This pattern is seen most clearly in Psalm 68, a psalm adapted for the Jerusalem sanctuary from older traditions of premonarchic times. If one may judge from other passages, the reputation of a poet was based on his brilliance in expanding this pattern with historical or pseudohistorical details—that is, historicizing the material.

One can see this clearly in Exodus 15:1-18, where the theme is that of the Exodus. In contrast the Song of Deborah has been historicized with imaginary details pertaining to a battle of Israel with the kings of Canaan. This subject continually slips into the more general interest in the conquest of Canaan as a whole. In his historicizing of the standard pattern the poet has not bothered to arrange all of his events in a fully natural sequence, much to the confusion of generations of scholars.

5:1-3. The prose ascription to **Deborah and Barak** in verse 1 did not originally belong to the poem, as shown by the allusions to these heroes in the second and third persons (verses 7, 12, 15). Verse 2c indicates the hymnic nature of the poem at the outset (cf. Psalm 68:26a, 35d). Verse 3 is a solemn rhetorical address to the rulers of the world, not to Israel's nobility. They are warned to learn from the song—and not to interfere with Israel lest they suffer the same fate as the opponents described in verses 19-21. Ancient Near Eastern rulers sometimes used similar expressions in the opening lines of monumental inscriptions which they set up for passers-by to see. Verse 3b-d is reminiscent of Psalm 68:4ab.

5:4-5. These verses are a solemn hymn of praise similar to Psalm 68:7-8. The allusion is not only to God as a storm deity but to the army of God (Israel) as well, which appears like raindrops. The poet has partially historicized this theological affirmation about God by suggesting the march of Israel through the wilderness before the settlement in Palestine. **Yon Sinai** in verse 5*b* should read "the One of Sinai" and be placed with the first half of the couplet.

5:6-11. Verses 6-9*b* are especially difficult to interpret because the text seems to have been altered. The poet attempts to introduce a historical prologue to the coming battle, but he deals chiefly in generalities. The names which he introduces only confuse the passage. On **Shamgar** as a judge see above on 3:31. In verse 9*c* a hymnic quality reappears, which continues in verses 10-11*c*. Riders, marchers, and musicians seem to be in a great procession (cf. Psalm 68:24-25), celebrating not so much a particular battle as the conquest of Palestine in general. The Revised Standard Version translation of verse 11 makes the best of an obscure passage. But the allusion actually seems to be to the antiphonal singing of **musicians** which rings out loudly and clearly in the procession, not at the **watering places** themselves. Verse 11*d* anticipates verse 13.

5:12. This verse seems to be out of sequence if the song is taken as a historical reminiscence. It appears to reflect the motif "Let God arise, let his enemies be scattered," which finds expression in Psalm 68:1. This motif also implies the exodus tradition (cf. Numbers 10:35).

5:13-18. These verses are reminiscent of Psalm 68:24-27. The setting there is that of a cult procession in which representatives of the tribes of Israel march in fixed order with **Benjamin** in the lead. Allusions to the coming battle are almost entirely lacking. In historicizing the description the poet seems to have in mind, not any particular battle, but the conquest of Palestine as a whole.

The tribes of Transjordan and the far north of Palestine are reproached for not participating. These are the ones which had a minor role in the conquest traditions. In its enumeration of those tribes to be praised and those to be castigated, the list is almost identical with the list of tribes for blessing and cursing given in Deuteronomy 27:12-13. The southern tribes, which do not figure in the Song of Deborah, are omitted, and verse 18 of the song is taken as an addition. **Machir** in verse 14 is the tribe of Manasseh. **Deborah** and **Barak** are awkwardly brought into verse 15*ab*, but the reference may preserve a genuine tradition that these heroes were from the tribe of **Issachar**; cf. 4:6, 10, which show only Naphtali and Zebulun going into battle. Verse 16*a* has an interesting parallel in Psalm 68:12*b*-13*a*. Verse 18 may have been introduced under the influence of 4:6, 10.

5:19-22. These verses are a historicizing of the motif which appears in Psalm 68:11-14 (cf. Exodus 15:1, 4-10). The poet has little information to draw on—perhaps none at all except the knowledge of the general locale of the battle. He is probably thinking of the whole conquest of Palestine, as the reference to the enemy as **the kings of Canaan** suggests. The region between **Taanach** and **Megiddo** had probably been celebrated as the scene of a great battle ever since Thutmose III of Egypt won a notable victory there centuries earlier. The allusion to **spoils** was a standard element in such songs (cf. Psalm 68:12*b*-13 and Exodus 15:9).

The description of the **stars** fighting **against Sisera** cannot be regarded as anything other than a poetic generalization indicating the hopelessness of the enemy's cause (cf. Joshua 10:12). Interpreters have usually taken the reference to the **torrent Kishon** sweeping away the enemy to be an allusion to a sudden flooding of the river near Megiddo. However, this should probably be understood as a figurative statement based on the theological motif of the destruction of Israel's enemies by God, a concept found most prominently in the traditions of the Exodus. It is related to the theme of God's coming with a flood of water (verse 4). The prose account of the battle knows of no such miraculous occurrence. Verses 21*c* and 22 are obscure both in content and in their position in the narrative.

5:23. The cursing of **Meroz** is an unexpectedly specific allusion. Unfortunately the original significance of this is unknown. The motif seems to be related to the enumeration of the tribes in verses 13-18. Cf. the curses implied against certain tribes in Deuteronomy 27:13.

5:24-27. Here the poet is exercising his—or her—skill to the fullest. The inspiration for this hypnotically repetitious stanza is probably that which finds expression in Psalm 68:21: "God will shatter the heads of his enemies, the hairy crown of him who walks in his guilty ways." The poet contributes essentially no information that is not in the prose account. His contribution is in the dramatic telling of the episode.

5:26-27. Jael improvises a murder weapon from bedouin equipment. Verse 26 seems to say that she grasped a **tent peg** in her left **hand** and a **mallet** for driving the peg in her **right** and so **pierced his temple**—as indeed the prose account describes (4:21). But here Sisera is apparently standing rather than lying asleep. On the other hand the word translated "mallet" is less precise than the English suggests, and the word translated "tent peg" might possibly be an editorial harmonization with 4:21. In poetic parallelism the two words could well be intended as synonyms for only one weapon. Similarly, **pierced** is evidently a synonymous parallel to **crushed.** On this basis the meaning seems to be that Jael used a single object as a club to strike the death blow. Most scholars have assumed this latter meaning. But it is possible that both the poet and the author of 4:21 were trying to interpret a tradition that Jael killed Sisera by driving a tent peg into his head.

5:28-30. The scene of women awaiting **spoil** is likewise a historicization of a familiar motif, one which appears in Psalm 68:12*b*-13 and Exodus 15:9. A simpler statement of the same theme has already appeared in verse 19*c*. The artificiality of the scene is evident. No Hebrew would have been present to witness the scene. Also, the mother's expectation of maidens and splendid garments would be appropriate if Sisera had been besieging a city but not amid the Israelite army.

5:31. This verse, taken by some scholars as a late addition, may be as old as the rest of the song (cf. Psalm 68:2-3, 35*c*; Deuteronomy 33:29).

E. GIDEON (6:1–8:35)

The story of **Gideon** is based on two or more old traditions. At least one of these seems to have concerned a warrior named **Jerubbaal** (6:32; 7:1; 8:29, 35; chapter 9), who was later identified with Gideon. The hand of the D editor can be seen only in 6:1 and perhaps in 8:33-35. Israel's new enemy is the **Midianites,** a nomadic or semi-nomadic people from the desert region southeast of Palestine who do not appear elsewhere in Judges.

6:1-10. *Midian's Oppression of Israel.* Verses 2-5 describe the Midianites' raids into the hill country of Palestine. The comparison of the invaders' army to **locusts** is an ancient one. 8:18-19 suggests some kind of feud between Gideon and the leaders of Midian, but of that nothing is said here. The **Amalekites and the people of the East** seem to be Transjordanians. Verses 8-10, apparently an addition to the story, contain the only reference to a **prophet** in Joshua and Judges. This fact does not necessarily mean that prophets were unknown in the period of the judges. The prophet's speech, which is a polished summary of God's salvation of Israel in the exodus and conquest, holds out no hope for the wayward Israelites.

6:11-24. *The Call of Gideon.* Gideon, of the tribe of Manasseh, is—like other early Israelites—a farmer by occupation and a soldier on occasion. Unable to thresh **wheat** openly, lest the dust cloud draw a raid from the Midianites, he beats out his grain by hand in the narrow rock-cut **wine press** in the floor of his father's house.

Gideon's divine call, which has similarities to the story of Samson's birth (chapter 13), seems to have been handed down in two traditions, one in verses 11-24 and another in verses 25-32. As Moses, prophets, and newly chosen kings often do, Gideon protests his inadequacy when the **angel** of Yahweh summons him to lead Israel. The authenticity of the divine revelation is attested by a **sign** not unlike that given to Moses (Exodus 3:2-5). Mingled with the motif of divine sign is that of hospitality which one offers to a guest and that of a ceremonial offering (verses 18,

20-24). The idea that seeing Yahweh was fatal appears several times in the Old Testament.

6:25-32. *Gideon's Attack on the Baal Cult.* This story shows Gideon acting much as a fiery prophet, but not yet as a military leader. The scene may be regarded as a variant tradition of the divine call of Gideon. The story presupposes that Gideon's family worships the Canaanite god **Baal,** for whom there was a household **altar** and an **Asherah** (a sacred wooden pole of some sort). Like the first account of Gideon's call, this episode shows Gideon erecting an **altar** to Yahweh (cf. verse 24). The use of a **bull,** the symbol of Baal, to destroy Baal's altar would strike the ancient hearer of the story as humorous and ironical.

The point of the story may be the idea that Gideon cannot hope to deliver Israel from its enemies unless the worship of foreign gods is purged from his clan. The story also serves to explain the reason Gideon was also known by the name **Jerubbaal.** The name actually means "Baal contends" or perhaps "establishment of Baal," and is clearly Canaanite in origin. The passage appears to be a harmonistic one which explains why Gideon had two names.

6:33–7:18. *Gideon's Preparations for Battle.* Manasseh's enemies approach and camp in the Valley of **Jezreel,** which slopes eastward toward the Jordan Valley. The reference to participation by the tribes of **Asher, Zubulun, and Naphtali** may not be original to the text. Gideon becomes divinely inspired (verse 34). He performs four acts of preparation for battle: he obtains an oracle, he selects his men, he scouts the enemy's camp, and he arms his men for the battle.

6:36-40. Gideon seeks to know if he has divine approval for the coming battle. Oracles before battles were commonplace. The use of **fleece** to obtain such prebattle oracles may have been an accepted practice. The first oracle is inconclusive, since fleece might well collect **dew** even if the **ground** appeared **dry.** The second oracle, in which the fleece is dry while the ground is wet, is regarded as conclusive proof that the outcome of the battle will be favorable to Gideon. There is no need to suppose that the story intends to describe a new call of Gideon.

7:1-8. Verse 1 uses the name **Jerubbaal** in a way which suggests that the story of the battle with Midian may have originally been told about that hero rather than Gideon. The second stage of preparation appears in verses 2-8, where Gideon selects a small band of men to participate in a daring ruse. The principle of selection has long puzzled readers, in part because the text of verses 5-6 has probably been expanded by an editor. The basic idea seems to be that Gideon chooses those who lap water like dogs—that is, those who are so reckless that they do not bother to keep a watchful eye as they drink. Possibly there is also an undertone of sympathetic magic here—lapping water like dogs being symbolic of the men's lapping the blood of their enemies as dogs would do. This stress on daring and viciousness well accords with the act which the soldiers will be asked to perform. Verse 8 seems to want to explain how the **three hundred men** got enough **jars** and **trumpets** to make the stratagem possible. They collected those items from the larger group of 32,000 men of the original fighting force.

7:9-14. The account of a **dream** which Gideon overhears during his reconnaissance is the sort of story which a commander sould gladly report to his troops to stir them up for the coming battle. This daring foray into the Midianite camp reminds one of stories told of heroes such as Jonathan (I Samuel 14:1-15) and David (I Samuel 26:6-12).

7:15-18. Gideon rouses his men and gives them their unusual weapons of **trumpets** and **torches** in **jars**.

7:19-23. *The Battle.* Creeping up to the Midianites' tents an hour or two before midnight, Gideon's soldiers create panic among the sleeping soldiers by blowing their rams' horns, breaking their jars, exposing their lighted torches, shouting, and charging about with drawn swords. Readers are likely to wonder how a soldier could possibly perform all these actions at once. The easiest solution is to suppose that two traditions of the attack have been interwoven, one of which spoke of horns and swords, the other of which knew only of jars, torches, and shouts.

Since Gideon's band was so small, the main purpose of the attack can hardly have been to kill the enemy. Presumably the original tradition understood that Gideon wished to chase the frightened enemy into the hands of a larger body of waiting troops. Verses 23-25 indeed suggest this, though the account is confused by the implied delay required for the new call to Naphtali, Asher, and Manasseh (cf. 6:35).

7:24—8:3. *Ephraim's Complaint.* This section apparently is from a separate tradition. Here it is the **men of Ephraim** who intercept the Midianites. Their irritation at not having been called earlier presupposes a covenant relationship between Ephraim and Manasseh which prohibited military action by only one of the tribes. The anger should therefore not be attributed simply to quarrelsomeness. Gideon's soothing words are a typical example of oriental diplomacy in which one flatters the offended person and deprecates oneself. The Midianite leaders **Oreb and Zeeb** appear only in 7:25 and 8:3.

8:4-21. *Gideon's Punishment of Offenders.* This passage comes from a different tradition from 7:24—8:3, with the result that Gideon seems to cross the **Jordan** a second time. It shows no knowledge of Ephraim's participation or of any troops other than Gideon's original **three hundred men.** Here the Midianite leaders, implausibly called **kings,** are **Zebah and Zalmunna.**

8:5-12. Pursuing the fleeing men, Gideon passes **Succoth** and **Penuel** on the east side of the Jordan. The elders of these cities refuse to supply provisions for Gideon's hungry men. Gideon continues his pursuit, successfully attacks the Midianite survivors and takes their leaders captive.

8:13-17. Returning to Succoth, Gideon plans punishment of the unfriendly cities. He accomplishes this with the aid of a learned **young man of Succoth,** who writes down the names of the city's leaders so that Gideon can later punish them. It is unlikely that the art of writing was widely known, if one may judge from this period in Palestine. But undoubtedly writing was used for commercial, governmental, and cultic records. Capturing Succoth, Gideon tortures its **elders** and ravages the city.

8:18-21. Gideon executes the captured Midianite leaders. He first asks his son to perform the act—as an honor to the son and a dishonor to the kings. When his son hesitates, he does the deed himself. According to this tradition Gideon goes to war to take vengeance on the Midianites for a specific act of aggression against his family (verses 18-19). Reference to blood vengeance of this kind can be found in Canaanite texts many centuries earlier. The **crescents** which Gideon takes from the slain kings' **camels** perhaps were amulets (cf. verse 26).

8:22-23. *Gideon's Rejection of Kingship.* These verses appear to be an editorial addition which prepare for the story of Abimelech in chapter 9. They tell briefly of the Israelites' wish to make Gideon **king** over them. Gideon refuses on the ground that Yahweh should rule. A similarly negative view of kingship is found in I Samuel 8 and 12.

8:24-28. *Gideon's Ephod.* Gideon collects a share of the jewelry of the defeated Midianites, who are here called **Ishmaelites.** As nomadic people the Midianites would carry a good deal of their wealth around with them. The **ephod** was a cult object used in obtaining oracles (see comment on I Samuel 14:2-3). The original story probably saw nothing wrong with Gideon's ephod, but the author of verse 27*b*, speaking from a later time, deplores the act. Like the Canaanite name Jerubbaal, the making of the ephod shows how different early Hebrew religion was from that of later times.

8:29-35. *Gideon's Later Life.* Gideon, or **Jerubbaal,** gives up his leadership of the army, which is presumably disbanded, and settles down at home. The number of sons attributed to him, **seventy,** is a round number especially popular in stories dealing with kings and nobles and may allude to Gideon's family as a whole. **Abimelech** is mentioned separately, perhaps in anticipation of the story in chapter 9. Verses 33-35 are an editorial transition to chapter 9—or perhaps they are the D editor's substitute for that chapter. The reference to **Baal-berith** in verse 33 is derived from the story which follows (see Introduction).

F. ABIMELECH (9:1-57)

These episodes show more clearly than perhaps any others in Judges the kind of activity in which some Israelite leaders were engaging during this period. **Abimelech** was an ambitious Israelite who apparently gained control of the countryside near the Canaanite city of **Shechem.** He maintained his headquarters in the insignificant town of **Arumah** and occasionally ventured out to conquer some vulnerable city in the region. His most audacious plan was to take over Shechem itself, which for centuries had been ruled by the dynasty of **Hamor.** This was not the first time Shechem had encountered Hebrews. As early as the fourteenth century the Habiru had been stirring up trouble in the vicinity, apparently less by battle than by persuasion and treachery (see Introduction to Joshua).

Like other Canaanite cities Shechem had lost much of its former vigor. The ruling house was so weak that Abimelech was apparently able to threaten, drive away, and kill its males to the point that none of them dared to occupy the throne. In his project he was aided by the report, true or false, that his mother was a Shechemite. Abimelech was proclaimed king by the elders of the city. He maintained his authority in spite of a rebellion by conservative elements which occurred a few years after he gained control. He finally met his end in an ignominious yet brave way at Thebez as he sought to put down a revolt there. Not without justification one interpreter has called Abimelech an early-day Macbeth.

Such, in brief, is the course of Abimelech's career as it can be reconstructed from the stories in this chapter. The stories themselves contain a number of obscurities, due in part to the storyteller's confusion about certain details and in part to the fact that at least two different traditions have been interwoven. Editors did not find Abimelech particularly commendable. The pre-D compiler regarded him as a wicked man (verses 1-5, 24, 56). The D editor may have omitted the account from his edition of Judges. The postexilic editor who reintroduced the story may have seen it as an example of the evils of kingship. The original story itself contained no suggestion that kingship, at least at Shechem, was evil or that Abimelech himself was acting wrongly.

9:1-21. *The Investiture of Abimelech at Shechem.* The pre-D compiler has greatly compressed the opening of the story. The details of Abimelech's rise to power at Shechem can no longer be fully understood. **Jerubbaal** (Gideon), Abimelech's father, was an Israelite. But the role which Jerubbaal and his **seventy . . . sons** play in verses 1-5 seems more appropriate as a description of what happened to the ruling dynasty of the sons of Hamor at Shechem. On **Baal-berith** see the Introduction. In any case, having been declared **king** by the **citizens of Shechem**, Abimelech goes to the sacred precinct in the city and is there invested with his new office (verse 6).

9:7-21. The storyteller presents Jotham's fable as a speech of the surviving son of Jerubbaal on hearing of the murder of his brothers. It is not unfavorable to Abimelech, but simply warns the Shechemites of their own duty to support Abimelech. Therefore, it is probably a speech originally thought to have been delivered by some prophet or priest at the ceremony of investiture.

The fable accurately describes the situation in which Shechem finds itself. Its ruling house (called **cedars of Lebanon**) cannot provide a man willing to rule—perhaps, one may suspect, because Abimelech has brought pressure to bear on them. A candidate of nonaristocratic birth (the **bramble**) is willing to be king. The point of the fable is that all will go well if the people serve Abimelech faithfully. Otherwise destruction will come upon them. The similarity of this idea to that in Samuel's speech at the investiture of Saul (I Samuel 12) is noteworthy. Verses 17-18 were not a part of the original story.

9:22-49. *The Revolt Against Abimelech.* Two traditions can be seen here. The first of these appears in verses 22-25, 42-45. The **men of Shechem** do indeed act **treacherously** toward Abimelech, without any apparent provocation on his part. (**Israel** in verse 22 should probably read "Shechem.") The outcome is that Abimelech ambushes the insurgents, slays them, and razes the city. Abimelech's sowing the city with salt is a graphic declaration that it should remain uninhabited. Archaeological evidence has thus far not supported this story, for there was no destruction of Shechem (modern Tell Balatah) during this period.

In the second account of the revolt, verses 26-41, 46-49, there is a great deal more specific detail. Here the rebellion is instigated by one **Gaal.** His appeal to the memory of the old ruling dynasty of **Hamor** suggests that he may have been one of that dynasty who had initially fled from Abimelech. As in the alternate tradition, Abimelech fights the insurgents outside Shechem and wins the battle.

Verse 41 is an intrusive editorial comment. The conclusion of the story seems to be found in verses 46-49, which tell of Abimelech's destruction of a large number of persons who have fled to city sanctuary for refuge (on **El-berith** see Introduction). Of the fate of the city as a whole the story says nothing. In every way this tradition seems to be the more historical of the two.

9:50-57. *Abimelech's Death at the Siege of Thebez.* The attack on the city of Thebez concludes the story of Abimelech. Like many another person in Judges, Abimelech meets his end in an unusual way. Struck by a **millstone** which a **woman** throws, he asks his **armor-bearer** to dispatch him lest he die disgracefully at the hands of a woman. Verses 55-57 are the work of one or more editors, who mistakenly suppose that Abimelech was supported by an army of men from all Israel.

G. Tola (10:1-2)

This is the first of two brief notices about otherwise unknown judges. Nothing is recorded about **Tola** except his ancestry, home, and length of judgeship. The family connections seem rather contrived. Genesis 46:13 names Tola and Puvah as sons of **Issachar** (cf. I Chronicles 7:1-2). Numbers 26:23 lists these persons as heads of clans.

H. JAIR (10:3-5)

Jair is a family name (cf. Numbers 32:41; Deuteronomy 3:14; I Kings 4:13) which appears here to have been individualized. Jair's **thirty sons** should perhaps be understood to be noblemen, not literally sons. The allusion to their **thirty asses** and **thirty cities** is stylized and is probably derived from an earlier tradition which spoke only of thirty cities. The implication is that Jair was overlord of a number of cities (or villages), each of which maintained its own government. Several Old Testament passages allude to the "cities of Jair," the number of which varies from twenty-three to sixty.

I. JEPHTHAH (10:6–12:7)

10:6-18. *An Editor's Transition.* This unusually long editorial statement anticipates the story of Jephthah. Like 2:11-23, which it resembles, the passage is largely D, though the editors use pre-D materials. Israel's enemies are now the Ammonites, dealt with in the following story, and the Philistines, who appear in the stories of Samson. The list of peoples from whom Yahweh has delivered Israel does not correspond to the enumeration of Israel's enemies in the stories of the judges. This indicates that the passage is not a summary of the contents of Judges. The **Maonites** were probably an Arab tribe living east of Edom. As usual, the editor presupposes that all Israel is involved in the oppression and deliverance rather than individual tribes.

10:17-18. This is a specific transition to the story of Jephthah. It seems to come from a different source from the rest of the passage (cf. verse 9). **Mizpah** is not the Benjaminite city but a cult center of uncertain location in northern Gilead.

11:1-11. *Jephthah's Rise to Leadership.* Jephthah has dubious family credentials. His father was an unknown Gileadite whom the storyteller calls simply Gilead and his mother was a prostitute. Rejected by his fellow tribesmen Jephthah turns to brigandry in the border region around **Tob.** He earns such a reputation as a leader that the **elders of Gilead** call on him as their deliverer when the **Ammonites** commence war against them.

11:9-11. Verse 11 alludes to an investiture of Jephthah in the sanctuary at **Mizpah** (see above on 10:17-18). The ceremony probably involved a covenant between Jephthah and the Gileadites in which each party agrees to certain conditions. The final words of the elders in verse 10 are similar to those used in the pledge between Jacob and Laban when they covenant at this same shrine (Genesis 31:49). It was customary to call on the deity to witness covenants and to punish any violators of the agreement.

11:12-28. *Jephthah's Futile Diplomatic Overtures.* Jephthah is acting as king in all but name. This section consists largely of a message he delivers to the Ammonites defending Israel's occupation of certain lands in Transjordan. It is clearly an editorial intrusion, for it speaks of all Israel rather than Gilead alone and of **Moab** more than Ammon. Jephthah's mild tone also contrasts with that in verses 29-33.

11:15-22. This historical summary is basically in agreement with Numbers 20–24. It shows how effectively Israelite archives could be utilized in international diplomacy. The message argues that the territory in dispute does not belong to either Ammon or Moab but is part of the former kingdom of **Sihon,** which the Israelites conquered under Moses. In style and content the passage seems to reflect conditions around 850, when King Mesha of Moab (see Introduction to Joshua) began to try to regain this territory. The land had belonged to Moab before Sihon took it (Numbers 21:26) and had been recaptured by the Moabites a time or two thereafter. It had been occupied by Israel at least since the time of David (cf. II Samuel 8:2). It is possible that we have here a transcript of a letter sent to Mesha by King Jehoram of Israel (cf. II Kings 3:4-7).

11:23-28. The Moabite god **Chemosh** is referred to as if he actually existed, and many interpreters have assumed that this represents Israelite thought of the time. However, if this passage is indeed a transcript of a letter sent to the king of Moab, it would necessarily be phrased in diplomatic language calculated to put the Israelite and Moabite gods on an equal plane.

Ostensibly **three hundred years** refers to the time between the conquest of the kingdom of Sihon and Jephthah's message, but the figure is too high to be historically accurate. It would be approximately correct as the time from Sihon to Mesha's day. The unusual reference to Yahweh as a **Judge** is an ancient expression which appears in Canaanite religious texts in connection with Baal.

11:29-40. *Jephthah's Sacrifice of His Daughter*. After the interruption of verses 12-28 the narrative takes up approximately where it was left off. Becoming divinely aroused for battle, Jephthah is willing to perform the most extreme of all prebattle rites—offering human sacrifice (see comment on Joshua 7). But Jephthah is also a shrewd man who does not wish to make his sacrifice in vain. He cleverly promises Yahweh a human offering only if he wins the battle. As yet a further safeguard Jephthah does not choose his victim in advance but agrees to sacrifice the first person who comes to meet him on his triumphal return home.

But Jephthah cannot cheat Yahweh. Having granted him victory, Yahweh arranges—one must suppose—that Jephthah is met by his virgin **daughter**. The storyteller heightens the pathos by presenting the girl as an **only child**. The whole episode, from Jephthah's attempt to cheat Yahweh to his final sad fulfilling of his vow, moves like a Greek tragedy. Indeed it has its parallel in the story of Agamemnon's sacrifice of his daughter Iphigenia.

It is evident that the story presupposes a primitive concept of what God demands of humans. One should not try to soften its hardness by emphasizing the fidelity with which Jephthah and his daughter carry out the grisly deed. One may legitimately point out, however, that the story is less a historical recollection than a moral tale teaching the futility of scheming against God.

It also seems to have served as a pseudohistorical explanation for the existence of ceremonially mourning—probably over the death of growing things which occurred each winter, here symbolized by the descent of a virgin to the realm of the dead (cf. the Greek myth of Persephone). Traces of a cult of this sort, sometimes involving a male who dies, can be found throughout the ancient Near Eastern and Mediterranean world. But this story lacks any allusion to the revivification of the slain person such as is presupposed in the ancient fertility myths.

12:1-7. *War Between Gilead and Ephraim.* This episode begins like 8:1-3. But because Jephthah makes no diplomatic overtures, the outcome is war between Gilead and Ephraim. Gilead is victor. Verse 4 is obscure but seems to allude to a covenant between the two tribes in which Gilead was the lesser party, forbidden to take unilateral military action. The Gileadites identify fleeing Ephraimites by their inability to pronounce "sh." Verse 7, which tells of Jephthah's death, is the compiler's conclusion to the Jephthah stories.

J. IBZAN (12:8-10)

This is the first of three brief notices concerning minor judges (cf. 10:1-5). **Thirty sons** is a conventional indication of the judge's importance. **Marriage** outside one's tribe or clan seems to have been a standard practice. Of Ibzan's acts of deliverance nothing is said. Since the stories in the basic collection in Judges concern only the northern tribes, some interpreters have suggested that **Bethlehem** here is not the well-known Judahite city but a locale in Zebulun. It is possible, however, that Bethlehem in Judah had an Ephraimite population, as the expression "Bethlehem Ephrathah" (i.e. "Ephraimite"; Ruth 4:11; Micah 5:2) seems to imply.

K. ELON (12:11-12)

All that one learns of this judge is that he was a **Zebulunite** whose home was in **Aijalon**—presumably an Aijalon other than that in central Palestine (1:35; Joshua 10:12). Possibly, however, the place name is not original to the account, since in Hebrew it is almost identical with the name Elon.

L. ABDON (12:13-15)

The author stresses the numerous sons and grandsons of this leader (cf. 8:30; 10:4; 12:9), a sign of his prominence in society. Abdon appears to have been an Ephraimite. The reference to **Amalekites** here is unusual. Elsewhere they are described as nomads ranging over an area south and southeast of Palestine. They are mentioned, however, as joining other groups in attacks on central Palestine from Transjordan (3:13; 6:3). Possibly on one of these occasions some of them settled in Ephraimite territory.

M. SAMSON (13:1–16:31)

The stories about Samson make up the most extensive cycle of traditions in Judges. They are heavily influenced by legendary, cultic, and folk elements. The result is that little or nothing can be said about Samson as a historical person. The Samson who does appear in these tales is a typical folk hero. He is a fascinating combination of roughness and gentleness, cleverness and naïveté, good-naturedness and irritability. Above all he has an extraordinary strength and passion for life.

The D editor evidently found little of interest in Samson. The pre-D compiler apparently did see a moral value to the stories and may be responsible for adding the account of Samson's birth. Samson is presented as a **Nazirite,** one who has made special vows to God. The reader will conclude that Samson failed to live according to his Nazirite calling when he contacted dead bodies, ate unclean food, drank wine, and allowed his hair to be cut—not to mention the times when he consorted with Israel's enemies, the Philistines. In the final story, in which the blind Samson pulls down the Philistine building, the compiler suggests that Samson finally was reconciled to God. His willingness to let the stories speak for themselves is notable, however.

The older materials which the compiler used may have originally circulated in poetic form. They show little or no concern with moral values, but there does seem to be a certain interest in old solar myths. Samson, whose very name seems to be related to the Hebrew word for "sun," appears suspiciously like a sun-god hero in several episodes. The extent to which one may legitimately discover this motif has long been debated by scholars.

What all scholars can agree on, however, is that these old stories contain a wealth of information about life in west-central Palestine during the period of the judges. Particularly valuable are the references to the Philistines, who are seen clearly for the first time as neighbors of the Israelites. The stories thus share much with the cycle of Samuel stories in I Samuel 1-12. Some of the Samson stories may have been influenced by Philistine traditions. In turn they may have influenced Philistine stories, which perhaps passed across the Mediterranean on Philistine ships to the Greeks. The legends about Hercules bear occasional resemblance to those about Samson.

13:1-25. *The Birth of Samson.* This chapter apparently belongs to the latest pre-D stage of the formation of the Samson cycle. It is prefaced by a D editor's formula in verse 1; thereafter no trace of D influence appears.

13:2-7. Samson's father, who is unnamed in chapter 14, is here called **Manoah.** He is of the tribe of Dan living in the town of **Zorah** on the western edge of the hill country. His unnamed wife, who is childless, prays for a **son.** The author probably supposes that the woman, like the childless Hannah not long afterward, goes to a sanctuary to make her petition (cf. I Samuel 1:9-18). An **angel** appears and directs her to rear her son as a **Nazirite,** one dedicated to an ascetic life (cf. Numbers 6). She herself must keep Nazirite purity until the child is born.

13:8-20. Manoah is also granted a vision of the angel. He offers the visitor the hospitality of a meal, but the food which he sets out is clearly an offering (cf. 6:19-24). The angel may originally have been thought of as a god, possibly even Yahweh himself. His name is so sacred that one dare not pronounce it (cf. verse 22). The angel's departure in the **flame** of the sacrifice has no close parallel elsewhere in the Old Testament.

13:21-25. The wife's reply to Manoah's expression of fear is refreshingly practical. In time she bears a son, Samson, who thrives under the Lord's blessing. As a transition to the story which follows, the storyteller adds an allusion to the divine power which begins to stir in Samson. This chapter, strongly influenced the infancy stories of John the Baptist and Jesus in Luke 1–2.

14:1–15:20. _Samson's Wife at Timnah._ These two chapters consist of a series of closely related stories which revolve around Samson's marriage to a Philistine woman.

14:1-4. Of marriageable age, Samson goes down the slopes a few miles to **Timnah**, which is apparently a Philistine city. The **Philistines** were a seafaring people who settled on the southern coast of Palestine around 1200. They are now living in close contact with the Hebrews to the east, over whom they exert both physical and cultural dominance. Samson does not hesitate to ask for a Philistine woman as a **wife**, but his parents hold the conservative view that he should marry among his own people. The storyteller justifies Samson's behavior on the ground that Yahweh put the idea into his mind for an ulterior purpose.

14:5-9. The story of Samson slaying the **lion** is suggestive of the ancient Near Eastern motif of a struggle between a hero-god and the lion as a sun symbol. It might also suggest Hercules' slaying of the Nemean lion. The lion image, however, was rather common. For example, the Canaanite god Baal was on occasion called a lion.

Samson's parents appear in this narrative rather awkwardly and should probably be removed from verse 5. The whole process of Samson's coming and going to Timnah is rather obscure, but much of the difficulty disappears if one regards this passage as originally having stood at the opening of the story.

Samson's eating **honey from the carcass of the lion** prepares for the episode which follows.

14:10-20. This passage tells of Samson's marriage. In good oriental style he entertains the party with a **riddle.** The seriousness with which the Philistines take the challenge indicates tension between the Israelites and the Philistines. When his bride eventually wheedles the answer to the riddle, Samson denounces the Philistines in a poetic couplet which is inapt but a not uncommon element of folk tales. Verse 20 prepares for the story which is to follow. The motif of the disloyal wife who cajoles a secret from her husband reappears in the story of Samson and Delilah (chapter 16).

15:1-8. Getting over his anger, Samson takes a gift and goes to Timnah **at the time of wheat harvest. . . to visit his wife.** Discovering that her father has given her to another (cf. 14:20), he plans revenge. He ties lighted **torches** to the **tails** of **foxes** and allows the distraught animals to run through the fields setting fire to the **grain.**

This episode has parallels elsewhere in the ancient world, particularly in a religious rite which the Romans annually performed. Behind such imagery, or perhaps reflecting it, may be the idea that the red-coated fox is a symbol of fire. The Greeks sometimes called the fox a "torch-tail." Such concepts and practices have suggested to some interpreters that this story is a historicized version of a harvest rite practiced among some of the ancient peoples of Palestine. The rite was perhaps connected with the concept of the sun as a scorching brand hurtling through the summer sky. Samson's deed sets off a fast-moving feud in which the Philistines retaliate by killing Samson's erstwhile wife and and her father. Samson returns the attack and then flees to the hills.

15:9-17. The Philistines seek Samson at the Judahite locality of **Lehi,** a few miles to the south. The men of Lehi find Samson and persuade him to let them hand him over to the Philistines. Brought to Lehi, Samson is seized by divine power, breaks his bonds, and slaughters the Philistines with a **fresh jawbone of an ass**. The bit of poetry in verse 16 may be a fragment of an older poem which perhaps alluded, not to an actual ass's jawbone, but to a curved sickle or scimitar resembling a large jawbone. Weapons were sometimes likened to objects in daily life.

15:18-20. In a further scene Samson, having grown **thirsty,** receives **water** from a rock which God splits open. Verse 20 is the compiler's summary of Samson's years as judge (cf. 16:31*b*).

16:1-3. *Samson at Gaza.* This brief story is not closely related to what precedes or follows. But, like the other episodes, it is built on one of Samson's amorous adventures. The story may be a historicized account of some now obscure cult rite or concept. Samson's picking up the **doors of the gates** of **Gaza** and carrying them some forty miles to the ridge of central Palestine may allude to the journey of the sun god as he daily breaches the gates of the underworld. Compare Samson's pulling down the two pillars in 16:23-30, an episode which is also said to occur at Gaza.

16:4-31. *Samson and Delilah.* Like the other episodes, Samson's third and fatal encounter with a woman involves the Philistines. His long hair attributed in 13:5 to his Nazirite vows, is here probably understood as the mark of a hero-warrior. There is a strong element of magic here. The story perhaps derived from a legend concerning the sun hero, whose fiery locks represented his strength. He was finally trapped when night (Hebrew *laylah;* cf. **Delilah**) wove his locks fast in a magic loom as he rested in the underworld, thus preventing him from rising. If this interpretation is correct—not all scholars would accept it—Delilah's third attempt to make Samson captive may be the one which originally succeeded. The fourth was added under the influence of the idea that Samson wore his hair long because he was a Nazirite.

The idea that Samson's strength was permanent and lay in his hair is at variance with the idea that he got his strength only on specific occasions by a divine infusion of power (14:6, 19; 15:14). The Philistines' blinding of Samson—suggestive of the idea of putting out the eye of the sun (cf. verse 28, whch speaks of one eye)—seems to imply a different idea as to how he could be rendered harmless.

The reference to the regrowth of Samson's **hair** seems to prepare for verses 28-30. There, however, the stress is on God's sending sudden power to Samson when he prays for it. Possibly this final story was the addition of the compiler, who wished to show that Samson was ultimately rehabilitated. Samson's seizing of the **two . . . pillars** is reminiscent of 16:3, also set at **Gaza.**

The god **Dagon** was a deity of grain. Dagon (or Dagan) is named a number of times in old Semitic texts. Verse 31 appears to be editorial (cf. 15:20).

III. SUPPLEMENTARY STORIES (17:1–21:25)

The stories in these chapters do not concern judges and are not included in the book's pattern of judgeships. But most of the materials seem to be as old as anything else in Judges. Chapters 17-18 and parts of chapters 19-21 may have been included in the pre-D edition of the book. Some interpreters believe that the D editor did not wish to use these materials and ended his edition with the Samson stories. If so, then a postexilic editor reintroduced this section, adding certain material of his own, especially 20:1–21:14.

The editorial statement that **in those days there was no king in Israel; every man did what was right in his own eyes** (17:6; 21:25; cf. 18:1; 19:1) seems to be a counterpart of the D formula that "whenever the judge died [Israel] turned back and behaved worse than their fathers, going after other gods" (2:19). The editor evidently felt that the deeds narrated in the stories were not commendable. Since they occurred during the times between judges, he apparently thought that the institution of kingship was a necessary stabilizing power in Israel. The statement appears only in connection with the earlier stories in these chapters. One may suppose that it is the work of the pre-D compiler, writing when the northern Israelite monarchy still existed, before 722.

A. THE ESTABLISHMENT OF THE DANITE CULT
(17:1–18:31)

17:1-13. *Micah and the Levite.* This story is based on two
differing accounts which an editor has interwoven—or,
according to some interpreters, a single account which has been
awkwardly expanded. It seems to serve chiefly as a background
for chapter 18. It is valuable, however, for its information about
religious practices in the period of the judges. One learns that at
least some families have household shrines at which the father,
or someone acting for him, officiates.

17:3-6. The **graven image** and **molten image** and the **ephod
and teraphim** all seem to be idols (cf. 8:24-27). It is possible that
the editor's comment in verse 6 implies disapproval of
household cults. But it is notable for its historical perspective;
he recognizes that customs have not always been as in his own
day.

17:7-13. A Levite from **Bethlehem** appears on the scene. This
man is a Judahite, which suggests that at this time **Levite**
denoted a profession rather than a tribe. Bethlehem may at this
time have been an Ephraimite settlement (see above on
12:8-10). Micah's concern to have a Levite as his priest suggests
that Levites were more skilled in cult matters than ordinary
persons.

18:1-31.*The Danites' Migration.* This story begins as though
it were a separate tradition. In any case it seems to consist of two
interwoven accounts. The Danites, an Israelite tribe which
lacked a well-defined territory of its own, were living crowded in
by Judah, Benjamin, Ephraim, and Philistia (cf. Joshua
19:40-48). The account tells how the Danites—or part of
them—migrated to the far north of Palestine. It forms a
concluding chapter in the story of the conquest of Palestine.

18:2-6. In an episode reminiscent of Numbers 13 the Danites
send out spies to locate a suitable land for conquest. Heading
north, the spies pass Micah's **house,** where they discover the
Levite and obtain a favorable oracle.

18:7-26. The Danites receive a good report from the spies and set out for the north. As they pass Micah's house they steal Micah's cult objects and the Levite who is his **priest.** Micah's cult objects and the Levite who is his **priest.** Micah pursues the Danites in vain, for their forces outnumber his.

18:27-31. Taking **Laish** by sudden assault the Danites settle, rename the city **Dan,** and establish a cult with the cult objects and the Levite. Verse 30, which names the Levite for the first time, is an editor's attempt to link the Danite cult with the mainstream of Hebraic cultic tradition. The reference to **the captivity of the land** suggests that the Danite cult continued until the Assyrian invasion of the region about 733. Verse 31 seems to be a different editorial conclusion. It is not known how long **the house of God was at Shiloh.** The allusion may be to the presumed destruction of Shiloh under the Philistines about 1050, to the centralization of the Hebrew religion at Jerusalem under David and Solomon—or just possibly to a destruction of Shiloh during the Assyrian invasion.

B. The War Between Israel and Benjamin (19:1–21:25)

19:1-30. *The Episode at Gibeah.* Here a new cycle of materials begins. To explain how the war between Benjamin and other Israelite tribes begins (chapter 20), the storyteller narrates how a **Levite** of **Ephraim** goes to Bethlehem for **his concubine** and on the way home stays overnight at the Benjaminite town of Gibeah. There he suffers a gross indignity which arouses first his anger and then that of all Israel.

19:10-15. Clearly **Jerusalem** was not yet under Israelite control. It is doubtful that the city was ever called **Jebus,** since extrabiblical texts of earlier centuries know only the name **Jerusalem.** The **open square** of Gibeah would be just inside the city's gate.

19:16-30. The details of the attempted assault by the men of Gibeah are reminiscent of the story of Lot at Sodom (Genesis 19); but the solution of the problem is unique. The Levite's anger does not arise out of compassion for his abused concubine, for whom he seems to show no personal concern. He is angered because his own dignity and property rights have been violated.

The distribution of **pieces** of the woman's body throughout Israel resembles Saul's distribution of the pieces of a yoke of oxen (I Samuel 11:5-7) It appears to be drawn from customs of covenanting (cf. Genesis 15:9-17). The implication is that the tribes of Israel must come to help the Levite take revenge, on penalty of suffering a fate like that of the dismembered woman. The earliest form of the story probably told only of a call to the men of Ephraim.

20:1-48. *Israel's Punishment of Benjamin.* This passage appears to be relatively late, since it shows Israel acting as a whole. It seems to be based on two earlier accounts of the same episode, traces of which appear from time to time. **From Dan to Beersheba** indicates the whole of Palestine. The tribes—except of course Benjamin—gather at **Mizpah** in Benjamin. Possibly an earlier version of the episode set the assembly at Bethel (cf. verse 18).

20:12-28. The Benjaminites stand solidly behind the offenders of Gibeah. Verse 16 speaks of the frequency of **left-handed** persons among them (cf. 3:15; I Chronicles 12:2) and their proficiency with the slingstone. The number of Israel's soldiers is vastly exaggerated. **Judah** receives the lot to go first (cf. 1:1-2 and Joshua 15), a convention which shows the southern background of the storyteller. When the men of Israel are defeated twice, they perform acts of penitence (verses 23, 26), and a divine oracle promises victory in the next battle. The parenthetical reference to the **ark** is a later addition; nowhere else in Judges is the ark mentioned.

20:29-48. Lured from the city in a maneuver reminiscent of that in Joshua 8, the **Benjaminites** see their city go up in **smoke.** Cut off, they are mostly slain. The details of this battle are not entirely clear. Some interpreters take verses 36*b*-44 as a separate and earlier version of the taking of Gibeah. Only **six hundred** Benjaminites escape, and the Israelites destroy **all the towns** of Benjamin. That such wholesale extermination of

Benjamin actually occurred is of course highly improbable. The idea is the work of the late editor who, long removed from the days of the judges, presents a highly stylized narrative.

21:1-25. *The Rehabilitation of Benjamin.* This chapter consists of two separate accounts. Both tell how the tribe of Benjamin survived after the near annihilation in chapter 20.

21:1-14. The first explanation, like chapter 20, is a late composition. It shows the tribes of Israel going to **Jabesh-gilead** in the Transjordanian territory of Gad and slaughtering every person in the city except **four hundred young virgins,** who become brides for a part of the surviving Benjaminites. Sparing virgins as spoil for warriors was not an unfamiliar practice. The account is highly artificial. Behind it may lie the remembrance that Jabesh-gilead, a city which had long had ties with Benjamin, was attacked as an ally of Gibeah.

21:15-25. These verses seem much nearer to old traditions, though they show late editorial influence. According to this account some of the Benjaminites got wives by capturing them at an annual vintage festival at **Shiloh.** The story hints that this practice was not entirely novel. Indeed it may be that during the period of the judges it was a regular practice for young men to choose partners from among the girls dancing at the festival—if not permanently at least for the duration of the celebration. Similar rites, known in many parts of the ancient world, had the serious purpose of attempting to induce fertility for the coming year.

THE BOOK OF RUTH

Herbert G. May

Introduction

The Story

The book of Ruth is an exciting short story, possessing almost rustic simplicity and charm. It may be compared for literary excellence with the story of Joseph. Unlike that story, however, it contains no note of dissension or intrigue. Unlike the story of Esther, it has no villain. It holds the reader's interest through the credibility of events and persons. The characters appear as real people, and the author has remarkable sensitivity in showing motivation. He draws no moral, but leaves his teaching obviously implicit.

The story is dramatic, but there are no spectacles. No miracles are wrought. The action shifts naturally from Moab to Bethlehem, from a day scene in the grain fields to a night scene on the threshing floor, from the gateway of the city to the home where a child is born. There are two heroines, Naomi the Jewess and Ruth the Moabitess. There is one hero, Boaz their kinsman. The other figures briefly play their parts and unobtrusively slip into the background. It is a story of tragedy overcome by love and loyalty—but also much more than that. The time is a quiet period in the hectic days of the judges.

The Purpose of the Story

Ruth is something more than a novel, even though it appears
to teach nothing directly. The author's main reason for telling
the story has to be determined from what seems to be its central
theme. It is the tale of a Gentile woman who is consistently
commended for her actions. She enters into the community of
Israel and becomes an important ancestress within that
community. She is a Moabitess who, in words that give the
impression of a keynote to the entire story, says to her Judean
mother-in-law: "Your people shall be my people and your God
my God" (1:16).

The author does not allow us to forget that his heroine was a
foreigner. His viewpoint clashes with that expressed in
Deuteronomy 23:3, that "no Ammonite or Moabite shall enter
the assembly of the Lord." It is contrary to that of Ezra and
Nehemiah, who led reforms in which foreign wives, including
women of Moab, were ousted from the community of Israel.

He would find Isaiah 56:6-8 more congenial. Here "the
foreigners who join themselves to the Lord" are welcomed into
Israel. And, though he was no legalist, he would agree with the
Priestly code in the Pentateuch, which prescribes "one law" for
both the sojourner and the native born (Numbers 15:15-16). He
would find support in the tradition that two leading tribes
sprang from the marriage of Joseph with the daughter of an
Egyptian priest, that Judah married a Canaanite woman, and
that Abraham took an Egyptian girl as a second wife.

He is not a theologian, intent on proclaiming the uniqueness
of one God whom all people should worship. He does not
envision a future when all peoples will acknowledge Israel's
God. He does not condemn Orpah for returning to her gods (see
below on 1:15-18). His is not a mission of conversion of Gentiles
to Judaism. Rather, he writes to answer the question whether it
is right and good that a Gentile woman be welcomed through
marriage into the community of Israel.

The author has several secondary motives. He wants to tell a
story about the ancestry of David. He intends his book to be a
part of the history of Israel in the period of the judges (see the

introduction to Judges). It is written as a continuation of that
which has gone before.

The setting in Bethlehem suggests that the allusions to David
were an original part of the story, although some scholars think
them later additions. David's family associations with Moab are
perhaps hinted in I Samuel 22:3-4. The author's contemporaries
doubtless found his message more meaningful because his story
concerned ancestors of the ruler from whose line they expected
the Messiah to come.

The book is also a story of the loyal friendship of two women,
Ruth and Naomi. It recalls that other great friendship tale in the
Old Testament, the story of David and Jonathan. Further, it is a
story of divine providence, a tale of what happens when one
seeks refuge in the shadow of the wings of the Lord. This theme
runs through the book.

The Date of Composition

One tradition holds that the author of Ruth was Samuel. The
book is obviously later than that, but modern scholars have
dated it all the way from the beginning of the Hebrew monarchy
to the third century B.C. The nature of the theme, the literary
style, the numerous Aramaic expressions in the Hebrew text,
and its position in the Hebrew Bible among the Writings—all
these when taken together speak strongly for an origin after the
Babylonian exile.

Although not written in a polemic spirit, it does involve the
issues at stake in the fifth century marriage "reforms" of Ezra
and Nehemiah. Many scholars have taken the book as a tract
written in opposition to those reforms. As noted above, the
viewpoint is congenial with the attitude of the postexilic writers
in Isaiah 56 and in the Priestly legislation. The general spirit is
consonant with that in Jonah. The author refers to a day long
before his own when he speaks of "the custom in former times in
Israel" (4:7). His opening sentence has almost a "once upon a
time" flavor. A late fifth of fourth century date of composition
seems most probable.

Despite its lateness, the book seems generally to be based on a solid historical tradition. The story of David's Moabite ancestry is hardly something that would have been invented in the postexilic period. The book does, of course reflect the author's religious viewpoint. He wrote it to teach his contemporaries by gentle persuasion.

The Place of the Book in the Bible

In our English Bibles which follow the Greek and Latin versions, Ruth is placed between Judges and I Samuel. This is in accord with the historical setting of the story. In the Hebrew Scriptures it is found among the Writings—those books which do not fall under the "law" of the "prophets." It is one of the five Scrolls (Song of Solomon, Ruth, Ecclesiastes, Lamentations, Esther), which are read at various festivals of the Jewish religious calendar. Ruth is appropriately read at the feast of Weeks, the harvest festival, which is also considered the anniversary of the giving of the Sinai covenant. The rabbis said that Ruth was used at this festival because it was at that time that the Torah—the law—which was intended for all, was given.

I. NAOMI'S BEREAVEMENT AND RETURN TO BETHLEHEM (1:1-22)

The mains sections of the narrative are adequately indicated by the chapter divisions. The first section introduces the situation for which the rest of the story is the unfolding solution. Naomi, bereaved of the husband and sons, returns to Bethlehem with her widowed and childless daughter-in-law.

1:1-5. *Naomi's Emigration and Loss.* As Abraham and Jacob went to Egypt in time of famine (Genesis 12:10; 47:4), so Elimelech with his wife Naomi and their two sons went to Moab, the land east of the Dead Sea. **Ephrathites** is a term also associated with Bethlehem in I Samuel 17:12 and Micah 5:2. **Elimelech** means "God is King" and **Naomi** "my pleasant one." The meanings of the other names are uncertain, although **Mahlon** has been taken to mean "weakness," **Chilion** "pining," **Orpah** "stiff-necked" or "rain cloud," and **Ruth** "rose" or "companion." It has even been noted that "Ruth" in Hebrew spelled backwards means "turtledove." These are not fictitious but real names and persons. "Elimelech" is found as early as the fourteenth century B.C. in Canaanite inscriptions.

The story carefully notes that Mahlon and Chilion married **Moabite**—that is, Gentile—women. The status of a childless widow was unfortunate, and the law demanded fair treatment of the widow. She is often classed with the sojourner and fatherless. God is the protector of widows (Psalm 68:5).

1:6-14. *Naomi Entreats Orpah and Ruth to Remain.* The three widows set out to return to Bethlehem. The solicitude of Naomi for the welfare of her Moabite daughters-in-law is notable. She seeks the blessing of her God, Yahweh, upon them, that Yahweh may **deal kindly** with them and grant that they **find a home** (rest and security) **each . . . in the house of her husband.** Thus she looks forward to their remarriage. The affection of Ruth and Orpah for their Judean mother-in-law is shown by their desire to go with her and by their tears.

1:11-14. Naomi's plea refers to the levirate marriage practice, the law for which is found in Deuteronomy 25:5-10. It involved marriage between the deceased husband's brother (or next of kin) and his childless widow. The first child born to the remarried widow was considered the son of the deceased husband. The story of Tamar, an ancestress of Boaz, likewise involves levirate marriage (Genesis 38), and Mark 12:19-23 also refers to it. Naomi's bitterness is not self-pity, but arises out of consideration for her **daughters.** The Lord has brought this calamity upon her. Orpah's decision to turn back sets in sharp relief Ruth's persistent loyalty. The parting may have been on the Plains of Moab before the Jordan River.

1:15-18. *Ruth Insists on Accompanying Naomi.* Naomi's persistence in trying to dissuade Ruth from accompanying her emphasizes her concern for Ruth's welfare. Naomi would have Ruth return, like Orpah, **to her people and to her gods.** The chief god of Moab was Chemosh. Naomi does not chide Orpah for returning to her own gods. Her interest is in her daughters-in-law, not in making proselytes. Ruth's motivation is not loyalty to Yahweh, but devotion to Naomi. The story moves on a personal rather than a theological plane, although there are, of course, theological implications.

1:16-17. These words of Ruth are regarded by some as poetry; at least they are poetic prose. In the Old Testament it is unusual for a Gentile to take an oath by the sacred name Yahweh (cf. the oath formula in I Samuel 20:13). Ruth affirms that Naomi's home, people, God, and tomb will be hers. Family tombs with multiple burials are frequently found in excavations (cf. the patriarchal family tomb in Genesis 23 and 49:29-33). Even in death Ruth would not be separated from Naomi.

1:19-22. *Naomi and Ruth Arrive at Bethlehem.* From Bethlehem Ruth could lift up her eyes and see the steep slopes of the hill country of Moab to the east beyond the Wilderness of Judah and the valley of the Dead Sea. Elimelech and Naomi had been persons of importance in Bethlehem. Naomi returns a childless, sorrowing widow, accompanied by her childless, widowed daughter-in-law. In verse 20 she uses an ancient name for God, Shaddai, translated **the Almighty. Mara** is an Aramaic feminine form. The change in name indicates a change in status, as when Abram became Abraham (Genesis 17:5) and Jacob became Israel (Genesis 32:28). So "my pleasant one" becomes "bitter." Like Job, Naomi accepts her lot as from the Lord (verse 21; Job 1:21).

1:22. The **barley harvest** came in late April or early May. A tenth century B.C. agricultural calendar found in Gezer designates a spring month as "his month of the harvest of barley." Barley ripened a couple of weeks earlier than wheat (2:23), could be grown on poorer soil, and was cheaper. The Hebrew word translated **return, turn back, go back** is a key word in this chapter, occurring twelve times.

II. Ruth Gleans in the Field of Boaz (2:1-23)

Boaz is the instrument for the resolution of the calamity set forth in chapter 1. As that chapter centered around Naomi, this one has Boaz as its key figure.

2:1-7. *Ruth Meets Boaz.* Boaz is a **kinsman** of Elimelech, but the story does not specify his exact relationship. He is a man of wealth and influence. There is no known connection between Boaz here and the name of one of the pillars of Solomon's temples (I Kings 7:21). Boaz appears in the genealogy of Jesus (Matthew 1:5; Luke 3:32). The meaning of the name is uncertain.

The widow and sojourner had a legal right to **glean**—that is, to pick up and keep the stalks of grain left by the harvesters (Leviticus 19:9-10; 23:22; Deuteronomy 24:19-22). The **reapers** cut the grain with small hand sickles, the blade of which was formed by a row of serrated flints set into a rounded haft. Ruth sought permission from Naomi to go gleaning. The obedient subservience of Ruth to Naomi is a part of the author's fine character depiction. Her industriousness receives special comment (verse 7). She **happened to come** into the field of Boaz; thus was the providence of God at work. Boaz singled out Ruth immediately. The piety of Boaz and of his people is evident in his greeting to the reapers and in their response. Compare Psalm 129:8, which also has a harvest context.

2:8-16. *Boaz' Solicitude for Ruth.* Boaz permitted Ruth to glean **close to** his **maidens** who were gathering up the sheaves to take to the threshing floor. Often reapers would yell at gleaners when they came too close (cf. verse 16), and gleaners would normally have to wait for a signal from the reapers before they could gather the leavings. Boaz also invited her to **drink** from the large water jars which were in the field for the use of the reapers. The water may have come from the well beside the gate at Bethlehem. Ruth's descendant, the battle-weary David, was to yearn for water from that well (II Samuel 23:15).

2:10-13. Ruth was surprised that she, a **foreigner,** should be so favored, but Boaz had heard of her loyalty to Naomi. His motive was more one of respect than of love. He was a devout, kindly, older farmer, and Ruth a humble, obedient, and grateful girl. In the name of the Lord, **under whose wings** she had **come to take refuge,** Boaz invoked a blessing on her.

2:14-16. The work day began at dawn. **Mealtime** was late in the morning, and there was a light repast. This gave Boaz opportunity to show further favors to Ruth. She was permitted to sit with the reapers and was given food and drink. She moistened the pieces of **bread** from the thin, flat loaves by dipping them into the fermented sour **wine** (or "vinegar," as the word is elsewhere translated). Boaz personally gave her **parched grain**—fresh heads of grain lightly roasted over the fire, from which the husks were then rubbed off. As she went back to her gleaning, she was permitted to **glean even among the sheaves.** The workers were instructed to **pull out** stalks from the sheaves to leave for her.

2:17-23. *Ruth Reports the Day's Events to Naomi.* As a result of the special treatment she received, Ruth returns to Naomi in the city with **an ephah** (about a half bushel) of barley. On learning the name of the man with whom Ruth has worked, Naomi invokes on him a second blessing from the Lord, **whose kindness has not forsaken the living and the dead.** Immediately she has seen in Boaz the solution to the problem of preserving the name of her dead son.

Nearest kin is a technical term. The Hebrew word *go'el,* literally means "redeemer." It may designate the one who redeems the name of the dead through the levirate marriage custom (see above on 1:11-13), or the one who redeems the property of a poor relative by buying it (Leviticus 25:25-28), or the avenger of blood (Numbers 35:12, 19-21). Both name and property are involved in this situation. *Go'el* is also a title used of God the Redeemer. The providence of God is working things out **for the living and the dead.** Keeping unobtrusively in the background, Naomi through her wise counseling helps the situation along to its desired end.

III. Ruth's Night Visit to the Threshing Floor (3:1-18)

In this threshing-floor scene Boaz agrees to act as next of kin and marry Ruth, providing the one who is actually next of kin should be unwilling to do so.

3:1-5. *Naomi Instructs Ruth.* Naomi again affirms her responsibility for Ruth's welfare (cf. 1:9). The barley sheaves were brought to the **threshing floor,** where they were crushed by a threshing sledge or by the feet of oxen. The **winnowing** was done toward evening, when the cool breezes were blowing in from the Mediterranean. The crushed sheaves were tossed into the air with a winnowing shovel or fork, and the wind blew the chaff away while the **heap of grain** grew larger near the feet of the winnower. Ruth was instructed to **anoint** herself and put on her **best clothes,** much as a bride. Boaz planned to spend the night at the threshing floor to guard the grain.

3:6-13. *Ruth and Boaz at the Threshing Floor.* After the evening meal, after the feasting and drinking which were a part of the happy occasion of a harvest, Boaz lay down at the end of the pile of grain on the threshing floor. As he slept, Ruth came quietly and lay down at his feet. She did not awaken him, and he discovered that she was there only when something startled him. It was then midnight, and Boaz could not recognize Ruth in the darkness.

Ruth's words were a clear request that he take her as his wife under the levirate marriage custom. He was her next of kin, her *go'el* (see above on 2:17-23). Cf. the use of the expression "to spread one's skirt over" in Ezekiel 16:8. The use of the words **young men** by Boaz suggests that he himself was not a young man. In verse 10 he calls Ruth his daughter. Although Boaz was honored by Ruth's **kindness** (Hebrew *hesed,* which also implies loyalty, faithfulness) in coming to him, he must give the nearer kinsman the opportunity to exercise his right. Boaz might in any case be reticent in expressing any emotional involvement with Ruth, since he could not yet be certain that she would be free to marry him.

3:11-13. The phrase **all my fellow townsmen** is literally "all the gate of my people"—that is, all the responsible citizens who have concern for community affairs, who might gather in the broad place before the city gate. Boaz requested Ruth to **remain** the rest of the night. Perhaps he feared she might be molested by the festal-spirited harvesters.

3:14-18. *Ruth Returns to Naomi in the Morning.* Boaz would protect Ruth's good reputation. Threshing floors were not always scenes of rustic innocence, especially at harvest festival time under the influence of Canaanitish fertility rites. Boaz would not let Ruth leave **empty-handed.** His gift of barley was perhaps both a present for Naomi and a token of the validity of his promise. **Six measures** were probably about one and a third bushels. The chapter ends with Naomi counseling patience, in confident assurance that before the day was over the matter would be settled. Thus the reader is prepared for the conclusion of the story.

IV. THE MARRIAGE AND THE BIRTH OF A SON (4:1-17)

The story comes to a satisfying end, with all the problems happily solved.

4:1-6. *The Next of Kin Refuses His Right.* Boaz went up (for Bethlehem is on a hill) to the city gate (see above on 3:11). There he chose **ten . . . elders** to act as a court of decision. This incident provided a precedent for the later view that ten men formed a quorum and was the smallest possible number for a synagogue.

4:3-4. Boaz presented the case to the next of kin, whose name is not given. For the first time it is noted that the case involves redeeming by purchase a **parcel of land** belonging to Elimelech which Naomi has put up for sale. See Leviticus 25:25-28 for the law of redemption of land by the next of kin; an illustration of the law in practice appears in Jeremiah 32. Naomi's control of the land seems inconsistent with the later law in Numbers 27:8-11, which presumes that the property of a man who dies without a son does not go to the widow.

4:5-6. The next of kin was apparently a man of limited wealth. He was willing to buy the land until he learned that it involved acquiring Ruth to restore the name of the dead to his inheritance. This would mean that the land would go to Ruth's son. He would thus diminish his own estate, and there would be less **inheritance** for his other sons. If Boaz had no sons, the son born to Ruth would perhaps be the legal heir of both the deceased and of Boaz. The situation is not entirely clear. In any case, the next of kin was not willing to take whatever loss there might be. **You are also buying Ruth** should perhaps be rendered "you are also acquiring Ruth." The verb has both meanings, and may be used in two senses in this verse. Ruth is not the property of anyone, but must go with the land, which will belong to her son.

4:7-12. *Boaz Assumes the Right of Redemption.* Through the ceremony of the removal of his **sandal** and presenting it to Boaz, the next of kin attested to his relinquishing the right of redemption. It was thus a symbol of renunciation and transfer of rights. A quite different custom is involved in Deuteronomy 25:5-10. There the widow pulls off the sandal of her husband's brother, who has refused to do the duty of a husband's brother, and spits in his face. There it is a symbol of disgrace. An earlier practice is represented in Ruth. In ancient Mesopotamia sandals or other articles of clothing might be used as tokens to validate special transactions. This is not quite the case here, for the next of kin is not the one who has bought something. Yet the action does in some way validate the agreement between the two parties. On **Ruth . . . I have bought** see above on 4:5-6.

4:11-12. Cf. the good wishes given to Boaz with those to Rebekah in Genesis 24:60 and especially those to the royal groom in Psalm 45:16-17. The people pray that Ruth may be like **Rachel and Leah,** who with their handmaidens had produced the ancestors of the twelve tribes of Israel. **Perez** was a son of **Tamar** (Genesis 38:27-30), and from him could be traced the line of David (cf. Matthew 1:3 and Luke 3:33). This suggests the author did intend to tell a tale about the ancestry of David. Tamar was also involved in a levirate marriage (see above on 1:11-13). She was probably a Canaanite woman and so, like Ruth, a Gentile married to a Hebrew.

4:13-17. *Obed Is Born.* The congratulations of the women of Bethlehem is set in deliberate contrast with their reaction in 1:19-21. This exemplifies the fine literary sensitivity of the author. Ruth was more to Naomi than **seven sons.** This was an ideal number of sons; the blameless Job had seven sons and three daughters. The women recognized the child as Naomi's, for through him the name of Elimelech had been redeemed, as well as that of Mahlon. Ruth has in part acted as a substitute for Naomi in the levirate marriage practice (see above on 1:11-13). Her son is also Naomi's. Naomi's action in verse 16 symbolizes and perhaps legitimatizes this fact.

4:17. The name **Obed,** meaning "he who serves," does not provide the usual play on words that one might expect (cf. Genesis 25:25-26). This has led some scholars to conclude that in the earlier form of the story there was a different name beginning with Ben ("son of") or one containing a play on Naomi's name. They therefore think the Davidic genealogy is an intrusion. On the other hand, the author may deliberately have avoided a word play to make more startling the punch-line of his composition: **he was the father of Jesse, the father of David.** Narrow-minded readers would get the point. Obed, the son of a Gentile woman, was the grandfather of David, who instigated the dynasty. God's covenant was with him, and from his line would come the Messiah.

4:18-22. *The Genealogy of David.* It is not known whether this is a later addition or the work of the original author. If the author wrote as late as the end of the fifth of the beginning of the fourth century, it may be his. He would then have had before him the genealogical lists in the Pentateuch, after which this genealogy is patterned. The list is obviously too brief by several generations to fill the period between the patriarchal age and the time of David.

The same genealogy, with differences in spelling, is presumed in I Chronicles 2:5-15. The Ruth and Chronicles lists have provided the data for the genealogical table in Matthew 1:2-6 and Luke 3:31-33. In Matthew 1:5 the mother of Boaz is identified with Rahab, a Canaanite woman of Jericho (Joshua 2). Through this genealogical list at the end of the book, the author or editor indicates that the story of Ruth is an important part of the sacred history of Israel.

THE FIRST BOOK OF SAMUEL

John William Wevers

INTRODUCTION

Originally the books of Samuel and Kings constituted one book. They were divided into two because of their length. The Septuagint further divided them into four and called them appropriately "Concerning the Kingdoms." The fourfold division has been adopted down to the present, but the name has not.

Name and Place in the Canon

The name "Samuel" for the first pair of books comes from the Hebrew text. It was probably chosen because Samuel is the first major character appearing in it. In the Hebrew Scriptures Samuel is grouped along with Joshua, Judges, and Kings to make up the Former Prophets. As opposed to Chronicles, Ezra, and Nehemiah, which constitute a priestly view of Israel's history, the Former Prophets show a prophetic viewpoint. In content they cover Israel's history from the conquest of Canaan to the destruction of Jerusalem in 586 B.C.

The Deuteronomic Edition

In its final form Samuel seems to have formed a part of a large work which contained also Joshua, Judges, Kings, and perhaps

Deuteronomy. This recounted the history of Israel from the conquest to the compiler's own day. It was put together by an editor (or editors) of the Deuteronomic school (see the Introduction to Joshua) during the Babylonian exile, around 560 B.C., as shown by the last event recorded in II Kings. Some scholars maintain that it was done during the reign of Josiah, around 610, with revision or supplementation by others of the Deuteronomic school about 560. The work of the Deuteronomic—or D—editor is not as apparent in Samuel as in Kings (see Introduction to I Kings). He adopted materials from various earlier sources without change, and only here and there did he add his own comments—for example, in II Samuel 7. He was, however, largely responsible for the present arrangement of the materials.

Earlier Sources
The problem of literary sources in Samuel is incredibly complicated. Only a sketch of these can be given. By the time the D editor began his work various collections of traditions were already in existence which in turn had been collected from earlier sources. Some of these sources are extremely early. Some are even contemporary with the events described—for example, the Military Source and the Succession Document described below. Certain lists and summaries of campaigns—for example, II Samuel 8 and 23:8-39—must go back to official court records kept in the time of David.

Local Traditions
Originally many of the early stories concerning Samuel and Saul were traditions connected with a particular area. Such sanctuaries as Mizpah, Gilgal, Ramah, and Shiloh in particular were centers of traditional lore about those ancient heroes. Sometimes the same story was told in two different centers. This resulted in both stories being taken over by later collectors of traditions and we get divergent or doublet accounts. This is particularly striking in the account of Saul's becoming king.

Involved are at least two, if not three, cycles of stories centered respectively at Ramah, Mizpah, and Gilgal.

Shiloh Stories

I Samuel 1–3 is obviously centered in the important sanctuary of Shiloh. It comes from an independent source, which in turn contains divergent traditions. 2:27-36 is an insertion from the D editor which parallels 3:10-14. The Song of Hannah, 2:1-10, is a hymn from monarchical times; verse 10, with its reference to the king, was inserted much later and put into the mouth of Hannah. The stories center about a permanent sanctuary with its cult and show no hint of its destruction. The picture of Samuel as a young ministrant to Eli finds no parallel elsewhere. Later Samuel stories contain no mention of his Shiloh apprenticeship.

Ark Stories

These stories are found in I Samuel 4:1–7:2 and II Samuel 6:1-19. They seem to be unrelated in origin to the Shiloh stories. The center of interest here is the fortunes of the ark and its holy character. Thus it is quite clear that the story of Uzzah in II Samuel 6:6-7 is of the same type as those in I Samuel 5 and 6:19–7:2 and belongs with them. It could not, however, be placed immediately after the capture of Jerusalem. The present form of II Samuel 6 is possibly an amalgamation of a tradition from the ark stories and one from the Succession Document, to which it also belongs. The stories were probably collected in the time of David.

Samuel Stories

These stories are found in I Samuel 7–12 and combine two quite distinct sources. Though both give the account of the origin of the monarchy, Samuel is the actual hero. He is the great judge, prophet, and charismatic leader; his words are definitive. Source A is in general unfavorably disposed to the monarchy, which its author views as rebellion against Yahweh. It probably originated in Mizpah, though chapter 8 details a

Ramah event. The following stories clearly belong to this source: 8:1-22; 10:17-27; and 12:1-25. Chapter 7, which has been somewhat editorialized, also belongs to this source. Samuel is judge over all Israel and universally respected, even though his advice is not heeded. The age of the stories cannot be determined. They come from the north, probably from the time shortly after the division of the kingdom in the tenth century. There is no good reason for considering these as a late source as many commentators do.

Source B, found in 9:1–10:16 and 11:1-15, represents a favorable view of Saul and the monarchy. Samuel is presented as a man of God only locally prominent, and Saul is a young man of great promise. The story of the charismatic actions of Saul against the Ammonites is an excellent sequel to God's giving Saul "another heart" in 10:9, as the Gilgal coronation is a sequel to Samuel's earlier instructions in 10:8.

Saul Stories

These are found in I Samuel 13–15; 28; and 31. Independent traditions concerning Saul are almost nonexistent in view of the dominance of David. Even the Saul stories in which David plays no part show a judgment on Saul's career quite at variance with the picture of him given in Source B of the Samuel stories. From the start the stories of his early successes against Philistines and Amalekites in chapters 13–15 are told under the shadow of his rejection and lack of good royal judgment. The D editor clearly shows that Yahweh's spirit was not on Saul, even though Saul was zealous for Yahweh.

Some of these stories have often been related to the Samuel ones, and this is possible. Thus the rejection of Saul twice told in different contexts (chapters 13 and 15) would fit with Source A. Both are Gilgal stories. However, the former is much more sympathetic toward Saul, whereas the latter is a complete rejection of a disobedient king. In all these stories the tragic figure of a rejected king is central. His reign begins in error (13:8-15) and ends with the despairing events at Endor and Gilboa (chapters 28 and 31).

I Samuel

Stories About David

The stories about David in I Samuel 16–27; 29–30; and II Samuel 1:1–5:5 present more difficulties than any others. These concern David's fortunes from his secret anointing by Samuel at Bethlehem to his election as king over the twelve tribes. The traditions are varied in origin and do not present a consistent chronological pattern. At time doublet accounts are given—for example, David's sparing Saul's life (I Samuel 24 in Engedi, but chapter 26 in Ziph; cf. 18:10-11; 19:8-10). At times stories that obviously belong in sequence are separated:

1) in I Samuel 17 verses 32-54 should follow verse 11;
2) the David and Jonathan story of I Samuel 20 cannot follow 19:24, but follows on 19:10;
3) the story of David at the Nob sanctuary is also out of order, properly constituting a sequel to 19:18-24.

There are numerous instances of contradictory accounts. In I Samuel, for example, David's flight to Gath (21:10-15) can hardly be harmonized with the story of his slaying of a Gath champion in chapter 17, or with his later stay near Gath in Achish's employ in chapters 27 and 29–30.

Nonetheless the stories must have been brought together by a collector of David stories no later than the time of Solomon. The collector's method was typically oriental. When variant accounts were found, all were written down so that no traditions would be lost. The arrangement of materials that resulted from this kind of collection is undoubtedly confusing.

The collector's motive is perfectly clear. He wanted to show that David's rise to power was not his own doing but strictly that of Yahweh. David does not fight Saul or his forces; he evades them. When David can easily stretch out his hand against Yahweh's anointed, he never does. In fact he reprimands those who wish to do so and kills those who do. His phenomenal popularity in his early days at court is due, not to his own planning, but to Yahweh's spirit.

Even in his military exploits he seeks oracles to ascertain Yahweh's will. He does not win the kingdom; it comes to him from Yahweh. After Saul's death at Yahweh's direction he goes up to Hebron, where the Judeans anoint him as their king. Later, after the death of Saul's heir, the united tribes anoint him as Israel's king. With few exceptions the David stories are basically Judean in origin.

The Succession Document

One of the finest historical sources which the editor took over is the account of court intrigues involving the problem of David's eventual succession. The core of this document is II Samuel 9–20, except for 10:1-19 and 12:26-31 (see the next section) and I Kings 1–2. It would seem likely that the document originally had parts of II Samuel 5–7 as a preface. Certainly some early version of God's covenantal promise of the prosperity of David's house—that is, of a succession (chapter 7)—must have preceded the document.

The document must have been composed by an eyewitness no later than the early years of Solomon's reign. Various names—Ahimaaz, Nathan, Gad, Zadok—may be suggested, but these are only guesses. Characteristic of the author is his failure to gloss over David's weaknesses as a husband and a father. That his chief interest is the royal succession is clear from his choice of stories. Ammon, the eldest, is rejected as immoral. (The second son, Chileab, probably died in early life; at least he is never mentioned beyond the list of sons born in Hebron, II 3:3.) After his death the third son Absalom attempts to take over the throne and is killed in the civil war that results. Joab subsequently has to save the kingdom for David. Finally Adonijah, the fourth son, attempts a coup d'etat but is thwarted by the Solomonic party (I Kings 1–2).

A Military Source

The author of the Succession Document uses the account of the Ammonite war in II Samuel 10:1-19 and 12:26-31 to give a proper setting for the David-Bathsheba story. Its vividness in describing the military operations and its lack of religious interest clearly brand it as a separate source. It probably constitutes an eyewitness account of the battle. In any event it is contemporary, earlier than the Succession Document.

Stories of Divine Affliction

The origin of two stories, II Samuel 21:1-14 and 24:1-25, is unknown. They seem to represent the same genre. In both Yahweh is displeased, in both some form of expiation is demanded, and in both Yahweh is appeased.

Poems

Four longer poems are inserted into the historical traditions. One, the Song of Hannah, has been discussed above. Two may well be Davidic in origin, the elegy over Saul and Jonathan (II Samuel 1:19-27) and David's last words (II Samuel 23:1-7). A fourth, found in II Samuel 22, is taken from the body of cultic poetry; it is a variant of Psalm 18. The origin of I Samuel 15:22-23 is not clear. Two other poems, I Samuel 18:7 and II Samuel 3:33-34, are popular refrains (cf. also I Samuel 29:15).

Religious Significance

Samuel stands in the middle of the Deuteronomic history. The historian's purpose was to show how Yahweh directed the course of Israel's affairs. Israel's God guided its destinies in a special way. Canaan was given to Israel under Joshua. After his death charismatic rulers judged Israel. Eventually Yahweh directed Israel through kings for whom the norm was David, the man after God's heart. Samuel shows the change from judge to Davidic king. Saul's reign was a misguided attempt to combine charismatic rule with kingship. David was the first genuine king.

But Yahweh's direction is based also on ethical demands. When David sins he is punished. Saul is rejected because he is disobedient. Eli's house is destroyed because of the immorality of his sons. On the other hand David's reign is prosperous because he follows the proper course of action. Before embarking on any venture he consults the oracles. He is not chosen for outward appearance, as Saul was, because Yahweh "looks on the heart." It is he who captures Jerusalem, the city where Yahweh has chosen "to put his name." He brings the ark there, not only making Jerusalem a political center but also turning it into Zion, the cultic center.

I. SHILOH STORIES (1:1–4:1*a*)

A. SAMUEL'S BIRTH AND DEDICATION (1:1–2:11)

1:1-20. *Birth of Samuel.* The story is laid in **Ephraim**, appropriately in **Ramah** ("height," verse 19) or **Ramathaim** ("two heights," verse 1). **Zophim** should read "a Zuphite" as in the Septuagint. The town was probably modern Beit-Rima, twelve miles west of **Shiloh**, not the better known Ramah five miles north of Jerusalem. The story concerns a favored but childless wife who is taunted by the other wife, who of course has children. Barrenness was considered the greatest of misfortunes. The occasion is the annual pilgrimage made by the family to **Shiloh**, modern Seilun, almost halfway from Bethel to Shechem. The ark was housed at this holy place. There **Elkanah** would offer a thank offering and the family would eat together at the feast. Finally the desperate wife, who can take the gibes of **her rival** no longer, rises and enters the sanctuary to pray.

1:9-20. Silently the distraught **Hannah** makes a vow to Yahweh **of hosts** (i.e., the armies of Israel), the full name of Israel's God. If he will give her a **son,** she will devote him as a Nazirite (cf. Numbers 6:1-21; Judges 13:2-14). **Eli,** the sanctuary priest, after an embarrassing misunderstanding is cleared up, blesses her. She is cheered, knowing that she has been heard.

In due time she has a son, whom she names **Samuel.** The explanation given is peculiar. Samuel means "name of God" rather than **asked.** However, "Saul" does mean "asked." An explanation of that name seems to have been inappropriately transferred to Samuel.

1:21–2:10. *Dedication of Samuel.* Until the baby **is weaned** Hannah stays home from the annual pilgrimage. But eventually the time comes for redeeming her vow. The story has been confused by the insertion of the Song of Hannah. Originally it must have concerned the woman only. The Revised Standard Version has hidden the difficulty by changing verse 28*b* to the plural. The Hebrew reads "he worshiped." Since Elkanah is not part of the story at all, "he" would have to refer to the infant Samuel. Originally the story must have read "and she worshiped Yahweh there and went home to Ramah" (2:11*a*). Hannah brings a particularly large offering for the occasion and leaves the child in Shiloh as a sanctuary servant.

2:1-11. The Song of Hannah is a hymn of praise to Yahweh, inappropriate in its present context. For similar insertions of a cultic poem compare the psalms of Hezekiah (Isaiah 38:10-20) and Jonah (Jonah 2:2-9). Its insertion here was no doubt due to the reference to **the barren.** It is clearly a later composition from the time of the monarchy, as the reference in verse 10 shows. The song is in praise of Yahweh's power, against which mortal opponents can do nothing. Life and death, honor and dishonor, and all these and more are under Yahweh's direction. God's power is not despotic, however. God will judge everyone by moral standards and will give strength to the Davidic king. This song was probably the model for the Song of Mary (Luke 1:46-55).

B. The House of Eli (2:12–4:1*a*)

2:12-17. *The Sins of Eli's Sons.* Though they are priests at Shiloh, Eli's sons are guilty of **contempt** for the **offering.** Apparently the **custom** at Shiloh was for the priest to take as much as could be **brought up** on a **fork** thrust into the vessel where the **meat was boiling.** Eli's sons, however, prefer to take **raw** meat. Most scholars feel that verses 13-14 should be corrected to read that the taking of the meat from the container was contrary to Shiloh custom and thus also evidence of the wickedness of the priests. However, such a change would be at odds with verses 15-16. On the priestly portion cf. Leviticus 7:28-36 and Deuteronomy 18:3-4.

2:18-21. *Hannah's Annual Visit to Shiloh.* Samuel does service in the sanctuary as a ministrant wearing the **linen ephod** appropriate for cultic service (cf. II Samuel 6:14). Each year Hannah visits her son and brings him new clothing, and she receives priestly blessing. On **the loan** cf. 1:28. The blessing is successful; Hannah has five more children.

2:22-26. *Eli's Rebuke of His Sinful Sons.* This passage, as well as verses 27-36, is intended to depreciate the house of Eli. Verse 22*b* is inconsistent to the narrative. It was probably added later to emphasize the immorality of the priests. The sanctuary here was not a **tent** but a building with doorposts (cf. 1:9). Eli's rebuke is ineffectual because Yahweh wanted **to slay them.** Even the sins of the Elids are part of the divine plan. In contrast to the evil sons Samuel is pictured as favored by God.

2:27-36. *House of Eli Denounced.* An oracle from an unnamed prophet is typical of the D editor (see Introduction to I Kings). The denunciation of the Elid house reflects the rivalry of the Zadokite and Aaronite priesthoods. Verse 28 refers to the choice of Aaron to perform the priestly offices (cf. Numbers 3:2-3). One of these offices was to carry (nor **wear**) the **ephod,** which is here an instrument of divination (see below on 14:2-3, 16-23) and not a garment as in verse 18. Because of the cultic sin of Eli's sons (cf. verses 15-17) Yahweh will destroy his house and raise up a **faithful priest,** Zadok, in his place.

2:32-36. Verse 32 is difficult. According to 4:18 Eli died, when he heard the news that the ark was taken and his sons were killed. What then is meant by **prosperity**? The text is probably corrupt. The **man** who alone is **spared** is Abiathar (see comment on I Kings 2:26-27). For the language of verse 35 cf. II Samuel 7. Verse 36 probably reflects the conditions of Josiah's reform (cf. II Kings 23:8-9).

3:1-4:1a. *Yahweh's Appearance to Samuel.* This passage combines the call of Samuel to prophethood with another denunciation of the house of Eli. The setting for the story emphasizes the rarity of such an oracle, the auditory and visual nature of which is emphasized (3:1). Samuel as a young ministrant is asleep when he hears his name called. Naturally he goes to Eli, his master, who on the third occasion realizes that Yahweh is **calling the boy.**

3:10-18. The oracle summarizes the divine intent to destroy Eli's house, not only because of the sins of his sons but also because of the father's slackness in rebuke (in contrast to 2:22-25). The sin is unpardonable.

3:19–4:1a. In the years that follow, Samuel's reputation as a **prophet** increases throughout **all Israel.** Note that elsewhere this word is not used of him; elsewhere it designates ecstatics (cf. 9:9; 10:5-6). The phrase **from Dan to Beersheba** means from the northern to the southern limits of the country (cf. Judges 20:1).

II. STORIES ABOUT THE ARK (4:1b–7:2)

The exact nature of the **ark of the covenant of the LORD of hosts,** as the D editor calls it, is not clear. It was probably a plain oblong box which dated from desert days before Israel's arrival in Canaan. It was in some special way a symbol of Yahweh's presence. Possibly it was intended to be the throne for the invisible deity. As such it was carried into battle, showing that Yahweh was the God of the armies of Israel. About its ultimate fate nothing is known.

4:1b-11. *The Capture of the Ark.* The site of **Aphek** is in the Plain of Sharon, near the border between Philistine and Israelite territory. **Ebenezer** must have been near by, though it remains unidentified (see below on 7:5-17). When battle is joined the Israelites are disastrously **defeated** but hold ground. Wise counselors suggest bringing the ark from Shiloh to insure Yahweh's presence.

4:4. The ark is given the full cultic name **ark of . . . the LORD of hosts, who is enthroned on the cherubim.** These were winged creatures (see comment on I Kings 6:23-28) who guarded the ark and served to support the divine throne. Possibly they were represented decoratively on the sides of the ark.

4:5-11. The Israelites, as well as their enemies, mistakenly confuse the symbol of the ark with the reality of Yahweh. The **Philistines** are full of superstitious dread—the storyteller even attributes to them an acquaintance with early Hebrew traditions of the plagues in Egypt. Nonetheless they are determined to fight **like men.** The results are again disastrous for Israel, especially the capture of the ark and the death of Eli's sons. That this is central to the story is clear from the failure of the author to refer to the fate of Shiloh, which was apparently destroyed by the Philistines (cf. Jeremiah 7:12-14; 26:6).

4:12-18. *The Death of Eli.* A Benjaminite runner with traditional display of mourning arrives at Shiloh with the news. Blind old Eli, alarmed at the outcry, inquires for news. He is sitting near the gate overlooking the **road.** When he hears about the capture of the ark he **fell over backward** in shock and **died.** The D editor, in accordance with the artificial scheme in Judges, speaks of Eli's serving **forty years** as judge. However, the original tale knows only of Eli as priest at Shiloh.

4:19-22. *The Birth of Ichabod.* Eli's **daughter-in-law** is pregnant. The news of the loss of the ark brings on **her pains** and she dies in childbirth. The **son** is named by the attendants, not by the unconscious mother. He is called **Ichabod,** meaning "there is no glory," to commemorate the disaster. Yahweh was Israel's **glory,** and the loss of the ark symbolized Yahweh's departure from Israel.

5:1-12. *A Terror to the Philistines.* The heathen take the sacred trophy to **Ashdod,** evidently at this time the chief of the five Philistine city-states. There they place it in the temple of their god. The name **Dagon** means "grain," rather than "fish" as formerly supposed, and indicates a vegetation deity. Yahweh, however, is not defeated. The first morning finds the Dagon statue in a position of obeisance before the ark, and the next morning it is shattered. Verse 5 is an antiquarian note to explain a Philistine **threshold** rite.

5:6-12. Shortly thereafter the city suffers a plague—possibly bubonic since mice are carriers of the disease (cf. 6:4-5). On consultation the Philistine **lords** decide to send the ark to **Gath,** another of their five cities. After the same dread result ensues, the ark is in turn sent to a third city, **Ekron,** where the inhabitants greet its arrival with **panic.** The plague, the **hand of God,** also breaks out there.

6:1–7:2. *The Return of the Ark.* The situation after **seven months** is critical. The experts—the **priests and diviners**—are consulted. They recommend its return together with a **guilt offering**—a kind of payment for infringement on the rights of deity. By sympathetic magic **five** (for the five city-states; cf. verses 17-18) **golden tumors and . . . mice** (symbolizing the plague and its cause) are to effect the deliverance.

To determine whether the plague is Yahweh-inspired or coincidence, the ark with the guilt offering is placed on a **new cart** drawn by a pair of fresh **cows.** If the cows leave their suckling **calves** and proceed to Israelite land, the plague is obviously from Yahweh. They do so, going directly to **Beth-shemesh,** about twelve miles to the east, and stopping near a large **stone.** Here the cows are sacrificed as a **burnt offering,** the cart being used for fuel. In verse 15 the interest of the author (or probably of a later editor) in correct cultic procedure is evident. Only **Levites** can handle the ark—though why they should be on the spot at the **wheat harvest** is not explained. Verse 18*b* is an antiquarian note identifying a large memorial stone as the site of this event.

6:19-21. The ark retains its dreadful power even on Israelite soil. Some people inspect (literally "looked at," not **looked into**) the holy object and are killed. The Hebrew text says 50,070 men, a fantastic number; **seventy** is likely correct. The ark is immediately transferred to **Kiriath-jearim,** about nine miles northwest of Jerusalem. Since Shiloh has been destroyed by the Philistines, this will be its temporary abode till David can transfer it to its permanent location in Jerusalem. Eli and his sons are now dead, and a new priest, **Eleazar,** is given **charge of the ark.** 7:2 is an editor's connecting link between the ark stories and the following section.

III. SAMUEL TRADITIONS (7:3–12:25)

In the main these stories have Samuel as their hero. They reflect two divergent views of the monarchy—one unfavorable (Source A), the other favorable (Source B; see Introduction). The D editor has also added his comments. Traditions about Samuel seem to have been numerous. He acts as priest, judge, intercessor, and prophet. As with Moses, a firm historical picture of Samuel is difficult to reconstruct.

A. SAMUEL AS LEADER OF ALL ISRAEL (7:3–8:22)

7:3-17. *Samuel the Last Judge.* This passage is based on Source A but has been rewritten by the D editor. The result is that it conflicts with other sources. Thus the picture of a Philistine rout and the idyllic recovery of lost **territory** contradicts the more historical accounts of continuous conflict. Verse 14 might be more accurately applied to David.

7:3-4. These verses are typical of the D editor and recall the framework of Judges (see Introduction to Judges). The Israelites are warned against idolatry and promised relief from the enemy if they will serve Yahweh only. They do so, and the stage is set for the great victory of verses 10-11. The people take part in a water-pouring ceremony apparently symbolizing repentance (verse 6).

7:5-17. Israel gathers at **Mizpah,** five miles north of Jerusalem in Benjaminite territory. Here Samuel **judged.** This probably means that he rendered legal decisions. On Samuel's intercessory powers cf. Jeremiah 15:1. The point of the story is that Yahweh is the victor; the Israelites simply engage in mopping up exercises. The location of **Beth-car** is unknown. The location given for the memorial **Ebenezer,** meaning "stone of help," indicates a different place from the town Ebenezer mentioned in 4:1*b*. However, some have suggested that this story reflects a variant tradition of the battle of 4:1*b*-2 in which an Israelite defeat has been turned into a victory. **Amorites** here is another name for Canaanites.

Apparently Samuel served as sanctuary judge in various places in central Palestine. On **Ramah** see above on 1:1-20. **Bethel** was a cultic center some ten miles north of Jerusalem. **Gilgal** here refers to a town seven miles north of Bethel, not the tribal center near Jericho prominent elsewhere in the Samuel and Saul traditions.

8:1-22. *The People's Demand for a King.* This account expresses most forcefully the bias against the monarchy which is characteristic of Source A. A group of **elders** comes to Samuel at his home in **Ramah** to plead for a **king.** Their plea is based on the misconduct of Samuel's own **sons** as judges in **Beer-sheba,** an important sanctuary in the far south. The point of the request, however, is to be **like all the nations.** Samuel recognizes this as a rejection of his own role as judge, but the narrator sees it as a rejection of God's kingship over Israel. This rejection is typical of Israel's past history from the time they became a people. It is characterized in the typical language of the D editor as idolatry (verse 8).

8:10-18. The picture that Samuel presents of royal prerogatives is not a reflection of later practice among the kings of Israel. Rather it describes the practice of oriental despots among **all the nations.** Such absolute monarchs despised their subjects' property rights and also impressed them into military and domestic service (cf. the strictures on kings in Deuteronomy 17:14-17).

8:19-22. The elders, however, insist on a king, since having such a leader will unite the people for military purposes.

B. SAUL'S ANOINTING (9:1–10:16)

All of this account comes from Source B. In contrast with the preceding Source A it considers Samuel a local leader only and views the founding of the monarchy as the means of saving Israel in a time of crisis.

9:1-4. *The Search for Lost Asses.* Saul is a Benjaminite of exceptional stature and fine appearance. He is in the prime of life (rather than **young**), and thus an ideal candidate for the kingship. He and a **servant** set out to find lost **asses** and travel for three days (verse 20). Both **Shalisha** and **Shaalim** are unknown. The text of verse 4 may well be corrupt, since obviously they start from **Benjamin** and arrive in **Ephraim**.

9:5-14. *Steps Toward Consulting a Seer.* When the travelers reach **Zuph**, the region of Samuel's home town of Ramah (see above on 1:1-20), the servant suggests a visit to the **man of God in this city**. The author builds up suspense by keeping him unidentified till the two actually meet him (verse 14). This man of God is reputed to be trustworthy; he can predict correctly (cf. Deuteronomy 18:21-22). When Saul brings up the fee customary for such consultation, the servant provides a small piece of **silver**. Verse 9 is an explanatory note on the word **seer**, which does not occur in the story until verse 11. In early times this term was distinct from **prophet**, which referred to roving ecstatics (cf. 10:5-13). The seer simply saw what others could not—that is, he had second sight. In the author's time the two terms had fallen together. Samuel traditionally was the father of prophecy, and as such was to anoint Saul to kingship.

9:11-14. Near Eastern cities were always on the hill, but the spring would be lower down the slope. Girls going for water tell the inquirers that the seer has just arrived (cf. 7:16-17). The **high place** was apparently outside the town walls on the brow of the hill. To slaughter meat was to **sacrifice** it, and Samuel as priest first has to bless it before the communal meal is eaten.

9:15-25. *Samuel's Encounter with Saul.* Samuel has received a prior revelation that Saul is coming and that he is to **anoint him** as the one designated by God to deliver Israel. Saul is invited to the sacrificial feast as the seer's special guest. The narrative throughout emphasizes Yahweh's direction of events. Saul is told not to worry about the lost asses; there are more important things in the wind. Samuel hints obscurely at Saul's future royal role in verse 20*b*, to which Saul replies with typical oriental modesty.

9:22-25. Saul is entertained in the **hall** of the high place—where the sacrificial feasts were held—and accorded the place of high honor. Who the other guests are is not indicated. They are probably important men of the city. Saul is also given a **bed** for the night on the **roof** of Samuel's home, a common place for sleeping in the Near East.

9:26-10:1b. *The Anointing.* At the **break of dawn** Samuel escorts Saul out of the city and anoints him secretly. The anointing of kings was a religious rite common among both the Egyptians and the Hittites. Though a priest or prophet could be anointed to office, it was the king especially who was set apart by this rite and sacramentally endowed with royal powers. In a real sense he became another man (cf. 10:6, 9). Now the obscure "all that is desirable in Israel" (9:20) is made clear. Saul is the divinely designated one to rule and **save** the people. It is clear that the kingship was set up in the first place to give military leadership in view of the Philistine crisis.

10:1c-13. *Signs Given to Saul.* Signs were often given as an attestation for what was otherwise incredible. Three are given to Saul, each of increasing value. First he **will meet two men by Rachel's tomb** (near Bethel; **Zelzah** remains unidentified). They will inform him about his domestic affairs. Next he will meet **three men** carrying provisions for a sacrificial feast at the **Bethel** sanctuary. They will give him **two loaves of bread,** which Saul is secretly to take as a guarantee of his future royal state. Finally he is to meet a **band of prophets** and temporarily become one of them. This is to occur at **Gibeath-elohim** ("hill of God"), probably simply his home town of Gibeah, three miles north of Jerusalem. The word translated **garrison** here and in 13:3-4 (differing from that in 13:23–14:15) is believed by most scholars to refer rather to an official, one of a number stationed by the Philistines throughout Israel for collecting tribute. In early times **prophets** were ecstatics, spirit-filled men, who used music to bring on a state of ecstasy during which they **prophesied.**

10:8. Samuel ends with instructions to **go down . . . to Gilgal,** the tribal center in the Jordan Valley near Jericho. There he is to wait for Samuel and receive further instructions. The author probably intended this to harmonize with the story of the popular acclaim of Saul as king at Gilgal (11:15; see below on 13:7*b*-15*a*).

10:9-13. All three signs are said to take place as Samuel has predicted, but only the third is described. The surprise of Saul's acquaintances at his joining in the ecstatic behavior of the **band of prophets** gives rise to a proverbial saying. What is meant is that Saul as a farmer has no business being a prophet (cf. 19:18-24 for another explanation of the saying). Verse 12 probably is intended to cast aspersions on prophets as a class whose parentage is unknown, whereas that of Saul is well known. **The high place** is probably a scribal error and should read "his house."

10:14-16. *Saul's Discretion.* Saul's uncle asks about the experiences of the journey. Saul reveals that they inquired of Samuel—apparently a familiar name to the uncle. But he refers only to the lost asses, keeping to himself the **matter of the kingdom.**

C. Saul's Election by Lot (10:17-27)

Source A resumes again with this story from Mizpah (see above on 7:5-17). It is quite at variance with the preceding tradition. If Saul were anointed he would hardly now have to be divinely chosen once again. The story may be a cult legend portraying the first coronation: the divine choice by lot, the popular acclaim, the recital of the privileges and duties of kingship and their incorporation into a book which was then deposited in the sanctuary. This passage originally followed 8:22*a*.

10:17-24. In distinction from the elders of chapter 8 all the **people** are involved here. **Thousands** in verse 19 has the sense of "clans." The sacred priestly **lot** is cast by Samuel, finally isolating Saul. The incident in verses 21*c*-23 is peculiar. Possibly it represents a variant tradition of the choice, like that in

16:6-13, in which the lot falls on no one. In the Hebrew text
Samuel asks, "Is there still another man to come here?" (rather
than the Septuagint **Did the man come hither?**). Saul eventually
becomes king by popular acclaim.

10:25-27. The final act in the drama is the "testimony" (cf. II
Kings 11:12) or recital which verse 25 relates. Apparently
coronation involved, at least in later times, such a statement of
royal **rights and duties.** For a similar recital which the D editor
would certainly know cf. Deuteronomy 17:14-20. This may well
be the D editor at work in keeping with the requirement set out
there. At the end of the passage we learn that the king is not
completely accepted by the people.

D. SAUL'S CORONATION AT GILGAL (11:1-15)

This section is from Source B and thus is a sequel to the secret
anointing of 9:1–10:16. It gives a variant Gilgal version to the
coronation described in 10:17-27.

11:1-4. The Ammonites were a nomadic people living in
Transjordan north of Moab and east of the Israelite tribe of
Gilead. **Jabesh** of Gilead, or **Jabesh-gilead,** was a town on the
eastern edge of the Jordan Valley. The besieged inhabitants ask
for terms, but the Ammonites make insulting demands instead
of the usual **treaty.** To highlight the general plight of Israel they
give a week's **respite** in which the **elders** can seek help.

11:5-11. Saul hears the news purely by chance. He has been
secretly anointed, but now the **spirit** of Yahweh falls on him, and
he becomes a charismatic leader like Samson (Judges 14:19;
15:14). For a parallel to Saul's symbolic act uniting all tribes in a
common venture cf. Judges 19:29–20:11. The result is a
universal **dread** of Yahweh—that is, Israel recognizes Saul's
action as divinely inspired. Failure to take part would mean
being under a curse. The numbers of verse 8 are incredibly
high. **Bezek** was thirteen miles northeast of Shechem on a hill
overlooking the Jordan Valley almost opposite the town of
Jabesh. It provided an excellent rallying place. The day began at

sundown; therefore **the morrow** means "that night." The **morning watch** was the final third of the night.

11:12-15. Verses 12-13 belong as a postscript to 10:27 and are out of place here. Verses 14-15 are the real point of the story. Samuel is pictured as summoning the people to **Gilgal** (see above on 10:8). At the sanctuary there the victorious Saul is made king by popular acclaim.

E. SAMUEL'S COVENANTAL DISCOURSE (12:1-25)

This chapter is from source A and belongs with 8:1-22 and 10:17-27. It has been rewritten in large part by the D editor.

12:1-6. *Samuel's Protestation of Integrity.* In contrast to 8:3-5 the mention of Samuel's **sons** is simply to show his age. The new institution of kingship has not been made necessary by the failure of the former charismatic leaders. Before God and the new king the people declare that Samuel has judged rightly.

12:7-15. *Yahweh's Redemptive Acts.* Samuel's survey of Yahweh's **saving deeds** includes not only the exodus and the gift of Canaan but also deliverance from the various enemies by the judges. **Jerubbaal** is another name for Gideon (cf. Judges 8:29). Also listed is Samuel himself, considered by the D editor to be the last of the great judges. Time and time again the people have rebelled, but always God has **delivered** them when they **cried** out. Now the Ammonites have threatened and the Israelites have demanded a king. This was quite unnecessary since **God was your king.** That this demand was occasioned by the Ammonite threat contradicts chapter 8.

12:16-25. *Samuel's Intercession.* Samuel shows his great power. He calls on Yahweh to bring on **thunder and rain** during the **wheat harvest,** a period when Palestine never sees rain. The people, fearing this phenomenon, are repentant and beg Samuel's intercession. For an interesting parallel of a prophet's intercessory power cf. I Kings 13:1-6. Samuel assures the people that they can cancel the effects of their sin by faithful adherence to Yahweh. Yahweh **will not cast away his people, for his great**

name's sake—that is, Yahweh's reputation is at stake. In typical D language the earlier admonitions of verses 14-15 are repeated in verses 23-25. Apparently the chapter reflects some kind of rite of contrition connected with the royal covenant. But beyond the materials of this chapter little is known of its character.

IV. SAUL'S REIGN AND REJECTION (13:1–15:35)

A. THE REVOLT AGAINST PHILISTINE DOMINATION (13:1–14:46)

13:1-22. *The Outbreak of Hostilities.* The original story of how Saul's war for independence from the Philistines began is found in verses 2-7a and 15b-18. The remainder consists of two additions by the D editor, verses 1 and 7b-15a, and a third passage, verses 19-22, which is probably an insertion.

13:1. The D editor has supplied the usual formula for kings' reigns, but textual corruption has produced an incomplete record. The number of years for Saul's age is lacking. The Septuagint has thirty years, but this may simply be a guess. His having a son with the prowess described in the following story, which clearly must be assigned to the beginning of his reign, indicates that actually Saul must have been forty or older (cf. 9:2). Similarly a word is obviously missing in the number for the length of the reign. Probably either ten or twenty must be inserted to make twelve or twenty-two years. Acts 13:21 has forty years, which is certainly too long.

13:2-4. Saul recruits an army of three thousand and assigns a third of it to **Jonathan,** who is here introduced for the first time. Later (verse 16) he is identified as the **son** of Saul. **Michmash** lay seven miles northeast of Jerusalem on the northern slope of a steep and narrow wadi (river course dry except in the rainy season). **Geba** lay on the higher southern slope, overlooking the pass where the action of 14:1-15 takes place. **Gibeah** was five miles southwest of Geba. The two places are confused at several points in chapters 13–14.

Jonathan and his troops are at Geba rather than Gibeah. He precipitates the revolt by killing the Philistine officer (not **garrison;** see above on 10:1c-13) stationed at Gibeah rather than Geba (cf. 10:5). Further textual corruption is evident in verse 3. Saul would not summon his compatriots in the name **Hebrews,** which in early times was a contemptuous term used primarily by outsiders (cf. 14:11; 29:3). The rumor spreading through **all Israel** assumes that the new king ordered his son's rash deed. On Gilgal (verse 4c) see below on verses 7b-15a.

13:5-7a. The Philistines gather an army to put down the uprising, and they occupy **Michmash.** The numbers are probably exaggerated; certainly **chariots** in this precipitous wadi would be useless. The Israelites are terrified. Many of them, fearing Philistine revenge, either hide or flee to Transjordan.

13:7b-15a. When the D editor took over this account he inserted a story to support his conviction that Saul's reign was rejected and that the acceptable rule began only with David, his successor. By adding a reference to **Gilgal** in verse 4 he gives the impression that Saul is in the Jordan Valley while Jonathan remains on the battlefield. It would have been military suicide to retire to such a distance at this time.

This Gilgal story gives one version of Saul's rejection as king by Yahweh. The D editor ties it in with Samuel's instruction in 10:8, which was intended to be fulfilled by Saul's coronation at Gilgal. In this story Saul is placed in an impossible position. The army is **scattering** but he must wait for Samuel. He waits the stipulated **seven days** (cf. 10:8) and then himself performs the necessary sacrifices. As soon as he has finished Samuel arrives and upbraids him.

Saul was being tested and has failed to meet the arbitrary requirement. Had he passed the test, Samuel says, the dynasty of the future would have been his rather than David's. For another version of Saul's rejection cf. chapter 15. The D editor may have placed the story in this context to prove that Saul was rejected before undertaking his first act of kingship. Could the two years of verse 1 then be intended as the length of time he ruled before his rejection?

114

13:15b-18. Desertions have reduced Saul's army to about **six hundred men.** They are at Geba on the southern side of the wadi (see above on verses 2-4). Opposite them at **Michmash** the Philistines send out most of their force in three companies of **raiders** to ravage the countryside to the north, west, and east respectively.

13:19-22. This parenthetical note may be part of the original story. But since there is no other indication that the Israelites were handicapped by lack of weapons, it is generally considered a later insertion. Even if they were ill equipped before, booty from the Ammonite war (chapter 11) must have provided a considerable supply. However, the note has a historical basis. Archaeology, has confirmed that at this period early in the Iron Age the Philistines far surpassed the Israelites in production and utilization of iron. Small weight stones incribed **pim,** used in balances to weigh silver for payments, have been found. This discovery underlies the Revised Standard Version reconstruction of verse 21 from the obscure Hebrew.

13:23–14:15. *Jonathan's Exploit.* From the height at Geba Jonathan sees across the wadi the **Philistine garrison** come out from **Michmash** to the north side of the **pass.** He suggests to the boy who serves him as **armor-bearer** a madcap venture. Of course he does not inform his **father** what he plans.

14:2-3. Saul with his reduced army is also at Geba (not **Gibeah;** cf. 13:16; see above on 13:2-4). **Migron** is unknown and may be a scribal error for "the threshing floor." **Ahijah** is the **son of Ahitub,** as is also Ahimelech, the father of David's priest Abiathar (chapters 21–22). The two names may identify brothers or, as many scholars believe, the same man. In either case the genealogy is probably intended to relate the prophecies concerning the house of **Eli** (2:27-36; 3:11-14) to Solomon's expulsion of Abiathar (I Kings 2:26-27). Ahijah is carrying, not **wearing,** the **ephod.** In this story the ephod is not a priestly garment, as in 2:18, but a container for the Urim and Thummin used to obtain oracles from Yahweh (see below on verses 16-23 and 36-46).

14:4-5. The jutting crags on either side of the forbidding **pass** have names. **Bozez** means "shining," that is baldfaced, and **Seneh** "thorny."

14:6-15. The slur **uncircumcised** is the regular Israelite designation of the Philistines, who alone among their neighbors did not share the practice of circumcision. In return the Philistines call the Israelites **Hebrews** (see above on 13:2-4). Jonathan proposes an arbitrary **sign** to his servant, who fully concurs. When the sign is positive, they clamber up the steep slope and with sublime faith fall on the garrison. Apparently the shock of the attack throws the army into panic. Yahweh helps the two attackers by an earthquake, which increases the panic even more.

14:16-23. *Defeat of the Philistines.* From Geba (not **Gibeah;** see above on verses 2-3) Saul's sentries, overlooking the enemy's camp, note the confusion. Saul immediately undertakes a roll call. Jonathan and his aide are discovered missing. The text of verse 18 is confused. Saul calls on the priest **Ahijah** to bring forward the **ark of God.** But at this time the ark was at Kiriath-jearim (7:2). The Septuagint represents a clearer tradition: " 'Bring hither the ephod,' for he was carrying the ephod at that time before Israel." Thus Saul asks Ahijah to bring the ephod (see above on verses 2-3) and secure an oracle. Observing the growing **tumult** among the Philistines on the other side of the wadi, he interrupts the priest's manipulation and orders an immediate attack.

The Israelites fall on the enemy camp, which is now in complete **confusion.** Their force of six hundred men is swelled by **Hebrews** who have been with the Philistines, as well as by stragglers who panicked earlier (cf. 13:6). Israel is victorious, and the Philistines flee. **Beth-aven** is unidentified but must have been west of Michmash in the direction of Philistine territory.

14:24-35. *Saul's Taboo.* The text of verses 24-26 is corrupt, but the general intent is clear. Saul is apparently concerned lest the people fail to set aside Yahweh's part of the booty first. Thus he imposes a taboo against eating before **evening.** It turns out to be a tactical error since the weakened troops find it difficult to pursue their military advantage with sufficient energy. Jonathan has not heard the **oath**. He breaks the taboo by eating some wild **honey** and is refreshed (**his eyes became bright**). The last sentence in verse 28 is probably copied from verse 31 by error.

14:31-35. The pursuit extends to **Aijalon**, about fifteen miles west of Michmash toward the Philistine border. By now the sun has gone down and the taboo is no longer in effect. The famished soldiers fall on the prey, eating flesh **with the blood**. This is forbidden practice (cf. Deuteronomy 12:16), and Saul is alarmed. A **great stone** is brought up to serve as **altar** and the people are ordered to **slay** their animals properly and then eat. Saul is much concerned with religious observance.

14:36-46. *The Silent Oracle.* Saul is determined to follow up his advantage and smite the enemy **by night. The priest** seeks an oracle from Yahweh and there is no **answer**. Saul realizes that someone must have broken the taboo that day. He swears an oath that the guilty **shall surely die**. The sacred lot is cast by means of **Urim** and **Thummin** (meaning "lights" and "perfections"). Exactly what these were is not known. Possibly they were flat objects carried in the ephod (see above on verses 2-3), perhaps dark and light on opposite sides.

The **lot** eventually falls on Jonathan, who confesses that he ate some **honey**. That he was unaware of the taboo makes no difference. He realizes that only his death will wipe out the effects. The people, to whom Jonathan is obviously the great hero of the day, stand between Saul and his son. They point out that if God really were displeased with Jonathan, he would hardly have saved Israel through him. A sense of fairness triumphs over superstition. Jonathan is **ransomed,** presumably by the sacrifice of an animal in his stead. Nonetheless the pursuit of the Philistines, which in Saul's eyes would demand the removal of the taboo, is abandoned.

B. CONCLUSION AND FINAL REJECTION (14:47–15:35)

14:47-52. *Summary Notices.* Verses 47-48 are a short summary, similar to that of David's reign in II Samuel 8. **Zobah**

was an Aramaean kingdom (see comment on II Samuel 8:3-8). That this is simply a summary is clear from verse 48*a*, which summarizes chapter 15 in a single sentence. Verse 52 refers to constant war with the Philistines and Saul's building of a standing army. Verses 49-51 interrupt the summary with genealogical notices concerning Saul's family. The list is incomplete, since 31:2 mentions another son, Abinadab. **Ishvi** (probably a textual corruption of "Ishiah," meaning "man of Yahweh") is evidently the same as Ishbosheth in II Samuel 2:10–4:12. His name was actually Ishbaal (see comment on II Samuel 2:8-11). **Abner,** Saul's commander of the army, was his cousin (cf. verse 51 with 9:1).

15:1-35. *Saul's Rejection.* To the D editor this tradition confirmed his belief that the real kingdom started with David. Therefore it was fitting that the David stories should follow immediately. The story has a parallel in 13:7*b*-15*a*. Here also the setting is **Gilgal,** but the occasion is changed to an Amalekite war of extermination. It presents the prophetic view on Saul and his kingdom.

15:1-3. Samuel is here a prophet. Through him Saul receives a divine mandate to conduct a holy war against the Amalekites in fulfillment of the curse in Deuteronomy 25:17-19. A holy war was a war of complete extermination presumably under Yahweh's orders. The **Amalekites** were nomads living in the wilderness area south of Judah. Saul may well have embarked on such a punitive expedition to insure Judean support of his throne.

15:4-9. Saul accordingly musters an army; note the overly large numbers. **Telaim** lay somewhere in the south of Judah. Its location is uncertain. Nor is the **city of Amalek** known—in fact Amalekites did not dwell in cities. This probably means a winter encampment. On the **Kenites** cf. Judges 1:16. The Amalekites are completely defeated and their chief captured. The dimensions of their territory are greatly exaggerated—from the boundaries of **Havilah** (Arabia) to those of **Egypt!** Saul, however, does not carry out the barbaric demands of a holy war. **Agag** is spared, as well as a large amount of cattle.

15:10-21. In the next scene Yahweh tells Samuel that he has rejected Saul because of his disobedience. Samuel's reaction is to be **angry.** Having anointed Saul he is disappointed and tries to change God's mind. **Carmel** (not Mt. Carmel) was seven miles south of Hebron, on the edge of Amalekite territory. There Saul has erected a vicotry stele, or **monument.** When Samuel and Saul meet at the Gilgal sanctuary, Samuel is not deceived. He hears all the **sheep** and **oxen.** But, says Saul, the people have saved some as a **sacrifice.** This is a lame excuse since all the cattle are under the ban—that is, declared profane and doomed to destruction, thus not fit for sacrifice. Samuel rebukes Saul, rightly placing all the responsibility on him as the **anointed** king.

15:22-23. This oracle of rejection has become classic as presenting the prophetic viewpoint over against the priestly. Cult is always second to morality. Sacrifice never takes precedence over obedience. Verse 23*ab* is difficult. The Hebrew text has: "The sin of divination is surely rebellion; and iniquity and idols a presumption." Their condemnation does not seem especially appropriate here. The three terms used are all connected with pagan cult, and Saul's sin seems to be compared with these evil practices. On the other hand **idolatry** here is literally "teraphim," and it has been suggested that originally **iniquity** read "ephod" (see above on 14:2-3). Thus the lines would condemn sin *against* divination by ephod and teraphim—that is, disobedience to the command of holy war against Amalek. At an earlier stage of the the tradition this command was received through divination rather than prophetically as now in verses 1-3.

15:24-35. Saul is portrayed as a pathetic character groveling before Samuel. For a symbolic act of tearing similar to that in verses 27-28 cf. I Kings 11:30-31. On the hidden reference to David cf. 13:14. The term **Glory of Israel** refers to Israel's God; it fits strangely with verse 11. Eventually Samuel gives in to Saul. For the sake of appearance he accompanies the king for the sacrifice. Possibly Samuel's killing of **Agag** was originally a separate tradition from that ending with verse 23. On the other hand verse 28 seems important to the story. What is clear is that after this the break is complete. Samuel never sees Saul again.

V. David's Rise to Power (16:1–II Samuel 5:5)

A. Introduction of David (16:1–18:5)

16:1-13. *David's Anointing.* It is appropriate that the collector of David stories should have begun with this one. It determines the outcome—David's succession to the throne—from the beginning. The story centers around Samuel, though the hero is David. Verse 1 connects it with the preceding chapter. Saul is **rejected,** and thus a new king must be chosen by Yahweh. **Bethlehem** is about five miles south of Jerusalem. The statement that Samuel **consecrated Jesse and his sons** refers to a purificatory rite otherwise unknown.

16:6-13. Seven sons of Jesse are successively viewed by Samuel. But none is **chosen** by Yahweh, who **looks on the heart.** Even so, when the **youngest,** a shepherd, is called, it is noted that he is **handsome** and **ruddy**—a word used also of the newborn Esau (Genesis 25:25). This has been interpreted by some to mean that both he and David were red-headed.

Samuel is told to **anoint** the youth. From verse 2 it appears that his real purpose in coming is to remain secret, but **in the midst of his brothers** would seem to make the anointing a public ceremony. Possibly the phrase does not mean "in the sight of," so that, as in the case of Saul, Samuel takes David aside. Or perhaps he performs the act in such a way that those present do not recognize what he is doing. Throughout the stories there is no hint that knowledge of it is public. Now God's **Spirit** inspires David—that is, makes him qualified to rule when the time comes. This ability is amply shown in subsequent stories.

16:14-23. *David's Arrival at Court.* The rejection of Saul means that God's Spirit has abandoned him; he is no longer qualified to rule. Saul was apparently a psychiatric case who progressively worsened. This is put in theological rather than psychological terms: **an evil spirit from the LORD tormented him.** His **servants** suggest the therapeutic value of music, and someone proposes David, who is described in glowing but exaggerated terms.

David arrives at court with his **lyre** and a present for the king from his father. The lyre was a stringed instrument later popular in the cult. David's musical therapy is successful, and Saul is enamored of his new servant, even making him his personal military aide. The story is only one version of David's introduction to Saul.

17:1-11. *A Philistine Champion's Challenge.* A Philistine army again is arrayed against Israel. This time the scene is in Judah, fourteen miles west of Bethlehem **between Socoh and Azekah. Ephesdammim** may be a site about four miles northeast of Socoh. The Israelite army is encamped by a wadi, the **valley of Elah.** Instead of beginning a pitched battle the Philistines send out a **champion** to challenge any Israelite to fight with him. This peculiar custom is well known from pre-Islamic desert days in Arabia. In II Samuel 21:19 it is stated that one of David's heroes, Elhanan, killed **Goliath** the Philistine giant. If that tradition is correct, it is likely that originally the champion of this story was anonymous. He was later given the name of a known giant. However, some interpreters have argued instead that a tradition of Elhanan's exploit came to be associated with the more famous hero David.

The giant champion is unbelievably huge and strong. He is about nine and a half feet tall and completely equipped with **bronze** armor of great weight and a large **iron** spear (see above on 13:19-22) which reminded one of a **weaver's beam.** Ancient weights were not standardized throughout the Near East. The figures given cannot be confidently translated into modern equivalents, but the impression given of impregnability and tremendous strength is intentional.

17:12-31. *Introduction of David.* This section contradicts chapter 16 and is not part of the story represented by verses 1-11 and 32-54. Along with 17:55–18:5 it is omitted by the Septuagint. Its author knew neither of David's anointing nor of his introduction to court. It thus is a doublet to 16:14-23. Its purpose is to bring David forward as Saul's legitimate successor, on whom God's favor rests. This is especially clear from 17:55–18:5, which belong to this same tradition.

17:12-16. David is introduced anew. Throughout the narrative editorial changes have been brought in to harmonize this account with the other. Thus reference is made to **eight sons** of Jesse, though the story presupposes only four. Verse 15 is also an addition to agree with 16:14-23, as though David is traveling **back and forth** from his **sheep** to the court. But verses 55-58 show that in this source Saul does not know David at all. Therefore verse 15 cannot have been part of the original story.

17:17-19. Jesse sends David with food for his three soldier **brothers** as well as a substantial present for their **commander.** And **ephah** is about a half bushel. Volunteer soldiers had to provide their own provisions. The **token** in verse 18 must be some agreed sign of their continued welfare. Verse 19 is part of Jesse's instructions and should not begin a new paragraph.

17:20-31. As David arrives the two armies are drawing into their **battle line,** as they do every morning, retiring to their camps at night. As usual the Philistine champion struts between the drawn lines challenging the Israelites. Rumor circulates that anyone who successfully defies him will receive a princess' hand in marriage—a common folk motif. No one dares to take up the challenge except the young visitor. David puts his finger on the real problem—the insult that this heathen should **defy the armies of the living God.** Like a typical older brother **Eliab** scolds David for his impertinence. Eventually Saul hears about young David's bold words.

17:32-54. *David's Victory.* The original story again is resumed. David offers his services as champion, but Saul is doubtful. David assures him of his prowess as a courageous shepherd. Furthermore Yahweh will fight for him, since this is really Yahweh's battle. Saul eventually gives in and tries to equip him as a soldier with armor. The term **his armor** in verse 38 hardly means Saul's own. David goes out as a shepherd, without armor, with **his sling.** The sling could be an extremely effective weapon (cf. Judges 20:16). David's lack of armor is important to the story. David is simply an instrument in God's hands.

17:41-47. As the unequal contestants meet, they both make speeches. The Philistine's is insulting and uncouth. It is a typical speech of a warrior who glories in his own strength and intends to put fear into the heart of an opponent. David's speech shows that the spirit of Yahweh is on him (cf. 16:13). His weapon is **the name of the Lord.** Yahweh will today defeat the Philistines through David.

17:48-54. Verses 50 and 51 both state that David **killed** the giant. In verse 50 it is with the **stone,** in verse 51 by decapitation. They need not be conflicting, since verse 51 simply supplies further details to the general summary of verse 50. On **Gath** and **Ekron** see above on 5:6-12. **Shaaraim** is unidentified. Verse 54 remains a mystery. **Jerusalem** was still a Jebusite city, and David could hardly have brought the grisly trophy there. Mention of David's **tent** conflicts with verses 12-31, but may be original. The Philistine's armor was later removed to the sanctuary at Nob (cf. 21:8-9).

17:55–18:5. *Postscript to the Story.* Saul again does not recognize David—in spite of verse 31! The story is another version of David's introduction to the court. This time he is not a musician (16:14-23) but a military hero. Saul's son **Jonathan** becomes attached to David. He makes a **covenant** of friendship with him, giving him clothing and **armor** as a seal on their friendship. Such a covenant was often made among Semites for mutual protection. It was intended as a covenant of clan adoption, as is evident from the one-sided gift of the wealthy prince to David. **Was successful** in verse 5 really means "acted wisely." Accordingly Saul gives him a military captaincy—which seems to please everyone.

B. Rivalry Between Saul and David (18:6–28:2)

18:6-16. *Saul's Jealousy.* The Revised Standard Edition rightly paragraphs this section as three stories. Throughout the narrative the tragic figure of the king whom Yahweh has abandoned is contrasted with the rising star of David whom Yahweh prospers. In the first story Saul's jealousy is aroused by the chanting of **women** giving greater honor to David than to himself. **Timbrels**, or tambourines, were commonly used by women to accompany dancing, as were the three-stringed lutes (**instruments of music**). The Septuagint has the women meeting David instead of **King Saul**, which makes better sense. Possibly the original reading had both.

18:10-11. The second scene is out of context since David is now pictured as a musician rather than a warrior. But an editor rightly felt that the tradition fitted the mood of Saul and David's relations. Verse 10 shows Saul's mental instability in an interesting way. When an evil spirit attacks him, he acts like a prophet—that is, **he raved**, a reference to the ecstatic frenzy of prophetic bands (cf. 19:23-24).

18:12-16. The last scene shows the king trying to solve his problem by getting rid of it. Saul sends David out as an army officer—at least he would not see the object of his hatred any more. But this too boomerangs. By being in the public eye David is fast becoming a popular idol. Small wonder that Saul is awestricken!

18:17-30. *David's Marriage to a Princess.* This section is composed of two stories, originally separate. The first acts as sequel to 17:25. It shows Saul breaking his promise to give his daughter to anyone defeating the Philistine giant. Saul promises David his **elder daughter Merab** as wife on condition that he remain a good soldier. The end of verse 17 may not be original to the story and may have crept in on the basis of verse 21a or 25b. Saul, however, gives her to someone else.

18:20-30. The second story concerns **Michal**, the daughter who does become David's wife. Saul wants to take advantage of the situation. He will incite David to a dangerous mission, hoping that he will be killed. A **marriage present** was a kind of bride purchase given by the husband to the father-in-law. Saul is again frustrated in his attempt to get rid of David. Saul is really powerless against David because Yahweh is with him. David is

now a most successful soldier as well as his **son-in-law.** Verse 21*b*
is editorial. The collector added this to harmonize the two
stories.

19:1-7. *Jonathan's Mediation.* Saul now comes out in the open
and gives general orders to **kill David.** Jonathan intercedes with
Saul successfully, and so David continues in service at court.
The passage seems to be another version of chapter 20. Probably
it was placed here by the collector of the David stories to show
why David is still in the court. The story is also confused. If
Jonathan spoke to Saul **in the field where you are,** why did he
have to inform David of his success afterward? And if Saul was
there, why must David be **brought** to Saul as though the latter
were at court?

19:8-24. *Saul's Attempts on David's Life.* The first attempt
(verses 8-10) is a doublet version of 18:10-11. That story belongs
here rather than in chapter 18.

19:11-17. The second attempt follows hard on the first,
according to the present arrangement. David flees to his home,
apparently on the city wall, and Michal lowers him **through the
window** outside the wall. To delay pursuit she puts **an image** in
the **bed** to deceive the casual onlooker. It is surprising that
Michal possesses an idol—if this is in fact the meaning of the
term, which is literally "teraphim" (see above on 15:22-23).
When Michal's ruse is discovered, she evades her father's anger
by a face-saving lie. David is now no longer safe. He remains at
large as an outlaw until Saul's death.

19:18-24. The third attempt finds David in **Ramah** under
Samuel's protection. The story is clearly legendary. It seems to
be a tale to give another explanation for the origin of the proverb
in verse 24 (cf. 10:10-12). The picture of Samuel as head of a
band of ecstatics is quite at variance with the Samuel stories of
chapters 7–12. Nor would one expect David to escape to the
north but rather to Judah. Three times messengers come to
capture David and remain to prophesy. Finally Saul himself
suffers a similar fate. Verse 24 gives a startling picture of the
uncontrolled frenzy of the prophets. **Secu** and **Naioth** are
unknown. Possibly the latter is simply the name for the dwelling

125

of the **company of the prophets.** The story probably came from the Ramah sanctuary and was eventually incorporated by the collector of the David stories.

20:1-42. *David and Jonathan.* The collector of these stories has connected the preceding story to this one by verse 1*a*. However, they do not follow chronologically. After the events of 19:17 it is hardly believable that Jonathan is unaware of his father's hostility toward David. It may be more believable after 19:9-10. Jonathan is astounded at his father's attitude. In accordance with his covenant of brotherhood (18:3-4) he is willing to do anything for his friend.

The following day will be a feast day—the **new moon,** like the sabbath, was a day of rest and of special religious significance. On the new moon David, as well as Abner and Jonathan, will be expected to eat with Saul. If Saul inquires about David's absence, Jonathan is to present his excuse—an annual family feast in Bethlehem. Saul's reaction will be definitive.

20:10-23. One problem occurs to David. If Saul is angry and suspicious, it will be impossible for the friends to meet. But Jonathan has a novel solution. They **go out into the field,** presumably somewhere near Gibeah. He suggests that three days hence David is to hide himself near a **stone heap** in the field. Jonathan will give the bad news by means of a code, and David can escape without endangering his friend. The phrase in verse 19 **when the matter was in hand** literally means "in the day of the affair," but the allusion is now lost.

20:14-17. Jonathan's instructions have been made considerably more difficult by a later editor's insertion of these verses. They are intended to explain David's later care for Mephibosheth (II Samuel 9:6-7; 21:7). Jonathan makes David **swear** that when he becomes king he will remain **loyal** to their covenant of brotherhood. Such a promise was not superfluous. It was a common Near Eastern custom for a new royal house to exterminate all members of the superseded house.

20:24-34. The arrangements are carried out without a hitch. On the first day Saul attributes David's absence to some ritual uncleanness. The following day he inquires concerning him.

The agreed excuse sends Saul into a rage, and he vilifies Jonathan. The real cause for his hatred slips out. He suspects that David will be the next king. When Jonathan tries to defend him, Saul throws **his spear** at Jonathan, who escapes.

20:35-42. The following morning Jonathan enacts his little scene with an unsuspecting partner in the hearing of David. Verses 40-42*a* are unnecessary to the story. If the friends could meet and speak, the shooting-arrows episode would be horseplay. This probably represents another version of the parting. David is now an outcast.

21:1-9. *David at Nob.* This story is a fitting sequel to 19:11-17. It contrasts with 19:18-24, where David seeks refuge with the prophets. Here it is with the priest. **Nob** was near Jerusalem, possibly on Mt. Scopus, in any event between Anathoth and Jerusalem. The priest there is **Ahimelech.** He is probably the same as Ahijah, who was descended from Eli and was formerly at Shiloh (see above on 14:2-3). David, unarmed and **alone,** presents a startling sight to the priest. He demands food under guise of being on a secret and hurried mission for the king.

Holy bread, which could only be eaten by those ritually clean, is provided on David's assurance that he (and his fictitious **young men**) have been sexually continent and thus are clean. **Bread of the Presence** according to the legislation in Leviticus 24:59 was renewed weekly and was reserved for the priests, but here there is no such reservation. David is given the weapon of the Philistine champion he killed (see above on 17:1-11). Present on this occasion is a certain **Doeg the Edomite,** of whom the next chapter relates dastardly action.

21:10-15. *David's Flight to Gath.* This is another version of chapter 27 and belongs at that point. It does not fit here. David has just received the **sword** of the Philistine champion and would hardly go to Gath with it. He is also called **king of the land,** which must be the reflection of a later situation—unless it is the Philistines' application of the song recalled in verse 11*b*. Possibly the tale is here retold in order to make certain that any possible idea of friendship with **Achish** is refuted.

22:1-5. *David's Brigand Band.* David now flees to **Adullam**, possibly a town ten miles southwest of Bethlehem, near the border between Judah and Philistine territory. Adullam is called a **cave** in verse 1, probably because of the many caves in that area. In verses 4-5 it is more appropriately a **stronghold**. According to verse 5 it is in Philistine hands. Here his relatives as well as a large number of malcontents and oppressed come to his support. David thus becomes the leader of a band of outlaws. His relatives naturally join him for fear of royal reprisal. Eventually a prophetic word orders him back to danger in **Judah**. This is intended to show that he must remain under Yahweh's protection rather than seek refuge in an alien land. The **forest of Hereth** is unknown but must have been in the southwestern part of Judah, northwest of Hebron.

22:3-4*a*. Inserted into this account is the strange reference to David's entrusting his parents to the care of the **king of Moab**. On the close relations of Bethlehem and Moab see the Introduction to Ruth. On the other hand David's severe treatment of the Moabites in II Samuel 8:2 makes this story questionable. **Mizpeh of Moab** is unknown.

22:6-19. *Saul's Revenge on the Priests of Nob.* This is the sequel to 21:1-9. Verse 6 was written by the collector as a connecting link. It also anticipates verse 9. Saul as king sits in the place of judgment, with the **spear** as symbol of royalty **in his hand**. He harangues his fellow tribesmen standing about.

22:9-19. In response **Doeg the Edomite** now informs on the priests of Nob (cf. 21:7). So Ahimelech and his fellow priests are summoned and accused of abetting the enemy. Ahimelech, who apparently knew nothing of the vendetta between Saul and David, stoutly affirms his good faith. The irrational Saul immediately condemns them all to death and commands his **guard** to carry out the sentence. They refuse, but Doeg is quite willing. He wipes out the entire priestly contingent and sacks their **city**. Saul is not only abandoned by Yahweh. He now uses holy war tactics against Yahweh's priests.

22:20-23. *A Priest's Escape.* Only one, **Abiathar**, son of Ahimelech, escapes the slaughter. He joins David's forces.

From now on Abiathar becomes David's close friend, personal priest, and confidant.

23:1-13. *David at Keilah.* Keilah was about nine miles northwest of Hebron and just a little south of Adullam (22:1-2). David is here portrayed in his later role of deliverer of Israel. The Philistines have come to raid the people of Keilah and take their harvest.

23:2-5. David twice inquires by the ephod (cf. verse 6; see above on 14:2-3, 36-46). Yahweh commands him to deliver Keilah. His men are dubious but David persists and is victorious. The Philistines are defeated, **their cattle** (for transporting the spoils) are taken, and the city is delivered.

23:6. According to this verse it is here at Keilah that Abiathar joins David (cf. 22:20-23). However, in view of verse 2 and 4 it seems more likely to have been prior to this. In any event the **ephod,** the means for inquiring an answer from Yahweh, is now no longer with Saul but with David.

23:7-13. Meanwhile Saul has heard of David's stay in Keilah. He is determined to attack the city and capture him. David asks two questions of Yahweh by means of the ephod. He discovers that Saul is intent on coming to Keilah and that its inhabitants will give him up rather than defend him. By now the number of his band has swelled to **six hundred.** From now on David is to stay out of walled towns and remain in **wilderness** areas. There David as a native has the advantage over Saul.

23:14-29. *Saul's Pursuit of David.* The **Wilderness of Ziph** is the rugged area east and southeast of Hebron around Ziph, which was about five miles from Hebron. **Horesh** was less than two miles south of Ziph. The emphasis in the story is on God's care for David so that Saul is frustrated throughout. The visit of **Jonathan,** though historically difficult, shows the increasing certainty of future events. David's succession to the throne is openly acknowledged (cf. 20:14-16). Jonathan will then take second place.

23:19-24a. The citizens of Ziph betray David's presence to Saul. The **hill of Hachilah** and **Jeshimon** are not identified but must have been south of Hebron, near Ziph. **Thousands** in verse

23 has the meaning of "clans." A more detailed doublet account of Saul's pursuit of David in the Wilderness of Ziph is found in chapter 26.

23:24b-29. David meanwhile has gone somewhat farther south to the area around **Maon,** three miles south of Horesh. Reference to the **Arabah** is out of order here. The Arabah was the great depression from the Sea of Galilee to the Gulf of Aquaba, and this event takes place in **mountain** territory. Saul is on the point of capturing David when he is recalled by news of a Philistine **raid.** After this hairbreadth escape David seeks refuge in the area around **En-gedi,** the wild mountain area overlooking the Dead Sea.

24:1-22. *Saul's Life Spared.* David and his men are in a large **cave** when Saul comes in alone unaware of danger. David's men are jubilant. They quote an oracle (verse 4) predicting David's victory over his enemy. But David refuses to harm Saul because he is Yahweh's **anointed.** Instead he removes a piece of Saul's outer garment as evidence that the king has been in his power. Verses 4*d*-5 should be understood as occurring between verse 7*a* and *b*. Saul remains completely unaware of what has happened until later, when David calls out after him and makes a speech of defense.

24:16-22. Saul settles the issue by admitting his own guilt and blessing David for his good action. Jonathan's statement in 23:17 is confirmed (verse 20). David promises that contrary to common Near Eastern customs, he will not kill off members of his predecessor's family. Then they go their separate ways. The point of the narrative is not merely to exalt David's fine character and show his respect for God's anointed. It brings out with increasing clarity the inevitableness of the establishment of the Davidic dynasty. For a more detailed doublet cf. chapter 26.

25:1-44. *David and Abigail.* Verse 1*a* gives an obituary notice of Samuel which seems out of place here and may have crept in from 28:3.

25:2-4. The **wilderness of Paran** seems to be a general designation for the desert area west of Edom, south of Judah, and extending down to Aqaba. It may be an error here. In any event David is once again south of Hebron near Maon (see above on 23:24b-29). A wealthy shepherd, **Nabal** (meaning "fool"), is engaged in sheepshearing at **Carmel,** about a mile northwest of his home in Maon. The Calebites were a small clan around Hebron, a subclan within Judah (cf. Joshua 14:13-14). Sheepshearing was occasion for a **feast day,** and the owner would be expected to provide liberally for the servants and guests. Now Nabal the dolt has a **wife** wise and **beautiful.** It is she who is the heroine, with David the hero, and Nabal the villain, of the story.

25:5-13. David sends **ten young men** to ask for a gift, a brigand's payment for protection. Nabal not only refuses payment but returns an insulting reply. David and his men are only renegade slaves, men of no account. Why should he give them anything? **Water** in verse 11 probably should read "wine." David in true oriental fashion immediately gives orders to prepare to wipe out the insult. Two thirds of his band are mustered for attack, the rest remaining to guard the baggage.

25:14-17. Meanwhile Nabal's servants tell **Abigail** of her husband's foolhardy retort to David's men. They insist that David's band deserves better treatment, having protected them against danger.

25:18-31. The next scene shows Abigail with a large present hurrying to intercept the hot-blooded David—without of course informing her churlish spouse. Meanwhile David has sworn an oath that he will wipe out the insult by blood. Suddenly the two meet, and Abigail intercedes for Nabal, asking David not to take revenge. Nabal is a fool indeed. She will bear his **guilt.** Accordingly she has brought a small gift; let David be generous.

She is Yahweh's instrument to keep him from incurring **bloodguilt,** which would be a stain on his record when he eventually becomes king. With perfect charm she ends her plea by asking for favor when Yahweh has prospered him—a harbinger of the romantic outcome of the story!

25:32-35. David can hardly resist the winsome charms of the heroine and blesses her for her intercession. He tells her of his previous intention of wiping out every male of Nabal's household before morning.

25:36-42. On Abigail's return Nabal is completely **drunk.** The next **morning** when he is sober Abigail gives him the full story. The shock apparently brings on a stroke, and a second stroke **ten days later** removes him. David sees Nabal's death as Yahweh's intervention through the good Abigail, who has kept him from bloodguilt. David thereupon woos and wins the widow.

25:43-44. David is becoming a man of parts in the area, also taking **Ahinoam** as wife. **Jezreel** is not to be confused with the famous northern city; it lay in the vicinity of Ziph. Meanwhile Saul has given **Michal,** David's first wife, to someone else. **Gallim** was a small town north of Jerusalem about a mile east of Gibeah.

26:1-25. Saul's Life Spared Again. This is another version of 23:19–24:22 (see comment). As in 23:19-20 the Ziphites are the informers. In this version Saul and his men are encamped. David and his nephew **Abishai,** whose mother, **Zeruiah,** was David's sister (I Chronicles 2:16) sneak **into the camp . . . by night,** into the tent of Saul. There lies the **sleeping** king with the upright lance beside him as a symbol of the presence of the king. As in 24:6 David will not harm Yahweh's **anointed** one. So they simply take the **spear** and a **water** jug from the tent and creep away unnoticed.

26:13-16. Once David is at a safe distance he shouts to **Abner,** taunting him with his failure to guard the king. The spear and the water jug are gone!

26:17-20. Meanwhile Saul has **recognized David's voice,** and David reproaches Saul for his pursuit of the innocent. The argument is somewhat different from that in 24:9-15. Who has caused Saul to pursue David? If it is Yahweh, may Yahweh be placated by an **offering?** That God could stir people up to sin is often said in the Old Testament. But **if it is men,** then may they be **cursed** in Yahweh's name. That David is being driven out of Yahweh's land means he cannot share in Yahweh's heritage. Only in Yahweh's land can he take part in the blessing of Yahwism. Popular belief had it that gods were closely allied to their land. In fact exile meant to **serve other gods,** because other lands meant other gods. All this anticipates the next chapter.

26:21-25. Saul's response, like that in 24:17-21, admits his guilt and David's innocence. They then go their separate ways, never to meet again.

27:1–28:2. *David's Service to the Philistines.* This passage shows no awareness of a prior visit of David to **Achish** (see above on 21:10-15). Aware that life in Judah is becoming increasingly dangerous for him, David goes to Philistine territory. There he offers his service to Achish, **king of Gath.** This is a daring step. To join the traditional enemy's side and be absent from the land may weaken his cause in Israel (see above in 22:1-5).

David now attempts a tightrope course. He uses his stay to persuade both Philistines and Judeans that he is loyal to their respective causes. He deceives his hosts by making numerous raids on Bedouin tribes, killing everyone—dead men tell no tales. Then he brings back booty and reports raids against Judeans. So successful is this deceit that Achish appoints David as his personal **bodyguard,** even in battle **against Israel.** He gives David the town of **Ziklag,** a border town about twelve miles north of Beer-sheba, as a reward for and token of his loyalty to the Philistines. Verses 5-7 are chronologically out of order and should be understood as following verse 12.

David is now free of Saul's persecution, and on foreign soil he is able to consolidate his position. His raids against the neighboring Bedouin tribes bring in wealth for both himself and Achish. The **Negeb** (cf. 30:14) refers simply to the dry steppe land extending from Beer-sheba over to the desert. Unfortunately David is overly successful in convincing Achish of his loyalty (28:1-2). What would have happened had David been put to the test is not known (see below on 29:1-11).

C. THE FINAL BATTLE OF SAUL
(I 28:3–II 1:27)

28:3-25. *The Witch of Endor.* This story concerns only Saul and is a fitting sequel to chapter 15. It is not really a part of the

133

David stories, but chronologically it does belong within their framework. Properly it should come between chapters 30 and 31. Chapters 29–30 continue the narrative of chapter 27. The advance of the Philistines also becomes reasonable if chapter 28 follows chapter 30. They are at Aphek in 29:1, go up to Jezreel in 29:11, and now encamp at **Shunem** (verse 4).

28:3. The notice of Samuel's death belongs here as a setting for this story rather than in 25:1. Also preparing for this story is the fact that Saul has earlier banished necromancy—communication with the dead—as an illegal and superstitious means of determining the future.

28:4-6. But the situation is now critical. The armies are drawn up in battle array. The **Philistines** are at **Shunem** overlooking the Jezreel valley on the southwest slope of Nebi Dahi. The Israelites on Mt. **Gilboa** at the eastern end of the valley. The fear-ridden king naturally wishes an oracle before proceeding to battle the next morning. But none of the legal means—**dreams,** the **Urim** (see above on 14:36-46), and **prophets**—give him an answer. Yahweh has now completely abandoned him.

28:7-14. So Saul seeks out a female necromancer at **Endor,** on the northern slope of Nebi Dahi, thus only a short distance away. Israel believed that people could have communication with the dead through mediums, though such communication was forbidden. The **medium** does not recognize the disguised king until he requests her to bring up the shade of Samuel. The narrator undoubtedly believed in the reality of the scene, but note that Saul never sees the spirit. The medium states that she sees the ghostlike figure (a **god,** literally "gods") of an **old man . . . wrapped in a robe.** Saul recognizes Samuel from her description.

28:15-19. Now the medium is no longer necessary. Saul tells of his distress; he can get no divine instructions. Samuel also refuses to give advice and says **tomorrow you and your sons** will die and Israel will be defeated. An editor expanded the original statement of Samuel by adding verses 17-19*a*, thus tying it in with chapter 15.

28:20-25. Saul is now without any hope. He returns to camp, a doomed man wrapped in despair.

29:1-11. *David's Dilemma Resolved.* This section is the sequel to 28:1-2. On **Aphek** see above on 4:1*b*-11. The **fountain . . . in Jezreel** ("spring of Harod," Judges 7:1) was probably at the foot of Mt. Gilboa. As the Philistine **lords** review their troops, David and his men pass by. The commanders recall his military prowess against the Philistines in former days. Naturally they are suspicious of his turncoat loyalties (on **Hebrews** see above on 13:2-4).

Achish defends David on the double ground that he is a Judean rebel and has proved his loyalty for the past two years (the Septuagint reading for **days and years**). The **commanders** overrule Achish. He advises David of his dismissal, assuring him of his own faith in his loyalty with an oath formula in the name of Yahweh, David's God. David protests this questioning of his devotion—doubtless with tongue in cheek. But Achish insists that he and his men leave the ranks before **morning.** The Septuagint amplifies verse 10 as an order to "go to the place where I stationed you and do not devise some evil plan in your heart because you are a good man in my opinion, and go directly."

30:1-6a. *An Amalekite Raid on Ziklag.* On their return to Ziklag, David and his men find it completely despoiled. All the women and children, including David's two wives (cf. 25:39-43), are **taken captive** by raiding Amalekites. The raid was probably retaliatory (cf. 27:8-12). Each bewails his loss, and then in anger the men turn on their leader David, a natural reaction. He had left no males to guard the town.

30:6b-20. *David's Rescue of the Captives.* David turns to the oracle for guidance. At his request **Abiathar,** his priest-friend (cf. 22:20-23), consults the **ephod.** Yahweh answers David affirmatively.

30:9-10. David immediately sets out with his band of six hundred men—in spite of the exhausting march from Aphek to Ziklag (around eighty miles) in less than three days which they have just finished. When they arrive at the **brook Besor,** a third of the band are **too exhausted** to make the crossing, and they are left with the baggage (verse 24). David continues with the remaining four hundred men.

30:11-15. Fortunately they find an **Egyptian** slave abandoned by the Amalekites. Abandonment in the desert meant inevitable death through starvation and thirst. Their kindness to him is amply repaid. Not only does he inform them of the extent of the raids but also leads them to the Amalekite encampment. On **Negeb** see above on 27:8-12. The Negeb of the **Cherethites** was at the southern end of Philistine territory, that of **Caleb** south of Hebron (cf. 25:1*b*-3).

30:16-20. The Amalekites are engaged in a great feast, probably a religious celebration because of their successful raids. It is not exactly clear when the attackers arrive. Verse 17 probably should read "from dawn" rather than **from twilight.** The point is that on the following day (they wait until dawn) they attack and the slaughter lasts until sunset. The **four hundred** cameleers escape; all the rest are killed. The captives are rescued and the spoil is taken. Verse 20 is not entirely clear. The intent seems to be to show that David took not only the spoil from Ziklag but also all that had been taken on other Amalekite raids (cf. verse 14). Verses 26-31 seem to suggest this as well. This spoil was considered to be the possession of the chieftan, who had absolute control over its division.

30:21-31. *The Division of the Spoil.* On the return journey the victors rejoin the two hundred men who stayed with the **baggage.** When it comes to the division of the booty, some men selfishly want the two hundred to have no share. David decrees that all shall share alike, quartermasters as well as warriors. This generous decision becomes binding precedent for later Israelite practice.

30:26-31. On arriving in Ziklag David repairs his political fences in southern Judah. He shares the **spoil** with leaders in the various places in the Negeb where he has been, symbolizing his identification with their situation. David has become the effective defender of the area. Not all the places mentioned in verses 26-31 have been identified, but all are in the same general area. **Racal** should probably be changed to "Carmel" as in the Septuagint.

31:1-13. *The Death of Saul.* This account is the sequel to chapter 28 (see comment). Battle between the two armies is joined and Israel is defeated. Three of Saul's four **sons** are killed—Ishbaal is not present at the battle apparently (see above on 14:47-52). Saul himself is hard pressed, **wounded,** and in despair. When his aide refuses to kill him he commits suicide, a rare occurrence among Israelites.

The Philistine success results in panic even across the Jordan. **Cities** and towns are abandoned by their inhabitants and occupied by the invading Philistines. Saul, in spite of his many shortcomings, had been the hope of Israel, and his death precipitated political chaos. Occupation east of the Jordan, however, must have been minimal. **Jabesh-gilead** (see above on 11:1-11) remained free. The parallel account in I Chronicles 10 omits reference to **those beyond the Jordan,** but this is not to be trusted.

31:8-13. The following morning the victors return to the battlefield to despoil the **slain** and find the royal corpses, which they strip of **armor.** Saul is decapitated (cf. 17:51). His armor is displayed in the **temple** of Astarte (**Ashtaroth**), probably in **Beth-shan,** a strong Canaanite city at the eastern end of the Valley of Jezreel. Astarte was the Canaanite fertility goddess, consort of Baal.

Saul began his reign with the rescue of Jabesh-gilead (11:1-11). Now it ends with the men of Jabesh as an act of piety taking his defiled corpse and those of his sons to Jabesh and interring them after cremation, an uncommon practice in Israel. It has been plausibly suggested that the Hebrew word for **burnt** in verse 12 actually means "anointed"; this would remove the difficulty. They then mourn for the dead Saul by fasting for a week.

THE SECOND BOOK OF SAMUEL

John William Wevers

INTRODUCTION

See the Introduction to I Samuel. The outline of the contents indicated by the headings continues that in I Samuel.

1:1-16. *News of Saul's Death.* This account is a sequel to I Samuel 30. An **Amalekite** messenger comes to David at **Ziklag** with signs of mourning to notify him that **Saul** and **Jonathan** are dead. His account conflicts with that of the preceding chapter. He is trying to gain favor by pretending to be responsible for Saul's death. Verse 9 is not clear. The word translated **anguish** may mean "giddiness" or possibly "fainting." The Amalekite must actually have been on the battlefield at Gilboa, since he robbed Saul's body of **crown** and **armlet** and brought them to David.

1:11-16. David's double reaction to this news (verses 11-12 and 13-16) has led many to think that two traditions are here intertwined. This theory is unnecessary if verses 11-12 are understood to follow verse 16. David's immediate reaction (verses 13-16) is anger against the Amalekite for daring to lay hands on Yahweh's **anointed.** The surprised Amalekite is killed forthwith at David's order (cf 4:10). The Amalekite is a **sojourner,** meaning a non-Israelite who lived in Israel. By his violent death the curse of Saul's death was wiped out. The second reaction (verses 11-12) is one of mourning for Saul, Jonathan, and the defeated Israelites—a mourning imposed on the entire camp for the day.

1:17-27. *A Dirge over the Fallen Heroes.* David's poetic genius is here beautifully shown. The **lamentation** was preserved in the **Book of Jashar** (see comment on I Kings 8:12-13). The poem is completely secular and is unquestionably from David's hand. It is full of difficulties, and the Revised Standard Version rendering is much clearer than the original. The Hebrew of verse 18*a* has "and he said that the people of Judah should be taught the bow," which makes no sense. Possibly the word for "bow" is a corruption for some word meaning a "dirge" or "poem."

1:19-21. David first bewails the defeat of the Israelites in battle. Israel's **glory** refers to its leaders, the **mighty.** Then he curses the place of battle (verse 21) as the place where the heroes were slain. There Saul's **shield** lies in the sun, its leather drying out for lack of **oil.** For **upsurging of the deep** the Hebrew has "fields of offering," which probably should be retained as a reference to productivity of the fields.

1:22-27. Here begins the actual dirge over Saul and Jonathan. They have been mighty warriors and now are together **in death.** The women normally led mourning as well as festal rites. Their grief is especially evoked since they have received costly booty from Saul's campaigns. But to David the loss of **Jonathan** is personal. With him he has had a covenant of brotherhood (cf. I Samuel 18:3-4; 20:42, 23:18), and the bond of love between them is now broken. **Weapons of war** in verse 27 refers to Saul and Jonathan.

D. DAVID'S ASCENT TO THE THRONE (2:1–5:5)

2:1-7. *David's Anointing as King of Judah.* With divine approval David can return to **Judah** now that Saul is dead. He is directed to **Hebron,** which is more or less central to the area where he has roamed and has in-laws. He is there **anointed** by

Judean representatives as king. Apparently the Philistines felt that David would extend their control over Judah. Later their eyes were opened to his real loyalties when he became king over the united tribes (5:17-25). The action described in I Samuel 30:26-31 immediately paid off.

2:4b-7. David begins strengthening his position immediately. The **loyalty** of the citizens of **Jabesh-gilead** (cf. I Samuel 31:11-13) to Saul's memory might create eventual trouble for his successor. David promises them his protection, a fairly clear statement of his ambitions. Protection of Jabesh from Hebron would be a meaningless promise!

2:8-11. *Saul's Son as King in the North.* A surviving son of Saul is **Ishbosheth.** His actual name was Ishbaal (Eshbaal in I Chronicles 8:33; 9:39), meaning "man of baal." In his time this was apparently used as a title ("master" or "lord") of Yahweh. Later editors replaced "baal" with "bosheth," meaning "shame," or in I Samuel 14:49 probably with "iah," meaning "Yahweh" (see comment on I Samuel 14:47-52). **Abner** now sets up Ishbaal as puppet king over the northern tribes. But his position is so insecure that he has to rule from **Mahanaim** in **Gilead** in Transjordan; its location is not known.

Ashurites probably means the tribe of Asher. **Jezreel** may be a general term for some of the northern tribes. Ishbaal's rule over these tribes, **Ephraim,** and **Benjamin** was certainly more nominal than real. The Philistines still occupied the land west of the Jordan. Verses 10-11 contain two difficulties. Ishbaal was certainly younger than **forty years** and, like his father, Saul, reigned more than **two years** (cf. I Samuel 13:1). He must have reigned about seven years. Ishbaal probably was too young to fight with Saul at Gilboa and was still a minor when Abner made him king.

2:12–3:1. *The Battle of Gibeon.* Gibeon was six miles northwest of Jerusalem. Here Abner's forces meet the Judean forces at the **pool,** a huge water cistern. The Judeans are led by **Joab,** son of David's sister **Zeruiah** (cf. I Chronicles 2:16). Joab is already in a commanding position, a position he is to retain throughout his uncle's reign. The two leaders agree to a jousting tournament, **twelve** to a side, as a form of sport. This leads to fatal consequences (just how all twenty-four could kill each other is not clear). Battle is then joined in which Abner's forces are beaten. The meaning of the place name commemorating the tournament is not certain (see the Revised Standard Version footnote).

2:18-28. Joab's younger brother, **Asahel,** is a runner. He is determined on military honors and tries to catch **Abner.** The seasoned warrior warns the youth, knowing that his death will start an undying blood feud with his brothers. Asahel nevertheless tries to take on Abner and is killed. The two remaining brothers, **Joab and Abishai,** take up the pursuit until sunset, when Abner is able to reassemble his forces on some defensible **hill.** Neither **Ammah** nor **Giah** has been identified, nor does the **wilderness of Gibeon** make good sense—after all the flight started at Gibeon. Possibly Geba should be read for Gibeon here; it lay five miles east on the way toward Jordan. Abner appeals to Joab to put an end to the blood feud and Joab agrees to the truce.

2:29–3:1. Both sides then return to their respective capitals. Abner's men are called Benjaminites, probably because most of Saul's support came from fellow tribesmen (cf. I Samuel 9:1). The concluding statement shows that David is obviously going to win the struggle.

3:2-5. *David's Sons.* This is the first list of David's offspring (cf. the supplement in 5:13-16). Six wives are listed (on the first two see comment on I Samuel 25:36-44), each with her first-born son. Oddly, one, **Eglah,** is specifically called **David's wife.** Only three of the six occur in later stories. **Chileab** is called Daluia in the Septuagint and Daniel in I Chronicles 3:1.

3:6-11. *Abner's Quarrel with Ishbaal.* When a king died, his harem became the possession of the new king. Abner, the strong man of the northen kingdom, has taken one of Saul's concubines, **Rizpah** for himself. Ishbaal (see above on 2:8-11) upbraids him for it. Abner then loses his temper and swears an oath to throw his support from Saul's to David's house. Abner is aware, as were Jonathan, Saul, and Abigail, that Yahweh intends David to rule over united Israel.

3:12-21. *Abner's Attempt to Fulfill His Oath.* Verses 12-16 fit badly into the context. Abner immediately seeks some agreement by which he will make David king over united Israel. David demands the return of **Michal**, his **wife**, whom Saul gave to another (cf. I Samuel 25:44), before he will negotiate. But then David makes the demand of Ishbaal, who agrees, and Abner is also involved in the removal of Michal from her second husband. Possibly these verses are a later insertion intended to make David's political action legitimate. As son-in-law of Saul he was a legitimate successor, and this needed to be established before he proceeded with negotiations. Abner meanwhile has a number of conferences with Israelite leaders, including the recalcitrant Benjaminites. He urges them to transfer their loyalties to David. With their agreement in hand he goes to Hebron, where he is festively received by David. Doubtless Abner expects something in return, but nothing is said about this.

3:22-30. *Joab Slays Abner.* Joab has been absent when David received Abner, possibly by David's careful arrangement. On his return from some successful raiding party he discovers what has happened and tells David it was foolish to let Abner depart peaceably. Unknown to David, Joab sends men to overtake Abner at the well of **Sirah**, a mile and a half to the northwest, and bring him back to Hebron. Pretending to speak with him privately, Joab treacherously stabs Abner in the **belly.** So Abner had fatally wounded Joab's brother Asahel (cf. 2:23).

The narrator insists that the murder is purely a brother's **blood** revenge and is not instigated by David. In fact David avoids the bloodguilt resulting from Abner's slaying by insisting that he himself is **guiltless** and calling an eternal curse on Joab's **house.** The involvement of **Abishai** in verse 30 seems secondary to the story. It is an editorial insistence that the deed is the result of a blood feud.

3:31-39. *Abner Mourned and Buried.* David completely dissociates himself from Joab's deed by ordering national mourning rites for the fallen leader. David convinces the people of his own innocence in various ways. He takes part in the funeral procession, he composes a dirge, and he fasts. The short dirge in verses 33-34 emphasizes the tragedy of Abner's death. A **fool** brings about his own death by folly. Abner did not die as a prisoner or in warfare but was killed by guile.

David again absolves himself from complicity in the guilt of his nephew (verse 39). Since it was a blood feud, he can hardly kill Joab, as was his normal practice (cf. 1:15; 4:12). He contents himself with a general curse on the **evildoer.** David realizes that this may well cause civil war and that his dream of ruling over united Israel has received a severe setback. His prompt action, however, averts further trouble.

4:1-12. *The Murder of Ishbaal.* The death of Abner precipitates a crisis in northern Israel. He has been the power behind the throne, and **all Israel** knows it. Ishbaal (see above on 2:8-11) is shortly thereafter murdered during the **noonday rest** by two of his officers. They take his **head** to David in expectation of reward. David, however, immediately has the two murderers **killed** and their bodies publicly displayed, thereby dissociating himself from the action.

4:2-3. The story has been amplified by a note explaining how Beeroth could be Benjaminite. According to Joshua 9:17 Beeroth was one of the four cities of the Gibeonite confederacy. It was probably about nine miles north of Jerusalem, though this location has been challenged. Why the citizens should have fled to **Gittaim** (location unknown) is not clear. Possibly David later took further revenge on the Beerothites for Ishbaal's murder, thereby causing their flight.

4:4. This verse is out of context here. It belongs to chapter 9, probably after 9:3. It refers to **Mephibosheth,** the son of Jonathan, and the reason for his lameness. His real name was Meribaal (cf. I Chronicles 8:34 and 9:40). As in Ishbaal, "baal" was changed to "bosheth" (see above on 2:8-11). "Mephi" is a scribal error for an original "Meri."

4:6. The text here is uncertain. The Revised Standard Version follows the Septuagint, rather than the Hebrew, which does not make good sense.

5:1-5. *David's Anointing as King of Israel.* Verses 1-2 relate how after Ishbaal's death the **tribes** gather to David at his southern capital. They plead his kingship on the basis of blood relationship, his past military leadership, and the divine prediction of his rule (cf. 3:9-10, 18). Verse 3 then specifies the actual kingmaking. The **elders** gather, agree to a **covenant,** and anoint David king over united **Israel.** The account is merely a summary of what was probably an involved negotiation and ceremony. Verses 4-5 are probably from the D editor (cf. the chronological notices in I and II Kings; see Introduction to I Kings). David's dreams are now fulfilled. God has made him king.

VI. EARLY SUCCESS AS KING OF ISRAEL (5:6-8:18)

A. MILITARY VICTORIES (5:6-25)

5:6-12. *The Capture of Jerusalem.* Obviously David could hardly rule the northern tribes from Hebron. Nor could he deny his own Judean kinsmen by moving his capital to the north. What he needed was neutral ground on the border between Judah and Benjamin. No better place could be found than **Jerusalem.** It was still in Canaanite (Jebusite) hands, and it was an easily defensible fortress. Jerusalem was an ancient city, mentioned in Egyptian texts of the nineteenth century. It is called Salem in Genesis 14:18. That Jerusalem was considered impregnable is clear from the taunting words of the inhabitants.

5:8. This verse would seem to be some explanation of the method of taking Jerusalem, but the text is full of difficulties. The original text has David saying: "Whoever would smite the Jebusite let him touch the lame and the blind, whom David's soul hates, in the water shaft." This makes no sense. The parallel passage in I Chronicles 11:6 has a simpler version, omitting all reference to water shafts and the lame and the blind. It is often suggested that the **water shaft** refers to an ancient tunnel known as Warren's Shaft. If this is understood as the path of the Judean entrance to the city, the feat was a tremendous undertaking. How the saying of David could explain the proverbial saying of verse 8*b* is also a mystery. Undoubtedly the text is corrupt.

5:9-10. On the **Millo** see comment on I Kings 9:15-23. **Zion** became the sacral name, whereas Jerusalem was the political name. Popularly it could be called the **city of David.**

5:11-12. The Phoenician **Hiram** (cf. I Kings 5:1) sends workmen and lumber to David to build a palace. David's reputation against the Philistines would be the basis for his gaining international respect. Hiram's actions are therefore more natural after verses 17-25.

5:13-16. *Postscript.* This note is certainly out of place, being a sequel to the list of David's sons in 3:2-5. **Solomon** was certainly born later since he was the son of Bathsheba (cf. 12:24). The list is probably taken from some later court record and inserted here to show David's royal status. Kings had many consorts.

5:17-25. *Defeat of the Philistines.* Two stories of Philistine defeat are here told serially in verses 17-21 and 22-25. But it is likely that the events of verses 6-10 intervened.

5:17-21. The **Philistines** did not mind David's ruling over Judah. However, as king over all **Israel** he threatened their control over Palestine. David realized that Hebron was hardly defensible and accordingly **went down to the stronghold.** This cannot refer to Jerusalem, which was on a hill. The stronghold must have been that of Adullam (cf. 23:13-14 and I Samuel 22:1-5), a favorite place of David.

The Philistines, however, go north to the plain of **Rephaim,** immediately southwest of Jerusalem. Probably they intended to cut the northern tribes from Judah. David as usual consults the oracle—probably the ephod at the hand of Abiathar (cf. I Samuel 23:6). He gets a positive response. He attacks and breaks through the Philistine army, thereby once and for all uniting the northern and southern tribes militarily. The place of breakthrough is memorialized by the name **Baalperazim,** "the Lord of the breaking through." It was probably about two and a half miles northwest of Jerusalem.

5:22-25. The second encounter—possibly after Jerusalem was in David's hands—is again in **Rephaim.** This time David receives divine instruction not to attack but to **go around to their rear.** He is to attack only when the divine sign is given. The rendering **balsam trees** is uncertain; some kind of shrub is undoubtedly meant. David is again successful, and the Philistines are driven back to their borders. **Gezer** was on the edge of the coastal plain. **Geba** should probably be Gibeon, as the Septuagint reads.

B. JERUSALEM AS RELIGIOUS CENTER (6:1-7:29)

6:1-11. *The First Move of the Ark.* This passage is the sequel to the taking of Jerusalem. It shows how David strengthens his new capital by making it a religious capital as well. He means to unite the northern tribes even more firmly to his rule by bringing their sacred symbol to Jerusalem. The account is full of obscurities.

6:1-2. The assembly of **thirty thousand men** seems grossly exaggerated; nor is it clear why **chosen men,** i.e. warriors, should take part in the ceremony. The ark has been housed in Kiriath-jearim (see comment on I Samuel 6:21-7:2), which according to I Chronicles 13:6 was also called Baalah. Somehow this latter name must have fallen out of verse 2 as the identification of the place to which **from there** refers. **Baale-judah** cannot be a variant form of Baalah, for Kiriath-jearim was not in Judah but in Benjamin. Rather the phrase should be translated "of the lords of Judah." On the cultic name of the ark see comment on I Samuel 4:4.

6:3-5. The name **Ahio** is strange and could simply be translated as "his brother." If this is correct, however, it is odd that the brother is unnamed. Apparently bringing up the ark was an important cultic ceremony, possibly connected with some feast. It seems probable that it gave rise to some later feast in which bringing up the ark became an important ritual (cf.

Psalm 24). Music and the sacral dance were part of the ritual (cf verse 14).

6:6-11. The unfortunate incident which puts an abrupt end to the festivities is particularly obscure. All that is clear is that **Uzzah** dies suddenly next to the ark. Apparently he does something thought to incur divine displeasure. The Revised Standard Version rendering of verses 6-7 is based on the parallel text of I Chronicles 13:9-10, which in turn was based on this passage. There is no word for **his hand** in either verse. The site of the tragedy is also unknown. In I Chronicles it is called Chidon instead of **Nacon.** In any event David is too terrified to continue. A nearby Philistine (**Gittite** means "man of Gath"), **Obed-edom** by name, is conscripted to care for the ark in his home.

6:12-19. *Bringing the Ark to Jerusalem.* The presence of the ark apparently has no further bad results, and so David resolves on its transfer to the Jerusalem sanctuary—that is, **the tent**. After the first **six paces** (not every six paces) a sacrifice is made by the king. God is apparently willing to let the ark proceed. David is clad, not in his royal robe, but in a **linen ephod** (cf. I Samuel 12:19). He performs some kind of whirling dance to the accompaniment of music and ritual shouting.

6:16-19. Verse 16 has been put into the story here to prepare for verses 20-23. David his prepared a **tent** and altar for the ark. Once it is housed he offers sacrifices and pronounces the benediction over the people. The king here performs priestly functions, since in the early monarchy the king could act as priest (cf. 8:18*b*). To end the festive occasion the people receive a royal gift of food.

6:20-23. *Micah's Quarrel.* This episode has been combined with the ark story but belongs to the Succession Document of chapters 9—20 and I Kings 1-2 (see Introduction). On David's return his wife **Michal,** Saul's daughter (cf. I Samuel 18:20-27), speaks sarcastically of his divesting himself of the royal robe. David's reply is corrupt in the Hebrew and must be corrected from the Septuagint to read "Before Yahweh I am dancing. Blessed be Yahweh who chose me. . . ." David is not interested in his wife's opinion of him as long as he remains popular with the common people. The quarrel apparently led to complete estrangement between the two. It is noted that there was no offspring from the union to perpetuate the house of Saul.

7:1-29. *God's Promise to David.* This story of Nathan's prophecy probably was placed here to follow the story of the ark's removal to Jerusalem in chapter 6. Its core belongs to the Succession Document of chapters 9-20 and I Kings 1-2 (see Introduction to I Samuel). The struggle for the succession presupposes the divine promise of a dynasty.

The chapter is composite and thus not fully consistent. There is a mixture of the promise to David with a statement concerning Israel's future. The D editor added the introductory words of verse 1 to give a setting for the story. He also added verse 13 to make the temple prophecy consistent with Solomon's building of the temple, and verses 22-24 as a hymnodic prayer praising God, who redeemed and established the people.

The source used by the D editor was not completely original. The oldest form is probably found in verses 2-7, 11*b*, 16, 18-21, and 25-29. According to this, David tells **Nathan** of his desire to build a permanent shrine for the **ark**. Nathan first approves, but later receives an oracle forbidding David to build a temple. Rather God will build David a **house**—that is, establish the Davidic dynasty, which will be unending. This promise became a cornerstone of the D editor's view of the history of the southern kingdom.

7:4-7. The argument used in the oracle is that Yahweh has never lived in, or demanded the construction of, a permanent **dwelling.** This is not strictly historical, since a permanent structure did house the ark in Shiloh (but Shiloh was destroyed and was not therefore permanent). The oracle probably means to say that Yahweh is not to be bound to a particular location or structure. A temple might endanger this belief.

7:8-17. Most of this section represents a somewhat later amplification of the original promise in verses 11*b* and 16. The point of view, however, is somewhat different. Though the promise of succession remains in verses 12 and 14-15, it is limited to Solomon rather than applied to an eternal dynasty.

The promise is also conditional on Solomon's good behavior—a principle which the D editor endorsed and used in his view of the Davidic dynasty. Furthermore the promise becomes somewhat secondary to national interests; the future greatness of Israel (is emphasized in verses 10-11a). Verse 13 refers to Solomon's building the temple and his (rather than David's) establishment of a dynasty. It ill fits the context and was not part of it before the D editor's time.

7:18-29. This is the royal prayer of praise to God for his promise. David goes **before the Lord**—that is, to the sanctuary. Not only has God blessed David wonderfully in the past; he has now given him a view of his descendants in the future. The end of verse 19 is textually corrupt. The Revised Standard Version has changed the Hebrew "this is the law of mankind" to **and hast shown me future generations,** which is only a guess. The prayer reflects the divine promise of a Davidic dynasty—except for 22-24, which are typically D and praise God for the redemption of the people. Verse 25 logically follows verse 21, since it asks confirmation of the knowledge given David in verses 19-21.

C. DAVID'S CAMPAIGNS AND CHIEF OFFICIALS (8:1-18)

8:1-14. *Summary of Davidic Wars.* This chapter belongs logically after chapter 5. It is a chronological record of David's various military successes which may at one time have concluded the source dealing with David's rise to power—though it has also been thought of as an independent record. In any event it does not belong after chapter 7, which presupposes "rest from all his enemies." The opening words, **after this,** can apply only to chapter 5, possibly to the taking of Jerusalem.

8:1. The first reference is to the subjection of the **Philistines. Methegh-ammah** is probably not a place name but a Hebrew phrase referring to sovereignty, "the reins of the metropolis."

8:2. That **Moab** was treated with particular severity is strange in view of I Samuel 22–3-4 (but see comment). Two thirds are killed—whether of captives, males, or the entire populace is not stated. On Moabite **tribute** cf. II Kings 3:4.

8:3-8. This account simply summarizes David's campaign against the Aramean states. There is a fuller parallel in 10:6-19. The locationn of **Zobah** is uncertain, though an area north of Damascus has been suggested by some. Others place it between the Lebanon and the Anti-Lebanon mountains. Since the territory of **Hadadezer** extended toward the **Euphrates,** the former is more likely. The numbers in verses 4-5 are exaggerated (cf. 10:6, 18). David cripples most of their **horses,** presumably capturing **a hundred chariots** and sufficient horses. Chariots were of little military value in the hilly regions of Palestine. Conquest of the state of **Damascus** and imposition of **tribute** on it marks David's military successes. The locations of **Betah** and **Berothai** are unknown.

8:9-12. The congratulatory message and gifts from **Hamath,** 120 miles north of Damascus, are a token of voluntary submission. Precious metals are all **dedicated** to Yahweh. Apparently Solomon used them in the building of the temple. The summary list of subjects (verse 12) includes **Amalek** (cf. I Samuel 27:8) and the **Ammonites** (cf. 10:1-19; 12:26-31). For Toi's son **Joram** I Chronicles 18:10 has Hadoram, which in turn is an error for "Hadad-ram." Joram is a Hebrew, not an Aramean, name.

8:13-14. David also is able to subdue **Edom.** Israelite prosperity could always be gauged by its ability to hold this land of nomads. It was not only difficult to hold—note that David keeps the land under occupation—it was also most important as giving access to the Gulf of Aqaba. For the **Valley of Salt** see comment on II Kings 14:7.

8:15-18. *The Chief Officials.* For a similar list cf. 20:23-26. David himself serves as ultimate judge by virtue of his royal office. The military is under double command: **Joab** is commander in chief of the **army,** and **Benaiah** is captain of David's foreign bodyguard, which is composed of **Pelethites,** i.e. Philistines. On **Cherethites** see above on I Samuel 30:11-15.

The **recorder** was probably some kind of press secretary and adviser on state affairs, whereas the **secretary** kept the official annals and records (cf. II Kings 25:19). The name of the secretary, **Seraiah,** is uncertain. In 20:25 it is given as Sheva and in I Chronicles 18:16 as Shavsha. In connection with the priests a curious error has crept in. **Zadok** was probably an earlier Jebusite king-priest. He is now placed on a par with "Abiathar the son of Ahimelech the son of Ahitub," David's old companion (see above on I Samuel 22:20-23). But the text has been disarranged to read **Zadok the son of Ahitub and Ahimelech the son of Abiathar.**

VII. David and His Court (9:1–20:26)

A. Some Royal Acts (9:1–12:31)

9:1-13. *David's Care for Jonathan's Son.* This chapter should come after 21:1-14 (see comment). David, probably recalling his covenant of brotherhood with Jonathan (cf. I Samuel 18:3-4; 20:42; 23:18), seeks information concerning possible offspring. A servant loyal to the **house of Saul** named **Ziba** informs him that the lame son of Jonathan lives in hiding in Gilead in Transjordan. **Lo-debar** remains unidentified. **Mephibosheth** was actually named Meribaal (see above on 4:4). He is brought to the court, and all Saul's former possessions are restored to him. He is kept under David's eye at court, where he is well treated. Ziba is appointed steward of Meribaal's restored lands.

10:1-11:1. *War with the Ammonites.* This section has been inserted into the narrative (see Introduction to I Samuel). On **Nahash** cf. I Samuel 11. David's ambassadors are grossly insulted. The **beard** was the pride of Semitic manhood, and nakedness was considered most shameful. Such an insult demands immediate revenge, and the Ammonites know it. They make hurried preparations by hiring various Syrian troops.

Beth-rehob lay near Dan in the north; its exact location is unknown. On **Zobah** see above on 8:3-8. **Maacah** was somewhere south of Mt. Hermon in the west of Bashan, whereas **Tob** lay further south in the Hauran, probably near the Yarmuk River. None of these sites is exactly identified. The numbers given are all exaggerated. **Joab** overcomes them with **the mighty men**—that is, the professional army.

10:9-14. As the battle lines are drawn, Joab is the victim of a pincer attack with **Syrians** on one side and the **Ammonites** on the other. The scene was probably at the entrance of **Rabbah** (11:1), modern Amman, the capital **city** of Ammon. Joab divides his army into two parts. He leads the force against the Syrians, **Abishai** the one against Ammon. The Syrians are defeated, and the Ammonites panic and retreat into the city. A siege being impractical, the Israelite soldiers return to Jerusalem.

10:15-11:1. This account of a subsequent attempt to fight **David** is parallel to that in 8:3-8. There are different and contradictory details—for example, verse 18 with 8:4. **Hadadezer**, with **Syrians** from the **Euphrates** region, comes to **Helam**, where David's army completely defeats them. The location is probably in northern Gilead. The Syrians now become subject to David. The **Ammonites** are isolated militarily for the next phase in the conflict, which is begun in 11:1 and continued in 12:26-31. **In the spring of the year** (11:1) is incorrect. The Hebrew means "at the turning of the year," which means fall, not spring. **Kings** did not do battle until after the harvest. This sets the stage for the David and Bathsheba story, which interrupts the account.

11:2-27a. *David's Great Sin.* David has not accompanied his army. **One afternoon** after the rest period he goes to the palace **roof** and sees **a woman bathing.** He learns that she is **Bathsheba,** probably granddaughter of his royal counselor Ahithophel (cf. 23:34) and wife of one of his professional soldiers. **Uriah** is a **Hittite** proselyte to Yahwism—as his name, meaning "Yahweh is light," shows. David commits adultery with Bathsheba, and she becomes pregnant.

11:6-13. In panic David tries to avoid the consequences of his sin. He recalls her husband, under the pretext of wanting news of the campaign, but actually to have him spend a night at home with his wife. But soldiers on an expedition were required to remain in a sanctified state. They could have no relations with women (cf. I Samuel 21:4-5), and Uriah simply beds down at the palace **door**. When the anxious David inquires, Uriah replies as a doughty soldier. David has him stay an extra night, making him drunk, but to no avail. The **ark** still accompanied Israel into battle (cf. I Samuel 4:3-9).

11:14-27a. David then sends Uriah with a **letter to Joab** ordering Uriah to be stationed in a place of danger. Joab obeys and Uriah is killed. After the traditional short period of **mourning** Bathsheba becomes David's wife. On **Abimelech** cf. Judges 9:50-57.

I Chronicles omits this entire story as derogatory to David. The account not only shows David's sin to be adultery and murder. There is also an implied criticism of failure to go to battle with his army.

11:27b–12:15a. *Nathan's Rebuke.* The account of David's sin was told—to show Yahweh's displeasure even though it was the one anointed who did wrong. Accordingly the court prophet **Nathan** is sent to David. Since David is in his royal capacity supreme judge (cf. 8:15), Nathan presents to him a blatant, though imaginary, case of injustice. David's anger is stirred at such injustice. He calls for **fourfold** repayment by this man, who really ought to **die**.

12:7-13a. At Nathan's reply, **You are the man** (verse 7a), David is conscience stricken (verse 13a). Intervening are later amplifications (verses 7b-12) which take subsequent disasters in David's life and explain them as punishment for this sin. The sin is one of despising Yahweh's word by doing evil. Verse 8 is the only reference to David's taking over his predecessor's harem (that of Ishbaal?). This was common evidence of royal dignity (cf. 3:7-11; I Kings 2:13-25). The punishment, according to the amplified version, is the trouble he is to have with his own sons (Amnon, Absalom, and Adonijah). On verses 11-12 cf. 16:20-23.

12:13b-15a. In Nathan's original prophecy David is restored

153

to favor with God—that is, he is forgiven. Nevertheless the actual effects of the sin cannot be voided. The **child** of the adulterous union must **die.** The Revised Standard Version translation of verse 14*a* is a conjecture. It probably should read "you have caused the enemies of Yahweh to blaspheme." Yahweh's cause has been degraded.

12:15*b*-25. *The Judgment Effected.* The punishment is the illness and eventual death of the child. David, by strict fasting and intercessory prayer, tries to dissuade Yahweh. Even the chieftains of his family are unable to persuade David to **eat.** When the child does die after six days, David's servants are afraid that he may be deranged by grief. But to their surprise, and contrary to oriental custom, he ends his fast, arises from the ground, washes, and changes. David explains his action by stating that he was hoping to sway Yahweh to spare the child. Now it is too late. Rather he will eventually join his child. David is now fully reconciled with God.

As signal of his atoned status David and Bathsheba have a second child, who is named **Solomon,** meaning "peace." A prophetic word by Nathan names the child **Jedidiah,** meaning "beloved of Yahweh." Nathan originally brought the divine condemnation and sentence. Now he brings the word that David is restored. The incident is closed.

12:26-31. *The Ammonite War Continued.* This is a continuation of 11:1. Joab eventually takes the walled capital city. **Royal city** should probably read **city of waters** as in verse 27. This would mean that he has captured Rabbah's water supply. Thus the actual taking of the city itself is a matter of course, which he diplomatically leaves to David. The citadel is taken and plundered, and the populace is reduced to slave labor. Particularly mentioned as booty is a **crown** of special splendor containing a gem of some kind which David takes for his own crown. The crown could hardly be **their king's** crown since it weighed a **talent**—about sixty-three pounds. Rather it belonged to their idol Milcom, confused with *malkam,* meaning "their king."

B. Family Struggles (13:1–14:33)

13:1-22. *The Rape of Tamar.* With this story David's family troubles explode. The crown prince **Amnon,** son of Ahinoam, has a sexual passion for his **virgin** half sister **Tamar,** sister of **Absalom** (children of Maacah; cf. 3:2-3). Marriage between half brother and sister was forbidden in later legislation but at this time was still acceptable. On the advice of a **crafty** cousin, **Jonadab,** he pretends illness. When David visits him, he asks his father for Tamar's attendance. Apparently Amnon has a separate dwelling with at least two rooms.

13:7-14. Accordingly Tamar is ordered to **prepare food** for her sick brother. When the food is set out he refuses to eat until all the servants clear out. Then when she brings the food he betrays his passion, which she renounces as both **folly** and against the social customs. If Amnon will ask for her, surely David will give her to him.

13:15-22. After he has had his way with her, Tamar as a violated woman is no longer eligible for marriage—hence her signs of mourning and her remaining **desolate** in her brother's house. Absalom is furious. He determines on vengeance, but cunningly he does not betray his feelings.

13:23-30. *Absalom's Revenge.* Only after **two full years** can Absalom wreak his revenge on Amnon. The occasion is his sheepshearing—a festival occasion—at **Baal-hazor,** six miles northeast of Bethel. He invites his father and brothers to attend. David declines but gives his blessing. When Absalom asks his father to send Amnon, David is suspicious, but on being pressed allows all the princes to go. At the festival Absalom orders his **servants** to **kill** Amnon as soon as he is drunk. When the deed is done, the other brothers flee for their lives, each on his **mule** (the animal for royalty). They probably assume that Absalom is intent on a coup d'etat.

13:30-36. Rumors quickly reach the court that Absalom has killed **all** his brothers. But David's nephew, the "crafty" **Jonadab** (cf. verse 3), advises him that only Amnon has been killed. Eventually the princes return along the road from

155

Horonaim (that is the two Horons, Upper and Lower Beth-horon, northwest of Gibeon).

13:37-38. The text of these verses is badly corrupt. Three times it is said that **Absalom fled** (verses 34, 37, 38). The first statement is out of place. Verses 37 and 38 are repetitious and do not fit with verse 39, which belongs with the next story. Verse 37*b* should precede verse 37*a*, with only the last phrase of verse 38 retained. **Geshur** was an Aramean state northeast of Galilee. Its king, **Talmai,** with whom Absalom sought refuge for **three years,** was his maternal grandfather (cf. 3:3).

13:39–14:33. *Absalom's Return.* David may be a brilliant military strategist and the anointed of God, but he is a poor parent, alternating between severity and laxity. He realizes that Absalom has incurred bloodguilt and should be put to death, but the three-year exile makes David long for his son. **Joab,** who always has David's best interests in mind, devises a plan by which David may be persuaded to do what in his **heart** he really wants. He sends for a **wise woman** of **Tekoa** (about six miles south of Bethlehem). She is to act as a mourning widow with an appeal case to present to David as supreme judge.

14:4-11. The woman tells David a fictitious tale about a fratricide son. His interest is awakened, and he promises that no one shall harm her or her son. When she still persists, he swears an oath in Yahweh's name that her son will not suffer.

14:12-17. Now the woman applies David's oathbound decision to the case of Absalom. David has become the family avenger in not allowing Absalom to return. Amnon is dead and cannot return. Verse 14*b* should be rendered: "but God does not simply take away life, but rather desires means not to keep an exile banished from him." That is, God is not interested in pure vengeance but rather in having the exile return. Having made the application, the woman returns to the original tale, probably to cover up her real aim.

14:18-24. David shrewdly sees through her subterfuge. He asks her bluntly whether she is speaking at Joab's direction. With crafty flattery and courtesy she compares his shrewdness to that of an **angel of God,** but fully admits Joab's direction.

David then informs Joab that he has won his case. Absalom may return to **his own house,** but must remain away from the court.

14:25-27. These verses interrupt the narrative but relate some popular rumors about the handsome prince—for example, the exaggerated fiction about his **heavy head of hair** (about 4 pounds). Reference to **three sons** conflicts with 18:18, where it is said that he has no sons.

14:28-33. After two years Absalom's non-recognition at court galls him. Twice he summons Joab, who refuses to come. Thereupon the imperious prince sets Joab's **barley** field on **fire.** When Joab comes to object, he is ordered to obtain full pardon from David for Absalom. Joab complies, and so the murderer is again fully accepted in court society.

C. ABSALOM'S REBELLION (15:1–19:8b)

15:1-6. *Absalom's Subversion.* Absalom is determined on a well planned coup d'etat. Amnon is dead. Chileab, the second son, has apparently died also, since he is not mentioned except in the list of David's sons born at Hebron (3:2). Absalom is the third son, thus in line for the succession (though the eldest was not necessarily the crown prince; cf I Kings 1:11-13). His princely state is shown by his obtaining a **chariot and horses** and runners—pomp which David has always avoided. Absalom cleverly puts himself forward as a man more interested than his father in the cause of the common people. This kind of propaganda naturally **stole** (i.e. won) **the hearts,** especially when he refuses obeisance and greets suppliants as brothers.

15:7-12. *The Coup.* Afer **four years** of propaganda Absalom is ready. **Hebron,** his birthplace, is to be the center for his move. Messengers secretly distribute invitations to take part in the revolt. **Two hundred** unsuspecting Jerusalem hostages accompany Absalom as **guests** at the rites used as a cover. **Ahithophel,** David's counselor, is summoned from his home at **Giloh,** about five miles north of Hebron, to serve Absalom. There was probably some dissatisfaction at David's removal of the capital to

Jerusalem. This may explain the reason for the choice of Hebron.

15:13–16:14. David's Flight from Jerusalem. When David hears the news, he immediately prepares to flee from the city—both to spare it and to choose his own form of defense.

15:16-23. At the **last house**—probably the extreme southern part of the city—David pauses to marshal his forces. **All the people** in verse 17 must refer to his forces rather than the populace. Accompanying David are his loyal officers, his mercenary guard, **his household** (except for **ten concubines**), and a special Philistine troop from **Gath** under **Ittai.** He and his followers leave the city, cross the **Kidron,** and proceed east up the **Mount of Olives** (verse 30) toward the Judean **wilderness.** On **Cherethites** and **Pelethites** see above on 8:18.

15:24-29. A second leave-taking scene concerns the priests and the **ark.** David orders the two priests to return to the **city** with the ark. Later they are to serve as spies for David in the city and send word to him secretly. The reference to **Levites** serving in this way in David's time is questionable. It may come from a later editor. Leaving the ark in Jerusalem is to be David's touchstone. His return to worship there will be determined by whether God is gracious to him. **Fords of the wilderness** refers to fords of the Jordan, probably those a few miles above the Dead Sea.

15:30-37. David's departure is accompanied by signs of mourning and distress (cf. 13:19). News of Ahithophel's defection is a staggering blow to David, since his wisdom and cunning were proverbial (cf. 16:23). At the **summit** of the **Mount of Olives** was a shrine (cf. I Kings 11:7). There **Hushai,** another wise man, comes as a loyal friend to David. The **Archite** clan was Benjaminite, living southwest of Bethel (cf. Joshua 16:2). David presents a plan by which Hushai is to return to Jerusalem and pledge false allegiance to Absalom. Thus he may counteract the **counsel of Ahithophel.** The sons of the two loyal priests are to inform David secretly.

16:1-4. Proceeding east beyond the summit David meets **Ziba** (cf. chapter 9). Ziba brings presents for the king but at the same time craftily intimates that his master, Meribaal (**Mephibosheth;** see above on 4:4), is also revolting. David naïvely believes the insinuation and gives him his master's property (cf. 19:24-30).

16:5-14. The final scene takes place at **Bahurim,** just east of Mt. Scopus. **Shimei,** a member of the **house of Saul,** heaps curses and insults on David. Obviously there still remained a great deal of hatred and bitterness in the followers of the former king. **Abishai** (on **Zeruiah** see comment on I Samuel 26:1-25) proposes to kill the offender, but David restrains him. He hopes that Yahweh may eventually grant him a blessing to offset the present **cursing.** The fleeing king and his supporters finally arrive at some place with water for refreshment, presumably the **Jordan.**

16:15–17:23. *Hushai's Advice.* Absalom and his followers have by now entered Jerusalem in triumph. Hushai also presents himself to Absalom and feigns adherence to his cause.

16:20-22. Absalom's first action, on the advice of his counselor **Ahithophel,** is publicly to take over the royal harem. He thereby symbolizes his succession to the throne (see above on 3:6-11 and 12:7-13*a*). The **tent** pitched on the **roof** was the wedding tent.

16:23–17:4. Absalom immediately convenes a council of strategy. Both Ahithophel and Hushai are invited to give counsel. Ahithophel's advice is to **pursue** David immediately and to concentrate on him **only.** Once David is killed, the followers will no longer oppose. Sound advice!

17:5-14. Hushai then proceeds to counteract Ahithophel's advice in order to win time for David. To pursue David now, when he and his **mighty men** are **enraged** like a mother **bear robbed of her cubs,** would be foolish. Besides the seasoned old campaigner is still wily. He would hardly be in an obvious place during the night. Should they attack now and some slaughter occur, it would be the unseasoned troops of Absalom who would panic since they are only too aware of the valor of David's bodyguard. Thus far the refutation.

Hushai's positive suggestion begins with verse 11. Let **all Israel** from north to south be collected together as one great

army. Let them be led **in person** by Absalom (subtle flattery).
Should David withdraw into a walled city, the great army will
simply dismantle the city. Bad advice! But Yahweh has **ordained**
that the **counsel of Hushai** should win the day.

17:15-22. Hushai has done his best for David, but he does not
know how effective his advice has been. Therefore he
immediately sends word to David not to stay at the **fords** of the
Jordan. On **En-rogel** see comment on I Kings 1:5-10. The
messengers are seen leaving the area and pursued. They
manage to escape through the connivance of a **woman** at
Bahurim (see above on 16:5-14). Details of the ruse employed
by the woman are obscure. The word rendered **grain** is
completely unknown, nor is her reply clear. **Brook** is purely a
guess. Since it is followed by **of water** it may be correct.

17:23. Meanwhile **Ahithophel** sees the handwriting on the
wall. The rejection of his **counsel** means the eventual triumph of
David. Rather than fall into David's hands, he goes home and
commits suicide.

17:24-29. *David's Arrival at Mahanaim.* Hushai's strategy
was sound. David has time to regroup and to entrench himself in
Mahanaim (see above on 2:8-11). Absalom has appointed
Amasa, a cousin of **Joab**, over his forces. Amasa's forebears are
not certain. In the Hebrew text his father is "the Israelite." I
Chronicles 2:16-17 says his father was Jether the Ishmaelite and
his mother Abigail, sister of David. **Daughter of Nahash** is
probably an error that crept in from the mention of Nahash in
verse 27.

17:27-29. David is greeted by friends with supplies. **Shobi**
was a brother of Hanun (cf. 10:1-5), king of the Ammonites. On
Rabbah see above on 12:26-31. **Machir** earlier provided
hospitality for Meribaal (9:4-5). **Rogelim** lay east of Mahanaim,
but its location is uncertain.

18:1-8. *The victory of David's Men.* David's forces are divided
equally under the command of faithful officers, **Joab** and **Abishai**
and the Philistine exile **Ittai** (cf. 15:19-22). The king is dissuaded
from taking part in the fight. He stays with the reserves in the
city. As the army leaves David gives orders to **deal gently** with

his rebel son. David's forces easily win the battle, and **twenty thousand** are killed. The field of battle is the **forest of Ephraim.** This designation of some Gilead woodland is surprising but not impossible. The treacherous forest contributes heavily to the casualties.

18:9-18. *Absalom's Death.* Trying to escape on his royal **mule,** Absalom loses control of the animal and is left helpless with his **head** wedged firmly in the branches of a large **oak.** When Joab hears of this, he puts common sense above sentimentality. David is guided by a father's heart, but Joab knows that only Absalom's death can bring stability to David's kingdom. Thus he takes **three darts** (literally "clubs," which could hardly be thrust into the heart) and smites him. Ten military aides then finish him off and Joab gives signal to stop the battle. The aides (**they** in verse 17 probably refers to the ten aides of verse 15) throw Absalom's corpse into a nearby **pit** and cover it with a large **heap of stones**—the mark of an evil person (cf. Achan's grave, Joshua 7:26).

18:18. This verse tells of a different type of monument to Absalom's memory. This stele was placed in the **King's Valley** (probably the Kidron Valley). The verse contradicts 14:27. Had the three sons born to him all died in infancy and this funeral stele been erected as **Absalom's monument?**

18:19–19:8b. *David's Reaction.* Zadok's son **Ahimaaz** has been David's faithful link with Jerusalem during the revolt. He again wishes to be bearer of **tidings** to the waiting David. But Joab, knowing his king, sends a **Cushite** (Ethiopian) slave. Ahimaaz is insistent, however, wanting to soften the blow. By choosing a better road he is able to reach Mahanaim first.

18:24–19:8b. Meanwhile David is waiting at the city entrance between the outer and inner **gates.** A **watchman** reports a solitary runner approaching, whom David rightly interprets to be a messenger (numerous men running would mean a flight). Ahimaaz, on arrival, informs the king of the victory but does not answer his question about Absalom's welfare. Not so the Ethiopian, who gives a full report.

David's excessive grief was as much for his own failure as

parent as lament for his dead son. **Joab** with characteristic bluntness rebukes the king. The king's lament in the hearing of the people is sheer ingratitude and dangerous for the future of the newly saved kingdom. Unless quick action is taken David will lose all popular support. Joab is right, and David's good sense takes over.

D. THE RETURN TO POWER (19:8c–20:26)

19:8c-43. *David's Return to Jerusalem.* The battle has been won, but the kingdom still has to be wooed. The first scene finds **Israel**—that is, the northern tribes—aware of the new situation: Absalom is **dead** and David is not. To gain some psychological and political advantage they make plans for escorting the king to the capital.

19:11-15. David has heard about the plans. The last clause of verse 11 belongs at the end of verse 10 and should be read "and the word of all Israel came to the king." With his old energy he quickly sends word to his **priests.** They are to persuade the Judeans who joined the revolt to be the first to welcome him back. His argument is based both on clan membership and on his promise to demote Joab in favor of **Amasa** (cf. 17:25). This strategy accomplishes two things: winning over Absalom's military commander and demoting Joab, over whom he has never had full control. The result is immediate capitulation. Judah is on hand to **bring the king over the Jordan.**

19:16-23. The next scene highlights a much-chastened **Shimei** (cf. 16:5-13), as well as the sycophantic **Ziba.** Ziba and his household assist in the fording of the Jordan, and Shimei apologizes humbly for his former cursing. Both of these attendants are Benjaminites, members of Saul's clan. When **Abishai** wants to kill Shimei, David declares an amnesty for him. Abishai, as brother of Joab, is hardly in favor with David. **House of Joseph** in verse 20 means the northern tribes.

19:24-30. Meribaal (**Mephibosheth;** see above on 4:4) also welcomes David and is upbraided for his earlier lack of support.

His defense contradicts the earlier statement of Ziba, and David gives final judgment on the property settlement (cf. 9:7-10 and 16:4 for earlier dispositions). The evidence of Meribaal's personal distress and his response to the king's questions demonstrate his real loyalties. Where this meeting took place is uncertain.

19:31-40. David's gracious but **aged** host, **Barzillai,** accompanies him to the Jordan (cf. 17:27-29). David urges him to come to the palace to live. But with courtly courtesy he declines and suggests that **Chimham** (probably a young son) serve as his substitute.

19:41-43. David's return is not without its difficulties. The northern tribes and Judah are equally eager to show their greater share in David's triumph. The stage is set for the revolt described in chapter 20.

20:1-22. *Sheba's Revolt.* Opposition to Davidic rule is spurred by Sheba, whose rallying cry is a return to tribalism. This was to be more effective after Solomon's death (I Kings 12:16). The call served temporarily to isolate Israel from Judah.

20:3. This verse is a digression, a note on David's dealing with the **concubines** defiled by Absalom (16:20-23). The phrase **living as if in widowhood** is a technical pharse for marriage without sexual relations.

20:4-13. The account of Joab's treachery is necessary to show why it was Joab who put down the rebellion rather than **Amasa,** his successor (19:13). Amasa is ordered to muster **Judah** but is ineffective. So David orders **Abishai** to take the professional troops and pursue Sheba to prevent his preparing adequate defense. For parallel strategy cf. 17:1-3. On the composition of the mercenaries (verse 7) see above on 8:15-18. Joab naturally accompanies his brother and automatically assumes command.

The details of Joab's deed are uncertain. Verse 8 seems to say that Joab has a **sword** sheathed and hidden in his **girdle.** Then as he approaches Amasa he greets him, taking him **by the beard with his right hand to kiss him.** Meanwhile the sword falls out into his left hand and with it he kills Amasa. Joab murders Amasa simply because he is a rival. Joab and his brother continue the pursuit of Sheba, and one of the men is left to deal with the dying Amasa.

20:14-22. Sheba meanwhile hurries north with his clan, the Benjaminite **Bichrites.** He holes up in **Abel of Beth-maacah,** four miles west of the city of Dan. The rebellion is now limited to a single clan. When the city is attacked, a **wise woman** intercedes with Joab. The city is spared when they give up the **head** of the rebel. The statement in verses 18-19 is difficult. Abel has apparently been a traditional center of wisdom. Why then use force when consultation at such a place will probably yield good results? **A mother in Israel** means a city with daughter villages around it—that is an important city.

20:23-26. *A List of Chief Officials.* A parallel list appears in 8:15-18 (see comment). Differences are the mention here of **Adoram,** chief of the **forced labor** (see comment on I Kings 4:1-6 and of an otherwise unknown **Ira the Jairite** (a clan in Manasseh). The list was probably placed here to show that Joab was again commander of the army.

VIII. APPENDIXES (21:1–24:25)

21:1-14. *Gibeonite Revenge on the House of Saul.* Chronologically this section belongs before chapter 9 since both chapter 9 and 16:7-8 presuppose it (see Introduction to I Samuel). A three-year drought needs explanation. David seeks an oracle concerning it and discovers that there is **blood guilt** in Israel (cf. a similar story about Achan, Joshua 7). In his early zeal for Yahweh Saul put to death Gibeonites, with whom Israel had a covenant of friendship (Joshua 9:3-27). This bloodguilt has to be removed before rain will come.

21:3-9. The Gibeonites demand retaliation. Seven of Saul's **sons** are to be delivered to them to be **hanged**—that is, exposed after execution as a public disgrace. The statement in verse 7 is a gloss to explain the action detailed in chapter 9. It also shows that the Meribaal (**Mephibosheth;** see above on 4:4) of verse 8 is not Jonathan's son. The victims are two sons of **Rizpah** (cf. 3:7) and five of **Merab,** Saul's elder daughter (cf. I Samuel 18:17-19). **Barzillai** is not to be confused with David's aged host in 17:27-29 and 19:31-40.

21:10-14. How long Rizpah kept the death watch is uncertain. Normally the **beginning of barley harvest** is in April and the fall rains do not begin until the end of October. But spring rains do occasionally come in May. The coming of the **rain** proves that the bloodguilt is removed. David's gathering of the seven corpses, along with the transfer of Saul's and Jonathan's bones from Jabesh (cf. I Samuel 31:11-13), is an act of piety. **Zela** is unknown. It is probably simply a rock tomb in Gibeah.

21:15-22. *Warrior Exploits.* Four successful exploits against Philistine **giants** are recorded. These events belong to the early period of the Philistine wars (cf. 5:17-25). These giants presumably belonged to the pre-Israelite occupants of Canaan, considered to be of large stature. The text of the first anecdote is corrupt. The name in verse 16 is simply a transliteration of the Hebrew for "and they dwelt in Nob," which makes no sense. Probably **Gob** (cf. verse 18) is intended. On the large **spear** cf. I Samuel 17:7.

Gob is still unidentified. **Hushathite** was probably a Bethlehem clan (cf. I Chronicles 4:4). On the conflict of tradition about **Goliath** see comment on I Samuel 17:1-11. I Chronicles 20:5 reconciles the two accounts by changing Goliath to "Lahmi, the brother of Goliath," but that is incorrect. The fourth giant is described as deformed.

22:1-51. *A Thanksgiving Psalm.* This psalm is almost word for word the same as Psalm 18. An editor has taken it as peculiarly appropriate to David after he was at rest from **all his enemies.**

23:1-7. *The Last Words of David.* This text has suffered a great deal. Whether is was written by David or not is uncertain, but it is an early poem celebrating his rule as a Yahwist king. **Sweet psalmist of Israel** should be "the favorite of Israel's songs—that is, the favorite hero of popular songs. Both as singer and as **anointed** he is the vehicle of divine inspiration.

Verses 3c-4 give the content of the divine message: God prospers the righteous and God-fearing ruler. The Hebrew of verse 4 reads literally: "Then he shall be as the morning light, when the sun shines, a cloudless morning—when because of the brightness due to rain grass comes from the earth." Then verse 5 applies this figure for prosperity to God's **covenant** with the Davidic **house** (cf. chapter 7). The last two verses show the fate of wickedness. The wicked are compared to the thorny bramble.

23:8-39. *David's Heroes and Their Exploits.* The parallel text in I Chronicles 11:11-47 is often better. The list of the thirty heroes is preceded by the exploits of the three heroes.

23:8-12. The name of the first hero in I Chronicles 11:11 is Jashobeam; originally it must have been Ishbaal. In verse 9 **when they defied the Philistines who** can be corrected from I Chronicles 11:13 to read "at Pasdammim when the Philistines." The site is unknown. The exploits of the three champions were all individual heroic deeds in the holy war against the Philistines.

23:13-17. These verses relate an act of bravery by three unidentified heroes. The occasion for the exploit is 5:17-21. The Philistines have a **garrison** at Bethlehem. In his **stronghold** David expresses longing for fresh **Bethlehem** water. The heroes **broke through** enemy ranks to fulfill David's wish. He then refuses to **drink** that for which men's lives have been endangered.

23:18-23. The commander of the **thirty** is **Abishai,** Joab's brother, of whom a heroic deed is recounted (cf. 21:15-17). Of **Benaiah,** captain of the **bodyguard,** a number of deeds are told. **Kabzeel** was in the southeastern part of Judah on the Edomite border but is unidentified. What **two ariels of Moab** were is unknown. Possibly the words "sons of" should be inserted after "two." The word "ariel" means "lion of God." Could it here mean "strong lions" in a view of the reference to **lion** in the next line?

23:24-39. The number of the mighty men is given in verse 39 as **thirty-seven** but the list contains only thirty-two. I Chronicles 11:26-47 expands the list to forty-seven. The number thirty-seven is intended to include not only the thirty-two but also the three of verses 8-11, as well as Abishai and Benaiah. The list does not include Joab, probably because he was commander of the army and thus not in the special list. It has been plausibly suggested that the list goes back to David's days in Ziklag and originally contained thirty, the last seven being added later.

24:1-25. A Pestilence from Yahweh. This story logically belongs with 21:1-14. The reason for Yahweh's anger is not given. I Chronicles 21:1 attributes the incitement to Satan in order to avoid charging Yahweh as the author of sin. The text, however, is the original. All historical movement was attributable to God, according to the ancients. Why a military census should be universally recognized in David's time (even by **Joab**) as sin is not clear. Yahweh did not save by large numbers, according to Judges 7:2-7. Possibly it was thought to be invading divine secrets.

24:5-9. The census is begun at **Aroer** on the Arnon river east of the Dead Sea. It proceeds north in Transjordan to **Jazer,** about ten miles west of Rabbah on the border of Ammonite territory. More likely than **Kadesh in the land of the Hittites** (i.e. on the Orontes in Syria) would be Kedesh in Naphtali, more or less on the way from **Gilead** to **Dan** and **Sidon.** In this case **Tyre** would be the northern point of the census. Then the commanders work their way south through western Palestine. The census ends at **Beer-sheba** on the edge of the **Negeb,** the arid region south of **Judah.** The final count is probably exaggerated, though not as much as in I Chronicles 21:5. The census lists in Numbers 1:46, often thought to be based on David's census, show a total of 603,550.

24:10-17. David's repentance follows the lengthy census, and God presents him with a choice of three forms of punishment. David rejects the second (flight before the enemy) and throws himself on Yahweh's mercy—either **famine** or **pestilence.** The severe pestilence throughout the land kills seventy thousand people before Yahweh relents. Verse 17 seems to have little to do with the context and may be an editorial expansion to enhance David's piety.

24:18-25. The point of the episode is to be found in the divine command to purchase the **threshing floor of Araunah** ("Ornan" in I Chronicles 21). He is a **Jebusite,** a pre-Israelite inhabitant of Jerusalem. There David is to build an **altar** and offer a sacrifice in order to stay the **plague.** On the typical oriental bargaining cf. Genesis 23:1-16. The importance of this purchase lies in the fact that the land is destined to be the site for the temple (cf. I Chronicles 22:1 and II Chronicles 3:1).

THE FIRST BOOK OF THE KINGS

John William Wevers

INTRODUCTION

The books of Kings were originally one book, the last of the Former Prophets. In fact the four books of the Former Prophets—Joshua, Judges, Samuel, Kings—were composed as a single history of Israel from Joshua's conquest of Palestine down to the exile. Its division into various books was probably only for convenience. The division of Kings into two books was introduced by the Septuagint.

Authorship and Date

In 622 B.C. the Deuteronomic—or D—Code was discovered in the course of temple renovations, and King Josiah inaugurated a thoroughgoing reform. The code was adopted as national law (see below on II Kings 23:3-20). Judah now had a word of God, a standard by which it might examine not only its practices but its history as well. Prior to this there had existed southern and northern sacred histories from earliest times to the conquest. These two documents are now known respectively as J and E. In the course of the seventh century the two had been united into a single JE history. But these were not yet accepted as part of the Hebrew canon, or holy scriptures, whereas D was now officially adopted as such.

It was thus necessary that the history of Israel be examined from this new D point of view. This task was undertaken by a historian who was thoroughly imbued with D ideas. A few passages (especially II Kings 22:20) seem to have been written during Josiah's lifetime. Some scholars thus maintain that the main body of the work was completed in the decade immediately following discovery of the D Code. It was then supplemented by others of a D school over the next half century. However, it seems more likely that the D historian lived and worked during the early years of the Babylonian exile and that he completed his history immediately following the last event he records (II Kings 25:27-30)—around 560.

Jerusalem, the sole legitimate sanctuary, had been destroyed in 586. The leading people of Judah had been exiled to Babylon. Now, after a reign of many years, the hated Babylonian king had died, and his successor seemed more favorably disposed toward the exiles. Perhaps he would allow a restoration. If so, it was appropriate, even imperative, that the history of the kingdoms be examined from the D point of view, giving the people guidance and warning.

The D historian had various sources available for his use. Some he adapted to his own ends and others he took over with little change. The result gives the appearance of an anthology of materials with a superficially imposed structure and point of view. He has combined materials from annals with prophetic legends, temple archives with popular stories and pure D creations.

The D Structure

I Kings 1-11 deals with the reign of Solomon. After his death the united kingdom was divided into the northern kingdom of Israel and the southern kingdom of Judah. Jerusalem was the capital of the southern kingdom, whose kings continued the line of David. The remaining chapters deal with the history of the divided kingdoms as a series of reigns of individual kings. Each reign begins with an accession notice giving the year of its beginning, its length, and an evaluation of it from the D viewpoint. The reign is then completely dealt with before the next reign—or that of the next king of the other kingdom—is taken up. This shuttlecock method is disconcerting but it was probably the simplest method available to the author-editor. Each reign ends with an obituary and succession notice and a reference to the "chronicles" of the reign for further details.

Various stories have been inserted into this formal structure. Not all of these are necessarily relevant to the reign in question. Thus not all the stories of Elisha (II Kings 2–8) are to be taken as part of the reign of Jehoram of Israel. Furthermore the story concerning Ahaziah of Israel in II Kings 1 probably belongs to the Elisha rather than the Elijah cycle.

Chronology. Kings of Israel and Judah

The United Kingdom

1020   Saul unites Israelite tribes as first king.

1009/8   Saul dies. David is chosen king of Judah in Hebron.

1002/1   David is anointed king of Israel, captures Jerusalem and makes it his capital.

970/69   Solomon anointed king. David dies.

The Divided Kingdoms

931/30   Rehoboam succeeds Solomon. Northern tribes secede, choose Jeroboam king of Israel.

913   Abijam succeeds Rehoboam in Judah.

911/10   Asa succeeds Abijam in Judah.

910/9   Nadab succeeds Jeroboam in Israel.

909/8   Nadab killed; Baasha usurps in Israel.

886/85   Elah succeeds Baahsa in Israel.

885/84   Elah killed by Zimri, who reigns seven days. Omri and Tibni lay rival claims to throne of Israel.

880   Omri overcomes Tibni, builds Samaria as his capital.

874/73   Ahab succeeds Omri in Israel.

873/72   Jehoshaphat co-regent with Asa in Judah.

870/69   Asa dies; Jehoshaphat sole ruler in Judah.

854/53   Jehoram (Joram) co-regent with Jehoshaphat in Judah.

852   Jehoram (Joram) succeeds Ahaziah in Israel.

848   Jehoshaphat dies; Jehoram (Joram) sole ruler in Judah.

841   Ahaziah succeeds Jehoram in Judah. He and Jehoram of Israel are killed in revolt of Jehu, who is anointed king of Israel. Athaliah seizes rule in Judah.

835   Athaliah killed; **Jehoash** (Joash) enthroned in Judah.

814/13   **Jehoahaz** (Joahaz) succeeds Jehu in Israel.

798   **Jehoash** (Joash) succeeds Jehoahaz in Israel.

796   Jehoash of Judah assassinated; **Amaziah** succeeds.

793/92   **Jeroboam II** co-regent with Jehoash in Israel.

792/91   Amaziah of Judah is captured. **Azariah** (Uzziah) is enthroned in his place.

782/81   Jehoash of Israel dies; Jeroboam II sole ruler. He frees Amaziah, who resumes rule in Judah.

767   Amaziah assassinated; Azariah sole ruler in Judah.

753   **Zechariah** succeeds Jeroboam II in Israel.

752   Zechariah killed; **Shallum** usurps, reigns one month; **Menahem** usurps.

750   **Jotham** co-regent in Judah when Azariah becomes leper.

742/41   **Pekahiah** succeeds Menahem in Israel.

740/39   Pekahiah killed in Israel; **Pekah** usurps, dates reign from 752. Azariah dies in Judah; Jotham sole ruler.

735   **Ahaz** co-regent with Jotham in Judah.

732/31   Pekah of Israel is killed; **Hoshea** usurps as Assyrian vassal.

Jotham of Judah dies; Ahaz sole ruler.

723/22   Fall of Samaria brings end to northern kingdom, exile to many Israelites.

The Southern Kingdom Alone

716/15   **Hezekiah** succeeds Ahaz in Judah.

697/96   **Manasseh** is co-regent with Hezekiah.

687/86   Hezekiah dies; Manasseh sole ruler.

643/42   **Amon** succeeds Manasseh.

641/40   **Josiah** succeeds Amon.

609   Josiah is killed. **Jehoahaz** succeeds, is deposed by Neco after three months. **Jehoiakim** is enthroned as Egyptian vassal.

598/97   **Jehoiachin** succeeds Jehoiakim in December/January about when Nebuchadrezzar besieges Jerusalem.

597   Jerusalem captured March 16. Jehoiachin and many leading citizens exiled; **Zedekiah** made regent as Babylonian puppet.

586   Wall of Jerusalem breached July 18; Zedekiah flees and is captured. Destruction of city and temple begins August 14 or 17.

The synchronization of reigns throughout gives the book an impression of scholarly exactness. Unfortunately this has created one of the most difficult historical problems. Many scholars have proposed solutions to the chronologies of the kings of Israel and Judah. Co-regencies, changes in dating systems (postdating and antedating), and textual errors have all been suggested.

Named Sources

Three sources are mentioned as providing materials for the history of the kingdoms:

1) the "book of the acts of Solomon" (I Kings 11:41);
2) the "Book of the Chronicles of the Kings of Israel" (I Kings 14:19, etc.);
3) the "Book of the Chronicles of the Kings of Judah" (I Kings 14:29, etc.).

These were apparently official court annals available at the time of composition but now lost. It should be noted that mention of a court annalist or recorder is first made for the reign of David (II Samuel 8:16).

The first of these sources may have contained not only extensive archival materials from Solomon's reign but also legendary biographical materials. These were intended to enhance the glory of his reign—for example, the stories of his wisdom (I Kings 3) and of his fabulous wealth and connection (I Kings 10). The chronicles of the two kingdoms are mentioned for all kings except Jehoram and Hoshea of Israel and Ahaziah, Jehoahaz, Jehoiachin, and Zedekiah of Judah. The last four are omitted because they were not buried in Judah.

These annalistic sources are especially important since they were contemporary. Such materials may often be recognized by the absence of editorial judgment, the use of temporal expressions such as "then," "in that day," "at that time," or of exact dating such as I Kings 14:25. These sources dealt mainly with such items as wars, amounts of tribute imposed, relations with other states, buildings and fortifications, alliances, commercial traffic, and lists of officials. One further source is mentioned in the Septuagint of I Kings 8:12-13 as being the "Book of Songs." This may be the same as the "Book of Jashar" of Joshua 10:13 and II Samuel 1:18 (see below on I Kings 8:12-13).

Prophetic Sources

Prophetic sources center largely around three figures: Elijah, Elisha, and Isaiah. These cycles of stories probably circulated independently at one time. The Elijah cycle (I Kings 17–19; 21; II Kings 1) was of special interest to the D historian. Elijah held a central position in the crucial struggle between Baalism and Yahwism under the Omri dynasty.

Like the Elijah cycle, the Elisha cycle (found mainly in II Kings 2–8) is basically northern in origin. It is far more folkloric in character. Most of the tales (excpt for the anointing of Jehu in II Kings 9:1-13) are miracle stories. Some of these parallel the Elijah stories (raising of a dead child to life, the unfailing cruse of oil, the parting of the Jordan waters). They were included by the historian to enhance the prophetic office.

The Isaiah cycle (II Kings 18:17–20:19) is repeated, with some variants and the additions of a complaint prayer, in Isaiah 36-39. This cycle is Jerusalem based and shows the position of the great prophet in the court of righteous King Hezekiah. As a historical source it is unreliable. The few historical facts have been extensively colored by legendary stories.

Other prophetic stories were kept alive by the "sons of the prophets." These are skillfully used by the author-editor to illustrate his D point of view. Such are the tales of Ahijah of Shiloh (I Kings 11:29-39), the unnamed prophets at Bethel (I Kings 13), and Jehu the son of Hanani (I Kings 16:1-4, 7; cf. also Jonah, II Kings 14:25). Not to be confused with this source are the references to prophets in II Kings 17:13 and 21:10-15, which are the creation of the D historian himself. Special mention should be made of I Kings 20 and 22. Though preserved by prophetic circles, these chapters are excellent historical sources, possibly from Ahab's own days. They are comparatively friendly toward Ahab, in contrast to the Elijah cycle into which they were inserted.

Other Sources

David's court memoirs come to an end with I Kings 2:46. These are a continuation of the Succession Document of II

Samuel 9–20 (see Introduction to I Samuel). Architectural description of Solomon's building operations—especially the temple and the temple furniture—in I Kings 6–7 is based on some contemporary official account. Such accounts were usually called temple archives. These documents may well have been preserved in the temple, but they included descriptions of other buildings as well.

Stories of cultic reform in Jerusalem may have come from the official chronicles. More likely they represent another source connected with the temple, though nonpriestly in origin. Thus the story of the revolt against Athaliah (II Kings 11:4-20) in one of its forms comes from this source. So do the stories of Jehoash's repair of the temple (II Kings 12:4-16), Ahaz' introduction of a Syrian altar (II Kings 16:10-16), and the finding of the book of the law (II Kings 22:3-20).

The D Point of View
The D historian wrote history from the point of view of the D Code. Central to its cultic demands was a purified cult at a single national sanctuary—namely the Jerusalem temple. Before the building of the temple the historian expresses no criticism of Solomon's sacrifices at Gibeon (I Kings 3). Even here, however, he has Solomon return to Jerusalem to stand before the ark and offer sacrifices at the end of the story. Once the temple is built he condemns all pre-D shrines outside Jerusalem and holds worship at such places to be illegitimate. He judges every succeeding reign by its fidelity to the cult of the central sanctuary.

After the division of the monarchy the northern kings remained officially Yahwist. But naturally, they did not worship at the Jerusalem temple, a shrine on foreign soil. For this the D historian condemns them all as doing "evil" in the eyes of Yahweh. He brands Jeroboam I as the one who "made Israel to sin"—that is, he encouraged worship at shrines in his own country. The historian even, regretfully, condemns Jehu, the ardent champion of Yahwism who ruthlessly stamped out Baalism (II Kings 10:28-31).

For the Davidic kings in the south the temple was the royal shrine. But in the eyes of the D historian these kings were not all faithful to the book of the law. He approves only the great cult reformers, Hezekiah and Josiah, as doing "right" in the eyes of Yahweh. Five others he conditionally approves as doing "right. . . . Nevertheless the high places were not removed." All others he summarily condemns.

The importance of the prophetic word is also characteristic of the D historian's point of view. Prophets again and again issue warnings and predict disaster, and events confirm their words. Thus Elijah predicts drought and the end of the house of Omri. Elisha predicts the end of famine in Samaria, Hazael's future harsh rule in Damascus, and Israelite victory over the Syrians. Ahijah foretells the division of the kingdom and the downfall of Jeroboam's house. Jehu the son of Hanani predicts the end of Baasha's house. Anonymous prophets predict the ruin of the Bethel sanctuary, Ahab's death, and the end of the Judean state.

The historical problem that particularly plagued the D historian was the end of the Davidic dynasty and the destruction of Jerusalem and the temple. God has promised David an eternal dynasty. True, this was conditional on the good behavior of David's descendants, but God had constantly been gracious. In spite of this the monarchy had come to a disastrous end. Furthermore the law demanded public worship at the Jerusalem temple only, and now it lay in ruins.

To this problem he found a solution in the reign of Manasseh. Manasseh's reign was so evil that Judah's existence could no longer be condoned. Even the reign of good Josiah could not avert the divine intention to destroy Judah and Jerusalem. Eventually God might restore the people, but for the moment they must bear the punishment.

I. SOLOMON'S SUCCESSION TO THE THRONE (1:1–2:46)

1:1-4. *David's Senility.* That the powers of a senile male could be restored by contact with a virgin was a common primitive belief. David's personal attendants provide such a girl, **Abishag the Shunammite.** She has often been wrongly equated with the Shulammite of Song of Solomon 6:13. The story emphasizes that she simply served as **nurse** to the aged king.

1:5-10. *Adonijah's Attempt to Seize Power.* Adonijah, the crown prince determines to take over the throne from his old father. He has the help of **Joab** and **Abiathar,** David's military commander and chief priest respectively. His tactics are similar to those of his late brother **Absalom** (cf. II Samuel 15:1). The court is divided in its loyalties. Those who do not take part in the attempt are listed in verse 8. They include the **mighty men,** i.e. the mercenaries. The planned coup d'etat is well supported by the court and Judean officials. It might have succeeded but for the prompt intervention of those of the pro-Solomon party, who are naturally not invited to the feast. **En-rogel** is usually identified with a spring near the juncture of the Kidron and Hinnom valleys.

1:11-31. *Nathan's Counterplot.* The prophet Nathan once reproved David for his relations with **Bathsheba** (II Samuel 12:1-15). Now he advises her as Solomon's **mother** to inform David immediately, since their lives are at stake, and to urge the king to immediate action.

1:15-21. Bathsheba informs David of Adonijah's attempt to seize the throne. She suggests that **all Israel** awaits royal direction in the matter. If affairs are allowed to drift, Adonijah will be successful. She and **Solomon** will, after David's death, lose their lives as unsuccessful pretenders to the throne.

1:22-27. Nathan enters. He asks whether this situation has David's approval and why the king's intimates have not been informed on the matter. This scene is separate from the preceding, since the queen has left. Nathan then also retires from the royal presence.

1:28-31. Bathsheba is recalled by the king. He repeats his oath and swears that Solomon is to **reign.** She leaves the scene after paying her respects.

1:32-40. *The Crowning of Solomon.* The king summons

Nathan and the faithful **Benaiah.** He gives them detailed instructions for the immediate coronation of Solomon. These steps are to be taken. Solomon is to ride on David's **own mule** and they are to go down into the Kidron Valley to the Spring of **Gihon.** There he is to be anointed (only **Zadok** as priest is to do the actual anointing; cf. verse 39). The **trumpet** is then to be blown and the coronation salute **Long live King Solomon** cried aloud. Finally the new king must come to the palace with his followers and take his place on the **throne** itself. To these instructions Benaiah makes a fitting response.

1:38-40. The royal wishes are immediately carried out. Those actually involved include Zadok, Nathan, and Benaiah, who represent priest, prophet, and soldier respectively. Also involved is the foreign bodyguard, composed of David's old comrades, **the Cherethites and the Pelethites,** i.e. Cretans and Philistines (cf. I Samuel 27). These have remained loyal to the old king and can be relied on to carry out his wishes. The **tent** is the shrine of Yahweh which David built earlier to contain the ark (II Samuel 6:17), and in which the Jerusalem cult has since been carried on. The coronation is popular with the people. They eagerly take part in the gala event, making a great deal of noise.

1:41-53. *Collapse of Adonijah's Attempt.* While Adonijah and his fellow plotters are prematurely **feasting,** they hear the noise accompanying Solomon's coronation. A runner brings the fateful news. He tells them that Solomon is receiving pledges of loyalty from his courtiers and that the bedridden David has given his blessing to the coronation.

1:49-53. This news quickly breaks up the feast. The ex-crown prince, fearing for his life, flees for sanctuary to the tent of Yahweh. There he touches the **horns of the altar.** By this symbolic act he invokes God's protection. Solomon is told of Adonijah's action. He sends a message promising him royal pardon for his treachery if he remains fully loyal to the new king. But at the first sign of **wickedness,** i.e. disloyalty, he will be put to death. Adonijah then pledges his loyalty to his brother, who dismisses him curtly.

2:1-12. *David's Dying Counsel.* This passage represents a favorite Hebrew literary genre (cf. Genesis 49; Deuteronomy 33; and Joshua 24). David, realizing that he is about to die, advises his son to continue his own **strong** rule.

2:3-4. These verses are the work of the D historian, reflecting on the later disastrous history of the dynasty. They contain typical D references to **statutes . . . commandments . . . ordinances . . . testimonies,** as well as to the **law of Moses.** The divine oracle probably refers to II Samuel 7.

2:5-9. David gives detailed instructions about three cases:

(1) **Joab** wreaked private vengeance in wartime (cf. II Samuel 3:27; 20:10). This endangered the security of the dynasty, since by this action guilt was attached to the royal house. Joab was David's appointee. Thus his act of barbarity involved the peace of his master's house. This breach of communal health can be healed only by Joab's violent death in turn.

(2) David owes a debt of gratitude to **Barzillai** which Solomon is told to pay to his family (cf. II Samuel 17:27-29 and 19:31-39).

(3) The curse of **Shimei** still lies on David's house (cf. II Samuel 16:5-14). In a moment of weakness David swore that he would not kill him (cf. II Samuel 19:18-23). Meanwhile the curse is still effective. Again only Shimei's violent death can remove the evil inherent in the curse. Since Solomon is not bound by his father's oath, he is told to take care of the matter.

2:10-12. *The D Editor's Note.* Both David and Solomon (cf. 11:42) are said to have reigned **forty years,** a round number meaning a full career. **City of David** now appropriately becomes the new term for Jerusalem.

2:13-25. *Adonijah's Death.* Adonijah wishes to have **Abishag** for his wife. He asks the queen mother to intercede with Solomon on his behalf. Bathsheba is somewhat leery of Adonijah but is willing to speak to her son on the matter.

2:19-25. Though Solomon accords his mother full courtesy, he chooses to interpret Adonijah's request as a challenge to his throne. Abishag has been a member of David's harem, and whoever inherits the harem is king (cf. II Samuel 16:22). On

179

Solomon's order **Benaiah,** the chief of his bodyguard, immediately goes out and kills Adonijah.

2:26-27. *Abiathar's Demotion.* Abiathar was a fellow conspirator with Adonijah. But because he is a priest and a close friend of David's youth his life is spared. He is removed from his position, however. Thereby the status of the Zadokites as sole priests of the Jerusalem shrine is consolidated (verse 35; see comment on II Samuel 8:15-18). The D editor adds a note stating that this was a divine judgment on the **house of Eli** (cf. I Samuel 2:27-36).

2:28-35. *Joab's Death.* Joab flees for sanctuary as did Adonijah (see above on 1:49-53)—but to no avail. Solomon orders Benaiah to kill him. Benaiah is somewhat fearful when Joab refuses to leave the shrine and returns to the king for further instructions. Solomon with a long apology commands Benaiah to violate the right of asylum. He justifies this on the basis of Joab's murder of the two commanders of the northern and southern armies. Bloodshed demands bloodshed in return before the health of the Davidic dynasty can be assured. Joab is therefore killed at the altar and buried on his own property east of Bethlehem (cf. II Samuel 2:32).

2:36-46. *Shimei's Death.* Shimei is told to remain in **Jerusalem** for life, in spite of the fact that he is a native of Transjordan. Should he as much as **cross the brook Kidron,** just outside the eastern wall of the city, he will be killed.

2:39-46. For **three years** Shimei obeys Solomon's order. But there comes a day when two runaway slaves of his are reported found in **Gath,** one of the Philistine cities where **Achish,** David's onetime ally, is still king. Shimei goes to get them. On his return Solomon uses this as a pretext for legally killing him. He is charged with violating his **oath** and disobeying the king's command. He is further reminded of his old **evil** (the curse) against David. Then Benaiah kills him. With these threats removed Solomon's position as David's successor is firmly **established.** The Succession Document continued from II Samuel 9–20 (see Introduction to I Samuel) comes to an end.

II. SOLOMON'S REIGN (3:1–11:43)

The actual account of Solomon's reign begins with the notice of his marriage to an Egyptian princess. To the D editor the building of the **house of the LORD**—the temple—was the great event of this reign, since through it the eventual centralization of worship at Jerusalem became possible.

A. HIS WISDOM AND RICHES (3:3–4:34)

3:3-15. *Solomon's Dream at Gibeon.* The D editor has a high opinion of Solomon's piety but admits that he worshiped **at the high places**—the ancient shrines. From the viewpoint of a later age this was an illegitimate act, since only Jerusalem was permitted as a true place of public worship. Solomon goes to **Gibeon,** an important shrine in Benjamin about six miles northwest of Jerusalem. The king's pilgrimage to Benjamin undoubtedly had political overtones as well. The story of his **dream** at the high place is certainly ancient, though the dialogue is typical of the D editor. The dream story is told to account for the wisdom attributed to Solomon. The earlier version (2:6) has it that the king's wisdom is an innate quality rather than a divine gift made at his own request.

3:15. On awakening the king returns to **Jerusalem** to engage in the proper cult practices—namely sacrifices before the **ark.** This would hardly seem to be original to the story but rather a D revision. The story originally may well have referred to the sacrifices and the concluding **feast** as part of the Gibeon pilgrimage.

3:16-28. *Solomon's Wise Judgment.* The gift of wisdom granted at Gibeon is immediately applied in this story of Solomon's judicial decision. The folklore motif of two mothers and one baby is a favorite one among various cultures, and it illustrates the Hebrew admiration for practical wisdom. The result of the king's wise decision is universal popular acclaim. The concluding verse emphasizes the Hebrew conception of

Solomon's **wisdom.** It is for rendering **justice** and its source is **God.**

4:1-6. *Solomon's Chief Officials.* The officials' names are given along with their offices. The reference to **Zadok and Abiathar** is an intrusion from the list of David's officials in II Samuel 8:17. The royal "cabinet" consists of the following officers: the **priest,** two **secretaries,** a **recorder** (probably the official court annalist), commander in chief of the **army,** head of the officers' staff, **priest and king's friend,** royal chamberlain, and chief of the **forced labor** corps. This chapter emphasizes Solomon's undoubted genius at organization.

4:7-19. *The Twelve Governors and Provinces.* Solomon divides his kingdom roughly along the lines of the old twelve tribal boundaries. The paragraph mentions thirteen districts, and may have suggested that **Judah** was outside the levy, being Solomon's own tribe. Admittedly the governor of Judah is not named. If this supposition is correct, it would mean that **all Israel** refers only to the northern tribes. But **Gilead** is mentioned twice, once with **Ben-geber** (that is, the son of Geber) as governor and once with **Geber.** Obviously one of these is repetitive and not original. The list is partially defective in that the first four governors' names are missing. Only their fathers' names are given ("the son of Hur," etc.).

4:20-28. *Solomon's Wealth.* The text is somewhat confused, since verses 27-28 are a conclusion to the previous section. Verses 20-21 and 24-25 give two ideal descriptions of the extent of Solomon's kingdom. Each states the extent of the royal supplies, the first listing the daily provisions, the second the number of **stalls of horses** and **horsemen.** The number given for the stalls is much exaggerated (cf. 10:26). A cor was five bushels. **Tiphsah** was the nearest point on the **Euphrates** to Palestine. **Gaza** was the Philistine city farthest south.

4:29-34. *Solomon's Wisdom.* The term **wisdom** refers to a particular type of oral and written literature consisting of **proverbs,** riddles, **songs,** and the like. These might deal with any subject. Particularly mentioned here is botanical and zoological lore. Just as a later age attached the name of Moses to law and that of David to psalmody, so it attributed wisdom to Solomon. The **people of the east** refers to the Arabs and Edomites, as well as the Egyptians, among whom were the wise men named in verse 31. These people were particularly noted for their wisdom.

B. THE BUILDING OF THE TEMPLE (5:1–7:51)

5:1-12. *Solomon's Treaty with Hiram of Tyre.* Chapter 5 serves as an introduction to the building of the temple. Preparations have to be made—especially wood, which is to be imported from **Lebanon.** The language has been expanded greatly by the D editor on the basis of II Samuel 7.

5:7-12. Hiram's woodcutters are to fell the timbers of **cedar and cypress** (perhaps pine) and ferry them as **rafts** down the Mediterranean coast (II Chronicles 2:16 says to Joppa, which seems the logical port). There Solomon's men are to **receive** them. In payment for the wood Solomon is to export **wheat** and **oil** to Lebanon. The number of **cors of beaten oil** required is not certain. The Hebrew of verse 11 says only twenty. **Twenty thousand** is taken, probably rightly, from the Septuagint and II Chronicles 2:10. A cor was five bushels.

5:13-18. *Solomon's Forced Labor Corps.* Solomon raises a **levy** of **thirty thousand men** to work in shifts every third month. The 150,000 workers added by the D editor in verse 15 necessitate **three thousand three hundred** foremen, in contrast to only 550 in 9:23. Solomon's laborers are skilled in **stone** but not in **timber.** Hiram's craftsmen are from **Gebal,** i.e. Byblos, a famous Phoenician seaport in ancient times.

6:1-10. *The Temple Structure.* The account of the building of the temple in chapters 6–7 is largely a contemporary document. There is not much evidence of later additions. One such is the opening chronological statement, part of which was adapted from verse 37. **Four hundred and eightieth** is an artificial number—twelve generations of forty years each. The actual interval from the exodus to the building of the temple probably did not exceed 325 years at the most. On **Ziv** see below on verses 37-38.

The temple dimensions are given as ninety feet long, forty-five feet high, and thirty feet wide—assuming the common cubit of about eighteen inches, though a long cubit of about twenty-one inches may have been used. To this must be added the vestibule, fifteen feet in width, running along the front or east side. On the sides are built **side chambers** three stories in height. The successive stories upward widened by correspondingly narrowing the main wall with **offsets.** These chambers were for use by the priests, probably for provisions and storage.

6:11-13. *A Prophetic Oracle to Solomon.* This passage interrupts the architectural description. It is a D addition based on II Samuel 7. The editor's concern for explaining how God could have permitted the exile of the people in his own day is clear. Solomon and his descendants did not keep God's ordinances and so God forsook the people.

6:14-22. *Woodwork and Other Decoration.* The temple proper consists of two parts, the **nave** or holy place, and the **inner sanctuary** or holy of holies. The latter is a thirty-foot cube and contains the **ark.** Emphasis is laid on the use of wood throughout, since wood, especially **cedar and cypress,** was scarce and therefore precious. The lavish use of **gold** overlay throughout as well as carved decorative motifs is described. Apparently everything in the **inner sanctuary**—walls, altar, and cherubim—is completely **overlaid** with gold.

6:23-28. *The Cherubim.* Canaanite and Mesopotamian carvings of **cherubim** (Hebrew plural of "cherub") show them as winged creatures, usually with human heads and animal bodies. They appear especially on the thrones of kings. Two such figures are said to have been placed in the **inner sanctuary.** Appropriately they fill the lower half of the western wall, their height being fifteen feet, and their outspread wings reaching from one side to the other. The empty upper half thus symbolizes the throne for the invisible deity. Other passages (for example Exodus 25:18-20; 37:6-9; Numbers 7:89) describe the ark as decorated with cherubs forming Yahweh's throne. These may represent a later tendency to seek earlier origins for features of the temple.

6:29-36. *Decorations and Doors.* There are not only carvings of cherubs, **palm trees,** and **flowers.** There is extravagant use of **gold** throughout, even to overlay all the **floor.** Both the five-sided **entrance** to the sanctuary and the **square** entrance to the nave have elaborate doors. Outside the temple is a court where the people congregate.

6:37-38. *Chronology of the Building.* The construction takes about **seven years.** This would be either six and a half or seven and a half since **Ziv** is April-May and **Bul** October-November. The use of these old Canaanite names shows the antiquity of the reference.

7:1-12. *Other Buildings.* Solomon's building continues for thirteen more years after the temple is finished (cf. 9:10). Since the architectural details are sparse and at times technical, it is not always clear what the records intend.

7:2-5. The first of these buildings is the **House of the Forest of Lebanon,** probably intended as an armory. It is one hundred fifty feet long, seventy-five feet wide, and forty-five feet high, thus considerably larger than the temple. It is likely that there were not **three** but four rows of **cedar pillars,** with the outer rows against the sides, forming three aisles. This would total sixty pillars in all, not **forty-five.** That this is correct appears from the reference to **three rows** and **three tiers** which have **windows**—an apparent allusion to the aisles. The building evidently received its name from its complete construction of cedar.

7:6. The **Hall of Pillars** may simply be a covered portico in the front of the preceding building—that is, an extension of it by **thirty cubits.** If so, verse 6*b* should read "even a portico in front with pillars and a roof over them."

7:7-12. The **Hall of Judgment** is apparently another part of this architectural complex. Solomon's palace and the house of **Pharaoh's daughter** (cf. 3:1) are in the harem complex, nicely called the **other court.**

7:13-14. *Hiram, Workman in Bronze.* This paragraph serves as an introduction to all the bronze furniture to be made for the temple recorded in verses 15-47. There is some doubt about the name of this Tyrian craftsman. II Chronicles 2:13-14 calls him **Huramabi** and states that his mother was from Dan rather than **Naphtali.**

7:15-22. The Two Pillars of Bronze. It was common practice in antiquity to erect two independent pillars flanking the entrance to a temple. Their precise purpose is unknown. The pillars for Solomon's temple are huge in size, each nearly six feet thick and about twenty-seven feet high. Each has an elaborately decorated **capital** of almost eight feet made of bronze three inches thick. The two pillars have names, **Jachin** (meaning "he sets up") and **Boaz** (meaning unknown, though with different vowels it would mean ("with strength"). Why these names were given and what they signified is unknown.

7:23-26. The Bronze Sea. According to II Chronicles 4:6 the huge **molten sea** is a basin for priestly ablutions. It is almost fifteen feet in diameter and eight feet deep and is made of **cast** bronze three inches thick. It rests on twelve bronze **oxen** facing outward, three in each direction. Why oxen were used is unknown. Some have conjectured that they were actually bulls and thus symbols of fertility, but the text gives no basis for this. The basin is set **on the southeast corner of the house.** Its capacity is much too great for the dimensions given and probably is an interpolation. **Two thousand baths** would be over ten thousand gallons according to fragments of jars marked "bath" which have been excavated.

7:27-39. The Stands and Lavers. Ten large wheeled stands are made, into which ten lavers are set. These are arranged five on the north and five on the south of the temple. The water in the lavers must have been used in connection with the sacrificial rites (cf. II Chronicles 4:6). Some of the technical terms of the description—**panels** and **frames**—are not understood. The dimensions and capacity stated seem to make the objects too large and heavy to be movable.

7:40-47. Summary of Bronze Objects. Not only the large objects described above but also many small vessels and decorations are made. All the bronze work is done in the **Jordan Valley**—in an area **between Succoth and Zarethan**. There **clay** is available to make molds for the casting.

7:48-51. *The Furnishings of Gold.* With the exception of the concluding statement in verse 51 this passage is a later reflection rather than a contemporary document. Possibly it was added by postexilic writers.

C. THE DEDICATION OF THE TEMPLE (8:1-66)

For an earlier parallel to this chapter see II Samuel 6. The **feast** of dedication is coincident with the feast of ingathering, or booths (cf. Deuteronomy 16:13-15). It has often been suggested that it was actually the New Year festival according to the calendar beginning in the fall. According to the later spring calendar **Ethanim** was the **seventh month**. In any event it was the month preceding Bul. Thus the feast was held either one month before or eleven months after the actual completion date (cf. 6:38).

8:3-13. *The Ark Brought into the Temple.* The main event is the pilgrimage with the ark, symbolizing Yahweh's invisible presence among the people, and its entrance into the **inner sanctuary**. The passage has been considerably amplified by later additions, especially verses 7-11. On the **cherubim** see above on 6:23-28. On the **cloud** cf. the late tradition in Exodus 40:34-35. Verses 12-13 are a fragment of a song which according to the Septuagint comes from the "Book of Songs" (see Introduction).

8:14-21. *Explanation for the Building Enterprise.* This is the D editor's interpretation of the fact that Solomon rather than David built the temple. It is an expansion of the first part of the dedicatory prayer in verses 22-26. Emphasis is placed on **David** as the object of Yahweh's choice rather than on a **city** where the temple was to be built.

8:22-53. *Solomon's Dedicatory Prayer.* This great prayer is also a late composition. It begins with praise for divine faithfulness to the terms of the Davidic **covenant** (II Samuel 7).

8:27-30. These verses are a general introduction. The temple is an effective place for prayer, since Yahweh has said that the divine **name shall be there.** Yahweh's name is the greatest gift that can be given, since by this Yahweh bestows power. This gift is divine condescension, for no house can **contain** the infinite deity.

8:31-34. The author believes that calamity is the result of sin. Accordingly, when the people suffer military defeat they must repent. When they confess their sins **in this house,** God may **forgive** and restore them **again to the land**—a phrase that seems to presuppose a knowledge of the Babylonian exile.

8:35-40. Similarly when natural calamities overtake the people—drought, **famine,** or other **plague**—they are the result of sin. They can be removed only by divine pardon following confession.

8:41-43. These verses are a prayer for the non-Israelites who may be attracted to the temple because of the fame of Israel's God. This passage is typical of a much later age—especially after the exile, when proselytes to the Jewish faith were much more welcome.

8:44-53. The last part of the prayer is a **supplication** for restoration from exile. Here the D editor interprets the meaning of exile as a national calamity. Such an event also lies under divine direction. By its emphasis on God's past deliverance of the **people** from **Egypt,** the prayer implies the hope that God will again restore them.

8:54-61. *Solomon's Benediction.* At the end of the prayers it is said that Solomon **arose.** This is in apparent contradiction to verse 22, where he stands and prays. II Chronicles 6:13 removes the contradiction by describing a bronze platform on which he first stands and then kneels for the actual prayer. Basic to this prayer is the realization that without divine help the people cannot keep God's laws (verse 58). Gradually what begins as benediction changes into a pleading with the assembly to remain faithful.

8:62-66. *The Feast of Dedication.* The feast of **seven days** is marked mainly by a large number (surely exaggerated) of sacrifices by which the building is officially dedicated. The passage, like the rest of the chapter, is editorial. It may actually describe postexilic practices.

The **middle of the court** probably means the area of the altar. Here occurs the first mention of the **bronze altar,** though the bronze furnishings were fully described earlier as being Hiram's workmanship. At least three kinds of sacrifices are mentioned. Only the **peace offerings** involved the common sacrificial meal. The **assembly** is described as representing the whole of ideal Israel, from the **entrance of Hamath** (the boundary of the city-state of Hamath on the Orontes in the north) to the **Brook of Egypt** (a seasonal stream about sixty miles southwest of Beer-sheba). The passage ends with the D editor's typical bias—the importance of the Davidic dynasty.

D. Solomon's Apex and Decline (9:1–11:43)

9:1-9. *Solomon's Second Vision.* Yahweh appears to Solomon in answer to his dedicatory prayer. The Lord states that the continuance of the dynasty and of Israel is conditional on the faithfulness of Solomon and his successors. Like chapter 8 this is D material. It constitutes the editor's explanation for the exile as due to the people's idolatry.

9:10-14. *Solomon's Bargain with Hiram.* The building operations are finally completed (see above on 7:1-12). Solomon's treasury is empty. In order to refill it he finds it necessary to sell Hiram **twenty cities in . . . Galilee** bordering on the state of Tyre for a huge amount of **gold.** An editorial parenthesis in verse 11a sugarcoats this unpalatable bit of history by implying that Solomon simply gave the villages in appreciation for past favors, but the building materials had already been paid for (cf. 5:11). The ceded area was named **Cabul,** the meaning of which is uncertain. An early folk etymology ("like nothing") has it that Hiram was dissatisfied with his new possession and gave it this derogatory name.

9:15-23. *Solomon's Labor Force.* This passage contradicts the true record in 5:13-18, which is confirmed by the complaint in 12:4. The levy of forced labor is here apologetically described as applied only to the non-Israelite population, with Israelites pictured as officers. Into the framework of this account has been inserted an early, probably archival, summary of Solomon's building operations (verses 15b-19). Solomon also builds up Jerusalem by extending the city **wall**—presumably northward to enclose the palace and temple structure. He also constructs the problematic **Millo,** which was some kind of stone or earth work in the city that needed constant repair—possibly a kind of stone terracing.

9:24-25. *A Miscellany.* Verse 24 is probably taken from Solomon's court annals. Verse 25 shows him as dutifully performing the major cultic rites—the celebration of the three annual feasts prescribed for all Israelites.

9:26-28. *Solomon's Navy.* The fleet is stationed at **Ezion-geber** at the northern end of the **Red Sea** (i.e. the Gulf of Aqaba). The control of this area was conditional on the subjection of **Edom.** The purpose of the navy was purely commercial. Various locations for **Ophir** have been proposed, but southeastern Arabia, where it is known that **gold** was produced, is the most likely.

10:1-13. *Visit of the Queen of Sheba.* This account describes a diplomatic visit by the monarch of a distant state to Solomon's court—no doubt to negotiate trade relations. Archaeologists have discovered that a highly developed Sabean kingdom existed in Solomon's time in southwest Arabia, and Assyrian inscriptions seem to confirm biblical references to Sabeans in northern Arabia. The interchange of gifts was part of oriental etiquette on such an occasion. There is no reason to doubt the historicity of the event, though details are probably exaggerated in order to enhance Solomon's fame.

10:11-12. The story is interrupted by these verses, which amplify the account of Solomon's commercial navy in 9:26-28. They call special attention to the importation of **precious stones** and **almug** wood. The meaning of the latter is unknown. It apparently could be used for making musical instruments.

10:14-25. *Various Laudatory Details.* Solomon's commercial exploits bring in a huge quantity of **gold** used for all kinds of displays. Since gold is a soft metal, the **shields** would be useless in warfare. They serve only to show the splendor of Solomon's reign. They are hung in the national armory (cf. 7:2-5). The **large shields** of verse 16 are long and curved to cover the body, whereas those of verse 17 are small and round. The location of **Tarshish** is uncertain. Tartessus, on the southwest coast of Spain, is most plausible.

10:23-25. This exaggerated summary of Solomon's **riches** and **wisdom** finds parallels in ancient oriental royal inscriptions. A later age made Solomon the wisest person of all times, a judgment contradicted by chapter 11.

10:26-29. *Solomon's Cavalry.* For **horsemen** in verse 26 read "horses." Trade in horses and chariotry was with Asia Minor. In verse 28 **Egypt** must be corrected to Musri, ancient Cappadocia. This region, together with **Kue,** i.e. Cilicia, was a center of horse breeding. It is possible that in verse 29 Egypt is correct as a center for chariot building, though this too may have been intended as Musri.

11:1-8. *Solomon's Large Harem.* The D editor has placed all of Solomon's difficulties in a final chapter, thereby creating the impression that these all occurred in the final years of his reign as a direct result of his idolatry. This is hardly true, as verses 21 and 25 show. Solomon's idolatry, the editor insists, was due to his large harem that included many foreigners. Many of them, primarily those of subject states, were probably political hostages. These foreign wives have their own **gods,** and Solomon provides for the cult of these gods.

Ashtoreth (Astarte) was the Phoenician fertility goddess. **Milcom** (meaning "the king" and sometimes shortened to **Molech,** "king," verse 7) and **Chemosh** were astral deities. For these last two he builds altars on the **mountain east of Jerusalem**—that is, the Mount of Olives (cf. II Samuel 15:32).

11:9-13. *Yahweh's Judgment on Solomon.* Here we have the D editor's explanation for the division of the kingdom at the end of Solomon's reign. Yahweh has warned Solomon in dreams against idolatry. Because of his disobedience Yahweh will remove all but **one tribe,** Judah, from the Davidic house after his death—a classic case of prophecy after the event.

11:14-22. *Hadad's Revolt.* Edom was conquered by David (cf. II Samuel 8:13-14). On that occasion the young Edomite prince fled first south to the desert of **Midian,** east of the Gulf of Aqaba. He then managed to make his way through the wilderness (or possibly oasis) of **Paran,** in the Sinai Peninsula, to **Egypt.** The circumstances of the Edomite invasion are not fully clear from the text. Obviously a general massacre occurred, though verse 16 is exaggerated—Edom was to remain for centuries! Hadad eventually intermarries with Pharaoh's house. He returns to Edom at the news of David's and Joab's deaths and apparently revolts against Solomon.

11:23-25. *Rezon's Revolt.* Syria was also defeated by David (cf. II Samuel 8:3-12; 10), quite thoroughly. On **Zobah** see comment on II Samuel 8:3-8. Rezon, who escaped from that slaughter, becomes a bandit chief. When the weaker Solomon becomes king, he is able to establish an independent Syrian state at **Damascus.** This city-state long remains a military opponent to Israel.

11:26-40. *Jeroboam's Revolt.* Jeroboam is from the north—an **Ephraimite** from **Zeredah,** the location of which is uncertain. Because of his ability he is given supervision of the **forced labor** in Ephraim, the **house of Joseph.** We do not learn what form his rebellion takes, but he is forced to flee to **Egypt.** There he becomes friendly with **Shishak,** the ruler. Into this story is inserted a prophetic story. **Ahijah** predicts the division of the kingdom. The language is characteristically D, with its emphasis on the continuation of the Davidic house in Jerusalem and the warning to keep the laws of God. The symbolic tearing action is typically prophetic (cf. I Samuel 15:27-28). It also reflects a later period when Judah had assimilated Simeon, thereby making **one tribe** out of two.

11:41-43. *Obituary Notice.* The regular D notice for change of ruler occurs here for the first time (see Introduction). **Forty years** is not an exact number (see above on 2:10-12).

III. HISTORY OF THE TWO KINGDOMS
(I KINGS 12:1–II KINGS 17:41)

A. THE DIVISION (12:1-24)

12:1-20. *The Revolt of the Ten Tribes.* The story as told here is strangely inconsistent. According to verses 2, 3, and 12 Jeroboam is a ringleader in the revolt, but verse 20 pictures him as summoned to the kingship. The Septuagint omits verses 2-3*a* and the reference to Jeroboam in verse 12, thus making a consistent story.

12:1-15. Significantly, and unlike Solomon, **Rehoboam** cannot be crowned at Jerusalem. He has to meet delegates in the north at **Shechem,** an old tribal shrine in premonarchic days. They demand an end to the forced labor levy as a condition of their loyalty. The young king-elect foolishly follows the advice of his contemporaries. The D editor adds an interpretative note (verse 15) that Rehoboam's foolishness was a fate divinely inspired in accordance with 11:29-39.

12:16-20. The result is immediate revolt against the Davidic dynasty by all the tribes except **Judah.** In verse 16 Sheba's old watchword is revived (cf. II Samuel 20:1). Rehoboam has to **flee** for his life to his capital. The ten tribes then elect **Jeroboam** as king, and the old rupture between Judah and the north is again complete. Politically the two kingdoms now go their own way, the south under dynastic rule, the north under a strong-man rule.

12:21-24. *An Attempt to Quell the Revolt.* Here the tribe of **Benjamin** joins Judah, reflecting the later extension of Judah to the north. Rehoboam's military action is stopped by a prophetic oracle intended to show that the Davidic dynasty was obedient to the divine intent.

B. EARLY HISTORY OF THE KINGDOMS (12:25–16:34)

12:25-33. *Jeroboam's Cultic Innovations.* The account of Jeroboam's reign in Israel is given first and at some length

(12:25–14:20). The first capital of the rebel kingdom is established at **Shechem.** The fortification of **Penuel** in Transjordan was probably intended both to interrupt the north-south trade route and to serve as a frontier post against invaders from the east.

12:26-33. The D editor is more concerned with condemnation of Jeroboam, "who made Israel to sin" by his attempt to break with the Jerusalem cult. Jeroboam realizes the danger to his new kingdom in the cultic dominance of Jerusalem. He seeks to promote local shrines, especially that at **Bethel,** known in Amos' time as "the king's sanctuary" (Amos 7:13). At at least two of these shrines he sets up golden **calves,** actually bulls, as images of Yahweh. Some scholars surmise that these figures were really thrones for the invisible Yahweh, like the cherubim in the Jerusalem temple (see above on 6:23-28). These symbols were particularly dangerous in view of the Canaanite use of the bull as a fertility symbol.

Other measures concern the clergy for these centers, or **high places,** as well as a change in the cultic calendar. Here the Judean bias is especially evident. The celebration of the **feast** (presumably ingathering, or booths) in the **eighth month** was simply an adherence to ancient custom, whereas the Judean observance in the seventh month was a later change (see above on 8:1-66).

13:1-10. *Jeroboam Warned by a Divine Word.* This is a prophetic legend not earlier than the time of Josiah, since the author is acquainted with the cultic reforms of 622. According to the story a Judean **man of God** utters an oracle against the **Bethel** altar, saying that one day **Josiah** will defile the **altar** by slaying the **priests** of the illegitimate shrines on it. The angry king tries to order the arrest of his rebuker, but his arm is paralyzed. The prophetic sign of the altar tumbling into ruins immediately takes place. On the holy man's intercession the king's arm is **restored.**

13:11-32. *The Sequel.* Obeying instructions the Judean holy man refuses to accept hospitality in Bethel. A Bethel **prophet** intercepts him and by a lying oracle persuades him to accept food and drink. The prophet then gives a true oracle reproving the holy man for his disobedience and predicting his violent death. The prediction is fulfilled. A **lion** kills him. The prophet buries him and mourns for him, requesting **his sons** to bury his own body in the same tomb. The story is homiletic and ties in with that in II Kings 23:17-20. On lying prophets see below on 22:5-28.

13:33-34. *The D Editor's Judgment on Jeroboam.* Not only has Jeroboam created an illegitimate cult but he has himself **consecrated** the illegitimate priesthood. To the D editor this is an unpardonable crime which can be corrected only by extermination of the royal **house.**

14:1-18. *Ahijah's Prophecy.* Another prophetic story is told to insure the complete denunciation of the renegade king. The long speech of Ahijah is the D editor's interpretation of the northern kingdom's ruin as due to its apostate cult. The editor considers it peculiarly appropriate that the prophet who predicted Jeroboam's rebel kingship many years previously (11:29-39) should now predict his doom.

The condemnation is put into the framework of a tale about a hopelessly **sick** child of Jeroboam. The queen disguises herself at the king's behest to seek guidance from the now aged and blind prophet. But the prophet has been divinely warned. He reprimands her and predicts the child's death before her return. The older form of the story is probably contained in verses 1-6, 12, 17.

14:15. The term **Asherim** (Hebrew plural of Asherah) probably refers to male and female fertility symbols associated with the worship of the Canaanite goddess Asherah.

14:17. The mention that the queen returned to **Tirzah,** if historically accurate, indicates that Jeroboam early in his reign moved his capital from Shechem to that city. Tirzah probably lay about seven miles northeast of Shechem. Some interpreters believe it was rather Baasha who established the northern capital at Tirzah (cf. 15:33), where it remained till Omri built Samaria (16:23-24).

14:19-20. *Obituary Notice of Jeroboam.* This is given in the usual annalistic terms (see Introduction): reference to the court records, the length of his reign, his death, and the name of his successor.

14:21-31. *Rehoboam's Reign in Judah.* Rehoboam's reign is introduced with the common formula giving his age at accession, the length of his reign, and his mother's name (given only for Judean kings). Rehoboam's mother is one of the foreign wives of Solomon, an **Ammonitess** (repeated by error in verse 31).

14:22-24. The particular accusations are sterotyped: the erection of illegitimate shrines, **pillars,** and **Asherim** (see above on verse 15) and the existence of **male cult prostitutes** (cult devotees in Canaanite religion). All of these were strictly forbidden in the later D legislation which guided the editor's evaluation.

14:25-28. Sheshonk, or **Shishak,** was the first ruler of the twelfth dynasty of Egypt. He was Jeroboam's patron (cf. 11:40), but his invasion was not to support Jeroboam. It was simply to gain booty, as proved by the well-known Karnak inscription with its long list of plundered Palestinian cities both north and south.

14:29-31. This is the usual obituary notice for Judean kings (see Introduction). Almost all of them are said to have been buried in Jerusalem. However, the site of the royal tomb area has not as yet been found.

15:1-8. *Abijam's Reign in Judah.* Abijam, the second king of Judah, reigns only **three years.** The name **Abishalom** is a variant form of Absalom and has sometimes been taken to mean David's son. This identification is supported by the appropriateness of **Maacah** as a name for the **daughter** of Absalom the son of David (see comment on II Samuel 14:25-27). Otherwise the identification seems unlikely for two reasons. First, any child of his would apparently be considerably older than Solomon's son Rehoboam. And second, after the rebellion his children would probably be in disfavor with the rest of David's family. Josephus, Jewish historian of the first century A.D., suggests a solution to the age problem by making Maacah the granddaughter of

Absalom through his daughter Tamar (cf. II Samuel 14:27). But it appears more probable that Abishalom was a different man from David's rebel son.

15:3-8. Abijam's rule is condemned as an evil one by the D editor. Typical of his point of view are verses 4-5, enhancing the promise of a dynasty to **David.** Verse 6 is a repitition of 14:30 and quite out of place here. Verses 7-8 give the usual obituary (cf. 14:29-31).

15:9-24. *Asa's Reign in Judah.* Asa is said to have ruled the southern kingdom **forty-one years.** A problem arises regarding the name of his mother, who is given the same name as the mother of Abijam, his father (see above on verses 1-8). Probably the explanation is that **Maacah** retained the status of queen mother, since Asa must have been a minor when he became king.

15:11-15. Because of the cultic reforms of his reign Asa is judged by the D editor to have done **right** in Yahweh's eyes. It must be noted, however, that he did not remove the shrines outside Jerusalem. The Canaanite practices have apparently been continued from the time of Rehoboam chiefly under Maacah's influence. The young king courageously demotes his grandmother from her harem leadership and destroys her idol. On **Asherah** see above on 14:15.

15:16-22. These verses describe Asa's military and political accomplishments. **Baasha** of Israel fortifies **Ramah**, only five miles north of Jerusalem. By a large bribe Asa persuades **Ben-hadad I** of **Damascus** to relieve the pressure by attacking the northern borders of Israel. The establishment of this treaty with Judah means breaking a similar treaty with Israel, a treachery which appeals to Ben-hadad's raiding instincts.

The attack on Israel's northern frontier is extensive, permitting Asa to regain the Benjamin territory in question. Instead of taking over Ramah as a fortress, Asa has it dismantled as a national work project. He uses the materials to fortify **Geba**—probably an error for Gibeah, Saul's old capital, two miles south of Ramah—and **Mizpah,** three miles to the north.

197

The passage ends with the usual obituary notice but adds that in his latter days he was **diseased in his feet.**

15:25-32. *Nadab's Reign in Israel.* Jeroboam I of Israel is succeeded briefly by his son Nadab. As a northern king he is naturally judged by the D editor as **evil.** After less than **two years** a military coup d'etat under **Baasha of Issachar** results in the assassination of Nadab along with the entire family of Jeroboam. Such wholesale wiping out of a royal house in order to destroy all possible opposition was common ancient practice. The D editor interprets it as the fulfillment of Ahijah's prophecy to Jeroboam's wife (cf. 14:14). Verse 32 is a repetition of verse 16. Either it is out of place or Nadab should be read for Baasha.

15:33-16:7. *Baasha's Reign in Israel.* Baasha is reported as ruling from **Tirzah** (see above on 14:17-18) for **twenty-four years.**

16:1-7. Nothing is told of Baasha's career except a prophetic doom oracle by **Jehu the Son of Hanani.** The oracle is similar to that of Ahijah against the house of Jeroboam (14:7-16) but briefer. The condemnation of Baasha's destruction of the **house of Jeroboam** in verse 7*b* is puzzling, since this was considered the fulfillment of the prophetic word according to 15:29. Possibly this is simply the judgment of the D editor.

16:8-14. *Elah's Reign in Israel.* Baasha is succeeded by his son Elah, who in turn is assassinated by one of his military commanders during his second year. Like Baasha, **Zimri** wipes out his predecessor's house. This is again interpreted as the fulfillment of a prophetic oracle.

16:15-22. *Zimri's Reign in Israel.* Zimri's assassination of Elah touches off civil war. On hearing of it **all Israel** (i.e. the army) elects **Omri** king. He immediately marches on **Tirzah.** Zimri, besieged in his castle, burns it to the ground and dies, having reigned only one week.

16:21-22. Omri's victory over Zimri is merely the first stage in his campaign. The people are **divided** in support of Omri and an otherwise unknown **Tibni.** Over four years of civil war end with Omri's victory, laconically described by **so Tibni died and Omri became king.**

16:23-28. *Omri's Reign in Israel.* Zimri's death is dated in the twenty-seventh year of Asa (verse 15) and Omri's reign is said to begin in the thirty-first year. Tibni presumably ruled during the interval (see Chronology in Introduction). That Omri was an extremely capable ruler is known from nonbiblical sources. He conquered Moab, made a marriage alliance with Sidon (i.e. Phoenicia), and built Samaria as the new permanent capital of Israel. A century later Assyrian kings still referred to the kingdom as the "land of Omri." The biblical writers recall only his purchase and building of Samaria midway during his reign. Samaria became as important politically for Israel as Jerusalem was for Judah.

16:29-34. *Introduction to Ahab of Israel.* Omri is succeeded by Ahab, in whom the D editor is particularly interested. Almost all the remainder of I Kings deals with events of his reign. Information concerning his period came to the editor mainly through prophetic stories. This passage is the only exception. It relates his unpardonable marriage with **Jezebel,** daughter of **Ethbaal king of the Sidonians.** According to Josephus she was a priest of Astarte. Her influence and ardor in attempting to substitute the worship of **Baal** for that of Israel's God evoked the wrath of later historians in Judah.

16:32-33. The title **Baal** (literally "master" or "lord") in earlier times was often used of Yahweh. At least from the time of Ahab on, it was used specifically of the Syrian god Hadad, worshiped as "Lord of the heavens." Under Ahab, because of the influence of Jezebel, Baalism became established in Samaria as an officially approved cult. On **Asherah** see above on 14:15.

16:34. This incidental historical note refers to the official refortification of **Jericho** by **Hiel.** He suffers the loss of two children, which the D editor interprets as the fulfillment of an ancient curse (cf. Joshua 6:26). Excavation of a foundation at Gezer has revealed skeletons of persons apparently sacrificed to secure divine favor for the construction. This has led many to conjecture that this verse records such a foundation sacrifice. But the text is more naturally understood as reflecting a popular interpretation of an unwary builder's double misfortune.

C. ELIJAH STORIES (17:1–19:21)

Chapters 17–19 and 21 contain a series of stories, largely miracle stories, in which Elijah is the chief figure. His name, which means "Yahweh is God," is the central theme.

17:1-7. *Elijah and the Drought.* The first scene shows Elijah, in obedience to Yahweh, predicting to Ahab a terrible drought. For this audacity he has to flee to an area beyond Ahab's jurisdiction, again by divine direction. He goes to the **brook Cherith** in Transjordan. There God commands **ravens** to feed him twice daily. This suffices until the drought dries up the brook.

17:8-16. *Elijah at Zarephath.* Again at divine bidding Elijah goes to **Zarephath,** about ten miles south of **Sidon,** to be fed by an impoverished **widow.** At his request she hospitably provides **water,** but she lacks sufficient food. Miraculously the **meal** and **oil** are multiplied in accordance with a divine oracle given by the prophet.

17:17-24. *The Revival of the Dead Boy.* When the widow's son dies, she is afraid of the prophet. Ancients felt that holy men could detect hidden faults as well as perform wonders and predict events. Elijah takes the child to his room and prays to Yahweh, protesting this seeming injustice. Elijah then performs a ritual prayer for the child's return to life. The revived lad is restored to **his mother,** who affirms her faith in Elijah's prophethood. This kind of story is a common folktale. A similar version about Elisha appears in II Kings 4:32-37.

18:1-19. *Elijah's Challenge to Ahab.* The drought is now to come to an end. But first the superiority of God over Baal must be decisively demonstrated. This occurs **in the third year.** Later Jewish traditions speak of a drought of three and a half years (cf. Luke 4:25 and James 5:17). As always Elijah moves only by divine order. Because of the severity of the famine Ahab orders his chamberlain **Obadiah** to help search throughout the land for food for the royal animals.

18:7-16. Later Elijah meets Obadiah, who is surprised that Elijah should openly appear in Israel. Ahab holds the prophet personally responsible for the drought and has conducted a frantic search everywhere for him. Elijah bids Obadiah summon the king, but the chamberlain reacts in fear. He knows that the prophet suddenly appears and disappears by the **Spirit of Yahweh.** He himself has been loyal to Yahweh rather than to Baal, and should Elijah again disappear he fears for his life. He obeys only when Elijah promises that he will remain, swearing by the full cultic name of the God of Israel—Yahweh **of hosts.**

18:17-19. Finally the two foes, king and prophet, meet. Ahab, full of animosity, calls his foe the one who troubles Israel. Elijah sternly places the blame for the famine directly on the king's idolatrous activities. Without further ado he orders Ahab to summon Israel, together with the prophets of **Baal** (see above on 16:32-33) and **Asherah** (see above on 14:15), to **Mount Carmel.** This famous mountain on the northern Palestinian coast was an old shrine, as appears from Thutmose III's reference to it as "the holy promontory."

18:20-40. *Yahweh versus Baal.* Ahab obeys Elijah and summons the assembly, which is to be judge and jury. The contest will be between Elijah and the Baal prophets. **The God who answers by fire**—that is, who lights the sacrifice without human instrumentality—is to be adjudged God. On Elijah's feeling of solitude see 19:9-18.

18:25-29. The prophets of Baal are to have the first turn. They engage in various cultic manipulations—a ritual limping dance about the unlit **altar,** wounding themselves with **swords** to produce **blood,** and calling on Baal ecstatically (**raved on**). Elijah, certain of the outcome, mocks the devotees. He suggests that their Baal is busy, **has gone aside** (to relieve himself), is traveling, or is sleeping. The Baalists persist until midafternoon, the time of the evening sacrifice.

18:30-35. Now Elijah's turn has come. As the people gather about, he prepares an **altar.** It is not clear whether this is a new altar (verse 32*a*) or an old altar that has been ruined, possibly through Jezebel's fanaticism (verse 30*b*). In any event verse 31 referring to **twelve** (rather than ten) **tribes** is a much later insertion hardly appropriate to a northern Israel story. To avoid any trickery the sacrifice and the altar are thoroughly drenched with **water.** Some have suggested that this was a magical rainmaking ceremony, but rather it is evidence of good faith.

18:36-40. The crucial moment is at hand. Elijah prays. Suddenly God's **fire** falls from heaven. God has spoken. The sacrifice, even **the stones, and the dust,** are consumed. Awestricken, the people render their decision: Yahweh is God. It is foolish to try to rationalize the story by calling the fire lightning. The whole point is the miraculous intervention, which to the Hebrews was the way God acts. In fact, in view of verse 44 it could not have been lightning at all. In the flush of this dramatic outcome Elijah has all four hundred and fifty **prophets** slain.

18:41-46. *The End of the Drought.* Now that Elijah's name, "Yahweh is God," has been vindicated, rain may be expected. Elijah goes to the **top of Carmel** to engage in a sevenfold rain ritual. Ahab is warned to hurry back to **Jezreel,** about seventeen miles to the southeast. Endowed with supernatural strength, Elijah is able to outrun Ahab's steeds. The rains descend. Yahweh's victory would now seem to be complete.

19:1-3. *Jezebel's Vow.* When Jezebel hears of the outcome at Carmel, she swears an oath by **the gods** that she will kill Elijah. She so informs him. In fear he flees **for his life,** passing through Judah and beyond **Beer-sheba** into the desert.

19:4-8. *Elijah in Despair.* Out in the desert the prophet sits in the shade of a **broom** shrub. Completely discouraged, he begs to be allowed to **die.** Falling asleep, he is awakened by the **angel** of Yahweh—that is, God appearing in human form. He eats divinely provided food and after another rest is told to continue. He is thus able to journey for **forty days and forty nights** without further nourishment. His destination is the holy mountain of revelation, called **Horeb** in the D sources.

19:9-18. *God's Revelation to Elijah.* On arrival at the holy mountain Elijah goes **to a cave.** There is some confusion in the story. Verses 13*b*-14 repeat almost word for word verses 9*b*-10. Furthermore verse 11*a* commands Elijah to stand outside, whereas verse 13 finds him still inside the cave. It seems best to consider verses 9b-11a as a later addition to the original story.

In the original story Elijah is in the cave when a **strong wind,** an **earthquake,** and a **fire** take place successively. But contrary to expectation Yahweh appears in none of these. It is the contrasting sound of a gentle whisper which Elijah recognizes as the voice of deity, causing him like Moses of old (Exodus 3:6) to hide **his face** lest he look on God. Yahweh inquires about his business here far outside Israel. He, in an orgy of self-pity, complains that all have forsaken God and that he is the sole true worshiper **left.** As though Carmel had never happened!

19:15-18. Before replying directly to Elijah's complaint Yahweh gives him a threefold mission. He is to anoint **Hazael** as **king of Damascus** (cf. II Kings 8:7-15), **Jehu** as **king** of **Israel** (cf. II Kings 9:1-10), and **Elisha** as his own successor. Since Elijah carries out only the last, it is possible that part of the Elisha cycle has here intruded into the Elijah story. In such case verse 17 is a judgment by an editor subsequent to that confusion. Finally Yahweh addresses himself to Elijah's complaint by correcting the facts. Elijah is far from being Yahweh's sole surviving worshiper.

19:19-21. *The Call of Elisha.* Elijah now carries out his third assignment. He finds Elisha, a young farmer, and throws on him his own hairy prophetic **mantle**—thought to be invested with great power (cf. II Kings 2:13-15). Elisha recognizes this action as a call to service and asks permission to say farewell to his parents. Elijah's peculiar answer is puzzling. It may be a mysterious way of saying: Do take leave of your parents if you recognize what I have done—that is, invested you as my successor.

D. War With Syria (20:1-43)

This chapter gives an account of the constant wars between Israel and Damascus around the middle of the ninth century. It comes from a source completely separate from chapters 17-19 and 21-22. It is the only account at all favorable to Ahab. There is no reference to Elijah and Elisha, though unnamed prophets are mentioned.

20:1-12. Ben-hadad's Demands. Ben-hadad of Damascus heads a large federation of troops, probably a group of minor Aramean kings. He has laid siege to **Samaria,** and it is in desperate straits. Ben-hadad sends in heavy demands, to which Ahab agrees. But then comes the malicious demand to open up the city to pillage. This is refused, and Ben-hadad states his intention to pulverize the city. Ahab answers defiantly with a proverb that means roughly "Don't count your chickens before they're hatched."

20:13-21. Israel's Victory. On the advice of an unnamed **prophet** Ahab determines on attack. At **noon,** an uncivilized time to begin a battle, a small group of **two hundred and thirty-two** men leave the city. They will draw out the besiegers. Then, when the "suicide squad" is engaged, the full army of **seven thousand** falls on the **Syrians,** and panic turns the tide. The Syrians flee, leaving their equipment behind them.

20:22-34. Ben-hadad's Second Attack. Ben-hadad's military council suggests two changes in strategy for the next campaign. First, they will attack on the **plain,** since Israel's gods are thought to be mountain **gods.** This rash statement brings on a divine oracle promising Ahab complete victory. Second, they will substitute military **commanders** for **kings** to lead the Syrian forces.

Accordingly battle is joined in the plain, at **Aphek.** The Syrians are completely routed, though the numbers in verses 29-30b are probably much exaggerated. **In the spring** can hardly be right. Warfare was not conducted until the fall, when the harvest was finished. The phrase probably should be rendered "at the beginning of the year,"—that is, in the fall.

20:30c-34. The surrender, though complete, is conducted with oriental cunning. Execution of a defeated king was normal procedure. Ahab, however, is flattered by the abjectness of the conquered. He not only spares Ben-hadad but courteously takes him into his own **chariot.** Ben-hadad then proposes economic concessions in his capital for Israelite merchants and the return of **cities** earlier taken by the Syrians during the reign of Baasha (15:20). **My father** in verse 34 has led many scholars to believe that this Ben-hadad is not the same as that in 15:16-24. But this is by no means certain.

20:35-43. *Rebuke of Ahab's Leniency.* An unnamed **prophet,** after having a comrade wound him, disguises himself so as to hide the prophetic brand on his forehead. He tells the king he was trusty for a Syrian captive who has escaped. Now he fears the consequences. Ahab refuses to listen to his appeal. Thereupon the prophet drops his disguise and predicts Ahab's death as penalty for having released Ben-hadad.

E. ELIJAH STORIES, CONTINUED (21:1-29)

21:1-16. *Naboth's Vineyard.* The story of royal violation of peasant property rights is told as a setting for the curse on Ahab and his house by Elijah. Thus it is part of the Elijah cycle. The scene of the incident is **Jezreel** (see above on 18:41-46). Naboth refuses to sell his patrimony to the king, who goes home in a fit of pique. His wicked queen takes the matter in hand by ordering trumped-up charges brought against Naboth by two false witnesses. Accordingly a **fast** is proclaimed—something done only in a great crisis. The false witnesses then present their charge that Naboth has **cursed God and the king.** This was a heinous crime, since a curse was thought by ancients to have inherent power. A spoken word was believed to be immediately effective. Such a curse could only be wiped out by stoning and state confiscation of goods. Thus Ahab takes over the coveted **vineyard.**

21:17-29. *The Curse on Ahab's House.* This story belongs to the Elijah cycle, as its introduction shows. **Elijah** is directed by a divine oracle to **meet Ahab** and pronounce doom on the king for his crimes. The D editor has expanded the original story by extending the curse to cover Ahab's **house.** In the process he dropped Elijah's original words which caused Ahab to show remorse.

21:27-29. Because of the king's outward repentance a second oracle mitigates the doom. The complete extermination of his house is postponed to a succeeding generation.

F. A Second Account of the Syrian War (22:1-53)

This chapter records Ahab's final battle. It must have taken place less than a year after the battle of Qarqar (853), in which Assyrian records report Ahab's fighting as an ally of Ben-hadad and the Syrians against the Assyrians.

22:2-4. The fact that **Jehoshaphat** is pressed into military service seems to indicate that Judah at this time was a vassal state of Israel.

22:5-28. *The Story of Micaiah.* Before going to battle people usually sought an oracle to see whether God would help them (cf. I Samuel 23:1-5). **Four hundred** prophets predict success for the venture. Jehoshaphat is suspicious of this. He asks whether there is **another prophet** who may be consulted. So **Micaiah the son of Imlah,** otherwise unknown, is summoned.

22:13-23. When the fearless Micaiah appears, he too, with tongue in cheek, echoes the reply of the four hundred. Commanded to speak the **truth** only, he poetically predicts the death of the king in battle. Then he continues with an account of a heavenly vision dramatizing a primitive view of the false prophet. God is sitting with the heavenly council, embarrassed by the continued existence of the evil **Ahab.** How can Ahab be misled into going to battle? Eventually one **spirit** has a suggestion; he will be a **lying spirit** for the band of prophets. Micaiah does not deny the sincerity of his fellow prophets. He simply states that they were intentionally misled by God.

22:24-28. For this treason Micaiah is **struck** by **Zedekiah,** leader of the false prophets who ironically asks how this lying spirit transported itself to speak to Micaiah. Micaiah replies that this will be clear when Zedekiah must flee for his life. Ahab then gives Micaiah into custody, to be held prisoner until his safe return. Verse 28*b* is a late editorial quotation from Micah 1:2*a*. It incorrectly identifies Micaiah with the prophet Micah of the late eighth century.

22:29-40. *Ahab's Death.* To avoid the dire fate predicted by Micaiah, Ahab goes into battle **disguised** as a common soldier. But to no avail. The chance shot of a bowman fells him. The prophetic word is fulfilled, and by **sunset** he dies. Ahab is **buried** in **Samaria,** and the account ends with the usual obituary and succession notice. The D editor added verse 38 to show the correctness of Elijah's prophecy in 21:19. **The ivory house which he built** refers to a palace decorated with ivory inlays. This has been substantiated by archaeological finds of the Samarian ivories.

22:41-50. *Jehoshaphat's Reign in Judah.* Jehoshaphat becomes sole ruler in Ahab's **fourth year.** He had been co-regent with **Asa,** his father, for three or four years which must be assumed to complete his total reign of **twenty-five** years (see Chronology in Introduction). On verse 44 see above on verses 2-4. Another early detail is described in verses 47-49. **Edom** is subject to Judah, being ruled by a Judean governor. Jehoshaphat's attempt to rebuild Solomon's fleet (cf. 9:25-28) is ill fated because of lack of naval experience. He astutely rejects an Israelite offer of help as interference.

22:51-53. *Accession of Ahaziah in Israel.* The accession date of Ahaziah is based on Jehoshaphat's sole rule and ignores his co-regency (see above on verses 41-50).

THE SECOND BOOK OF
THE KINGS

John William Wevers

INTRODUCTION

See the Introduction to I Kings. The outline of the contents indicated by the headings continues that in I Kings.

G. ELIJAH STORIES, CONCLUDED (1:1-18)

The chapter begins with a statement taken from 3:5. Except for the obituary and succession notice at the end, the remainder is a story from the prophetic cycle. In general tone it is far more like the Elisha stories than like those of the Elijah cycle.

1:2-16. *The Sickness of Ahaziah of Israel.* The occasion for the tale is Ahaziah's illness. This is the result of a fall, and consequently he seeks an oracle from Baal instead of from Israel's God. Probably the name here given Baal was originally Baal-zebul (cf. Beelzebul, Mark 3:22, where he is called "prince of demons"). It was perhaps intentionally changed in early times to ridicule the idol by calling it **Baal-zebub**, meaning "lord of flies." **Ekron** was the Philistine city nearest to Samaria.

1:5-16. The king's messengers are intercepted by a man who pronounces a doom oracle. Ahaziah recognizes Elijah. He sends two consecutive military detachments to apprehend the impertinent prophet, with disastrous results. A third, whose **captain** pleads with the prophet, is spared. Elijah then predicts death to the king in person. The tale is another stage in the story of Elijah as Yahweh's prophet in the struggle between Israel's God and the Canaanite Baal.

1:17-18. *Obituary of Ahaziah of Israel.* The succession notice states that Ahaziah was succeeded by **Jehoram, his brother,** in the second year of **Jehoram** of **Judah.** But 3:1 states that this took place in the eighteenth year of Jehoshaphat. Apparently Jehoram of Judah had begun a co-regency with his father, Jehoshaphat, during the preceding year (see Chronology in Introduction to I Kings).

H. ELISHA STORIES (2:1–8:29)

2:1-12*b*. *Elijah's Ascent into Heaven.* Though Elijah is the central figure of this story, it really belongs to the Elisha cycle. **Elisha** is here introduced as the successor to Elijah's **spirit.** He receives Elijah's **mantle** with its mystic powers. He also receives the legacy of a firstborn son, a **double portion** of his spirit. He thus becomes the leader of the prophetic bands.

2:1-8. The two prophets walk **from Gilgal . . . down to Bethel . . . to Jericho . . . to the Jordan.** Gilgal here can hardly mean the well-known sanctuary site near Jericho. It must refer to the town of this name about seven miles north of Bethel. When they reach the Jordan, Elijah, like a second Moses or Joshua, miraculously parts the river by striking it with **his mantle.**

2:9-12*b*. Suddenly the fiery **horses** and **chariot** come and Elijah is transported heavenward. Elisha cries out in despair; Elijah is equal to Israel's entire cavalry. The story of Elijah's miraculous ascent probably originally had something to do with the myth of the chariots of the sun. In later legend Elijah is ranked with Moses as one whom God personally cared for. For this reason no one knows their graves (cf. Deuteronomy 34:6).

2:12c-18. *Elisha as Elijah II.* Elisha is now Elijah's successor and is fully endowed with his spirit. This is clear from his miraculously parting the Jordan with Elijah's **mantle**.

2:15-18. On Elisha's return to Jericho the prophetic band recognize him as their new leader. In spite of his warning they send a group to search for the departed Elijah. Yahweh's **Spirit** has often removed Elijah suddenly in the past.

2:19-22. *The Healing of the Waters.* This is the first in a series of miracle stories about Elisha. **Water** from the Jericho **spring** is blamed for making women barren. Elisha heals the waters by means of **salt** and a divine oracle. Note the point of view of the later writer in the phrase **to this day**.

2:23-25. *The Curse on the Jeering Boys.* Elisha has his head shaved as a sign of his prophetic function. When **boys** of **Bethel** jeer at this prophetic mark, he utters an awful **curse** in Yahweh's name. The curse is immediately effective when **two she-bears** kill forty-two of the lads. The legend emphasizes the awful consequences of profaning that which is holy, whether it be God or God's prophet.

3:1-3. *Accession of Jehoram in Israel.* On the accession date see above on 1:17-18. The usual judgment on northern kings is made. One mitigating fact is mentioned—his removal of the Baal image made by his father Ahab.

3:4-27. *War Against Moab.* The famous Moabite Stone was a monument erected by **Mesha** to celebrate his accomplishments, especially against Israel. According to this monument, Moab was conquered by Omri and remained a vassal state for forty years. Mesha rebelled in the days of Omri's "son"—evidently to be understood as meaning "grandson," i.e. **Jehoram.**

3:4-8. Israel required a huge annual tribute of Mesha. When he rebels, Israel naturally has no intention of giving up this lucrative income without a struggle. Jehoram invites **Jehoshaphat** of Judah and the latter's vassal, **Edom,** to help him put down the rebellious shepherd king of Moab. The invitation was a polite way of actually ordering a vassal state.

3:9-12. Perhaps because of fortifications in northern Moab which Mesha boasts of on his monument, the allies make a

circuitous march. They apparently go around the southern end of the Dead Sea through Edom, in order to attack Moab from the south. On the border of Moab the expected **water** supply does not materialize and the attackers are in desperate straits. Jehoshaphat inquires whether any **prophet** is present, and Elisha is discovered.

3:13-20. The prophetic story is again tinged with the miraculous. **A minstrel** is brought to play in order to induce ecstasy—a practice common in various cultures. The oracle given by Elisha predicts **water** in the **dry stream-bed,** or wadi, without benefit of **wind or rain.** Victory over the Moabites is also predicted. Elisha further commands complete destruction of Moab, even cutting down trees and despoiling all water holes. At dawn the stream is rushing with water.

3:21-25. The **Moabites** are encamped on the northern edge of the wadi. When they look down on the unexpected **water** it looks **red**—probably a word play on the word "Edom," which means "red." They rush down to plunder, but are badly beaten and flee in panic. The ensuing devastation of the countryside is told in terms of the prophetic command in verse 19. Finally only one fortress is left to Mesha in southern Moab, **Kir-hareseth.** This is "attacked," not **conquered,** by the **slingers** of the allies.

3:26-27. Mesha sees that even this stronhold is on the point of falling. He makes a strong effort to break through the line of besiegers but fails. He then determines on a desperate course. In full view of the attackers he sacrifices **his eldest son,** the crown prince, as a **burnt offering** to Chemosh, his god. This action causes the attackers to panic, and the siege is lifted. On the sacrifice of offspring cf. 16:3; see comment I Kings 16:34.

4:1-7. *The Unfailing Jar.* Here begins a series of prophetic miracle stories which show Elisha as a worker of wonders. Some of these have parallels in the Elijah cycle. On this story cf. I Kings 17:8-16. Enslavement for debt was practiced in Israel, though later legislation mitigated the practice.

4:8-37. *Restoration of the Dead Boy.* This story is much more elaborate than the parallel from the Elijah cycle (I Kings 17:17-24). **A wealthy woman** of **Shunem,** i.e. a **Shunammite,**

provides a specially built and furnished guest room for Elisha. For this kindness Elisha wishes to repay her, but she proudly asserts her independence. **Gehazi,** Elisha's **servant,** notes that **she has no son, and her husband is old.** Elisha then promises her a son **when the time comes round**—that is, after a normal period of pregnancy. The city of Shunem was about twenty-five miles west of Mount Carmel.

4:18-25a. The next scene shows the young lad out in the field. He is suddenly stricken with sunstroke and taken to the house, where he dies in his mother's arms. She lays the corpse on Elisha's **bed** and immediately sets out for **Mount Carmel.**

4:25b-31. When she arrives, Elisha sends his servant with his wonder-working **staff,** which he is to **lay** on the **face** of the corpse. He is to maintain complete silence on the journey so as to lose none of the wonder-working power of the staff. The magic, however, does not work. Meanwhile the woman with correct intuition has refused to leave the prophet.

4:32-37. In the final scene Elisha enters his chamber. There he both prays to Yahweh and performs a magical life-transference rite, which is finally successful.

4:38-41. *The Poisoned Food.* Elisha is visiting **Gilgal** (see comment on 2:1-8) in a time of **famine.** There at the confraternity of **prophets** a common meal is being provided. A large **pot** of vegetables is being cooked, but unfortunately someone has by error collected some poisonous **gourds** (probably colocynthis). Elisha throws in some good **meal,** thereby rendering the food edible.

4:42-44. *Multiplication of Loaves.* Again the prophetic confraternity's food is involved. Custom demanded that Yahweh receive the **first fruits** of the harvest at the shrine. Apparently in early days a prophet as well as a priest might receive this offering. **Baal-shalisha** was probably a village southwest of Shechem.

5:1-19a. *The Healing of Naaman.* Naaman is military **commander** of Damascus. He is in **high favor** with his **master,** an unnamed **king of Syria—but he was a leper.** Leprosy was a term used to designate a wide variety of skin diseases. It is doubtful whether modern leprosy (Hansen's disease) was prevalent in ancient Palestine or Syria.

5:2-7. An Israelite slave girl mentions to her mistress, **Naaman's wife,** that a **prophet** in **Samaria** can **cure** the leprosy. Elisha is pictured as having a house there. The Elisha stories have various locales throughout the north—Mount Carmel, Shunem, Gilgal, Jericho, Dothan, and the Jordan. Naaman proceeds to Samaria with a fabulous load of presents. He comes to the **king of Israel**—apparently a Syrian vassal—to whom he gives his master's **letter** ordering the healing of Naaman. The Israelite king is greatly disturbed at this impossible demand.

5:8-14. Elisha meanwhile hears about the king's distress. He sends an ironical note bidding the leper come to him. When Naaman arrives, the prophet simply sends him a message to bathe **seven times** in the Jordan. Naaman is indignant. Rivers in Damascus—the **Abana** and the **Pharpar**—are far finer than the muddy Jordan. Better counsel prevails, however, and he carries out Elisha's prescription. He is cured.

5:15-19a. Naaman now recognizes Yahweh as the true God and vows to be a worshiper. The story here involves some curiously primitive ideas. He wishes to take Israelite **earth** along to Damascus so that he will be able to worship Israel's God there—the theory being that a god could be worshiped only on its own soil. He asks pardon for one exception to his vow—he must accompany the Syrian king to worship his god on state occasions. **Rimmon** was a Syrian title (meaning "thunderer") of the god Hadad (see comment on I Kings 16:32-33).

5:19b-27. *Gehazi's Greed.* Elisha has refused to accept any gifts from Naaman. Gehazi secretly follows the Syrian and by means of a falsehood secures for himself money and clothing. He hides these presumably in his own quarters though exactly what is meant by **hill** (verse 24) is not known. Elisha's prophetic sight reveals the deception. As punishment Gehazi is to be afflicted with Naaman's **leprosy,** a fitting retribution. In line with the ancient idea of corporate involvement in guilt this leprosy is to be suffered by his offspring as well.

6:1-7. *A Floating Axe Head.* On an expedition to get logs from

the banks of the Jordan a **borrowed** axe head made of **iron** falls
into the water. Elisha by his magical powers makes it **float,** thus
enabling the borrower to recover it.

6:8-23. *Capture of a Syrian Army.* This is another miracle
story about Elisha's second sight. The Israelite king inexplicably
and repeatedly learns of Syrian military plans. The **king of syria**
naturally suspects treachery. On inquiry he is told that Elisha is
the informer. When he discovers that Elisha is in **Dothan**—
about ten miles north of Samaria—he dispatches a large force to
besiege the city and seize the informer.

6:15-19. The following morning Elisha's **servant** is dismayed
at the sight. At Elisha's prayer the servant is able to see the
horses and chariots of fire (cf. 2:11-12*a*) surrounding and
protecting the prophet. Again at Elisha's prayer the Syrians are
struck **with blindness** and **led . . . to Samaria.**

6:20-23. The Syrians are now helpless captives. At Elisha's
word their sight is restored. Elisha orders the king to treat them
hospitably and release them. The story has a happy but quite
unhistorical ending. The Syrians do not remain at peace with
Israel after this.

6:24–7:20. *Siege of Samaria.* In contrast to the statement in
verse 23, **Ben-hadad** (perhaps not Benhadad I but the son of
Hazael; cf. 13:24-25) lays siege to **Samaria.** The city is in
extreme straits. Prices have soared, and people are paying
exorbitantly for garbage. A **kab** was slightly more than a dry
quart. The king's reply in verse 27 is better rendered "No! may
Yahweh help you." A story of cannibalism incites the distressed
king to swear an oath that he will kill Elisha. For unexplained
reasons he holds Elijah responsible.

6:32–7:2. Immediately someone is sent to capture Elisha. But
the prophet, aware of the situation by second sight, has already
barred the **door.** The **king** follows his **messenger** and is
apparently allowed to enter. He expresses complete skepticism
of any divine help. Elisha then gives an oracle that within
twenty-four hours the siege will be lifted and food will be on sale
at normal prices. A **captain** of the king expresses disbelief, and
his death is predicted for the following day.

7:3-15. During the night rumor spreads through the Syrian camp that **Hittites** are approaching to help the Israelites (for **Egypt;** see comment on I Kings 10:26-29). The rumor has been divinely inspired in order to fulfill the prophet's oracle. Panic sets in. Abandoning all their arms and provisions, the Syrians flee without the besieged city's knowing it. Meanwhile at daybreak **four . . . lepers** go over to the Syrian camp (**twilight,** verse 5, refers to the first break in the night's darkness, in contrast to **morning light,** verse 9, which means the full dawn). They find it deserted and eat their fill and gather some plunder before reporting the **good news** to the city. The king suspects a trap. But in view of the desperate situation he is persuaded to risk a few cavalrymen for reconnoitering. They report that the Syrians are nowhere in sight.

7:16-20. So the siege comes to an end. There still remains the skeptical **captain** to deal with. He is on duty at the gate that day and loses his life in the trample of the excited people. So the word of the prophet is again vindicated.

8:1-6. *Restoration of the Shunammite's Property.* Elisha had warned his hostess at Shunem (cf. 4:8-37) of **famine.** Therefore she has spent **seven years** in Philistia. When she returns she finds her possessions confiscated. She happens to appeal to the king at the exact moment when **Gehazi** tells him of Elisha's restoring her son to life. She confirms the story, and the king orders the return of her property, including its **produce** during her seven-year absence.

8:7-15. *Elisha in Damascus.* The aged **Ben-hadad** is ill. Hearing that the great prophet Elisha is in the city, he sends **Hazael** to him for an oracle. That a fee had to be paid for such a service is clear from I Samuel 9:5-10, but the gift in this story seems much exaggerated. Elisha replies ambiguously with an oracle which probably means "the sickness is not fatal." He predicts Hazael's succession and his cruel treatment of Israelites in future warfare. Hazael politely protests but nonetheless returns to the palace and carries out Elisha's prediction. He reassures the bedridden king with the ambiguous oracle. The following day he assassinates him and assumes the Syrian throne.

8:16-24. *Jehoram's Reign in Judah.* The name **Joram** is a shortened form used of both Jehoram of Israel (cf. 3:1-8) and Jehoram of Judah (verses 21-24). The accession notice takes no account of the co-regency indicated by 1:17 (see comment).

8:20-24. Politically the reign of Jehoram of Judah was calamitous, as two historical notes from contemporary annals show (verses 20-22*a*, 22*b*). **Edom** revolts and throws off its vassalage in a battle from which the king extricates himself with difficulty. Apparently the Israelite army is surrounded, the infantry deserts, and the kings and the chariotry manage to break through and escape. The location of **Zair** is uncertain. Some have placed it near Hebron, but the context points rather to the southern end of the Dead Sea. **Libnah** was a frontier town on the Philistine border. Later it seemingly was regained by Judah (cf. 19:8 and 23:31).

8:25-29. *Ahaziah's Reign in Judah.* For the accession dates see Chronology in the Introduction to I Kings. Ahaziah's mother was **Athaliah,** Ahab's daughter. **Son-in-law** is not to be taken literally, since it was his father who was son-in-law to Ahab. The son is then said to be **son-in-law to the house of Ahab.** Verses 28-29 are a doublet to 9:14-16.

I. JEHU'S REVOLT (9:1–10:28)

9:1-13. *Jehu's Anointing as King of Israel.* The first scene describes the secret anointing by an emissary of Elisha (cf. I Kings 19:16). Jehu is a commander of the Israelite army on guard duty at **Ramoth-gilead.** Prophets were often involved in anointing—for example, Samuel (I Samuel 10:1; 16:12-13) and Nathan (I Kings 1:34). Elisha's command in verse 3 is carried out by the young **prophet** in verses 6 and 10*b*. But the D editor has inserted an addition (verses 7-10*a*) based on I Kings 21:21-24.

9:11-13. After the ceremony Jehu returns to the meeting of the chiefs of staff from which he has been summoned. He is eventually persuaded to tell his comrades about the anointing. They thereupon proclaim him **king** on the spot (cf. I Kings 1:38-40). The prophet is called a **mad fellow** since prophets were held in some contempt because of their ecstatic behavior (cf. I Samuel 19:18-23).

9:14-29. *Jehu's Successful Attack.* Since the success of a revolution depends in part on surprise, Jehu asks his followers to guard the secret. He immediately sets out in **his chariot** for **Jezreel,** where Joram is convalescing in his palace. **Ahaziah** of Judah is also there visiting his royal cousin.

9:17-26. Jehu and his company are seen at a distance by the **tower** guard. Two successive advance scouts are sent, who desert to Jehu. The guard finally recognizes the party because of Jehu's mad **driving.** The royal cousins then go out in their chariots expecting news from the Ramoth-gilead front. When Joram meets Jehu he realizes his danger for the first time, calls out a warning to his cousin, and tries to flee. Jehu kills him and orders the corpse thrown into Naboth's vineyard. This is appropriate to the prophetic doom predicted to Ahab.

9:27-29. In the meantime Ahaziah of Judah flees toward **Beth-haggan,** seven miles south of Jezreel. He is shot on the way between there and **Ibleam,** a mile farther south. The wounded king changes his course to the northwest and dies in **Megiddo,** almost twelve miles away. His body is brought to **Jerusalem** and **buried.** Verse 29 does not belong here.

9:30-37. *Assassination of Jezebel.* The proud queen mother, realizing that she is not to escape, takes great pains to beautify herself for death. When Jehu approaches, she taunts him. She is flung from an upper **window** and her crushed body is **trampled** by the **horses** and chariots. Later Jehu orders her burial, but only remnants of the corpse remain, in accordance with Elijah's word (cf. I Kings 21:23).

10:1-17. *Extermination of the House of Omri.* The capital city of **Samaria** is not yet in Jehu's hands. So a **letter** is sent to the military and civil authorities, as well as to the palace officials, challenging them to civil war. The officials immediately capitulate.

10:6-11. Jehu now demands that they bring him the **heads** of all the king's **sons** within twenty-four hours. This gruesome demand is complied with, and the heads are thrown in **two heaps at the entrance** of the city, the traditional place of judgment. Jehu attributes this slaughter to an act of Yahweh and proceeds to a bloodbath of the **house of Ahab** in Jezreel.

10:12-17. Now Jehu can proceed to the capital city itself. On the way he meets some relatives of **Ahaziah** of Judah, who are all ruthlessly killed. Shortly thereafter he meets **Jehonadab,** a prophet and leader of the Rechabites. The Rechabites were a seminomadic clan, strongly opposed to urban life. They were particularly bitter opponents of Canaanite culture and natural foes of the house of Omri. Jehu is assured of cooperation. On arrival he kills off **all that remained to Ahab** in Samaria.

10:18-28. *Massacre of the Baal Devotees.* Jehu assembles all the officials—**prophets** and **priests** (omit **all his worshipers** from verse 19)—together in the Baal temple which Ahab built (cf. I Kings 16:32). Ostensibly an important cultic feast for Baal is to be held. To make his ruse more convincing the king himself offers the sacrifice. Once it is clear that only Baal devotees are present, the order is given to slaughter them all. The temple and all its cultic paraphernalia are destroyed and defiled.

J. FROM JEHU TO THE FALL OF SAMARIA (10:29–17:41)

10:29-36. *The Remainder of Jehu's Reign.* Because of Jehu's effective destruction of the Baalists the D editor's judgment on him (verses 29-31) is not as condemnatory as the other northern kings. A prophetic oracle in verse 30 promises dynastic succession to the **fourth generation** for his zeal.

10:32-36. Jehu's reign marks the beginning of Syrian incursions on Israelite territory. All of Transjordan is lost to **Hazael,** not to be retaken until the reign of Jeroboam II (cf. 14:23-29). Jehu reigns **twenty-eight years.**

11:1-3. *Athaliah's Interregnum in Judah.* Ahaziah's mother, Athaliah, daughter of Ahab, seizes the throne by killing off the entire royal family. Only the infant **Joash** (see comment on 12:19-21) escapes the bloodbath. The baby's aunt, **Jehosheba** (wife of the priest Jehoiada according to II Chronicles 22:11), hides the baby in the priestly quarters of the temple. Athaliah rules for **six years,** unaware of the crown prince's existence.

11:4-20. *Athaliah's Overthrow.* This account is based on two contemporary sources. One is official (verses 4-12, 18*b*-20) and the other popular (verses 13-18*a*). Both describe the slaying of Athaliah. Verse 20 actually says "the city was quiet and Athaliah they slew with the sword." The two accounts supplement each other nicely.

11:4-8. The coup d'etat is thoroughly planned by **Jehoiada** the priest. The **Carites**—the mercenary elite—are organized for the revolt and sworn to secrecy. Apparently **on the sabbath** a third of the guard is on duty and stationed at three posts (the two gates are named but their location is unknown). The other two groups are to remain on duty in the temple to protect the young **king.**

11:9-12. Only when the stage is fully prepared is the crown prince brought out and the public coronation rite enacted. The meaning of **testimony** is uncertain. Possibly some scroll delineating the covenantal responsibilities of the ruler is meant.

11:13-18*a*. The popular account adds details concerning the killing of Athaliah, the royal covenant, and the religious reform sparking the restoration of the Davidic king. Only the **noise** of the public coronation ceremony makes the queen aware that her plans have gone awry. She is roughly seized as she approaches the temple and led away to an area near the palace. There she is executed.

11:17. Here is the first mention that coronation in Judah involved a covenant ceremony. It is presented as twofold:

(1) a sacral bond renewing the covenant between Yahweh and the people;

(2) a popular contract between **the king and the people.** It is not certain what this latter involved, but from now on **the people of the land** (the populace) take a more important part in political affairs.

11:18*a*. The renewal of the sacral bond is immediately applied when the people demolish all the cultic objects and shrines associated with Baalism. The chief **priest of Baal**—whose possible Phoenician background is apparent from his name, **Mattan**—is also slain.

11:18b-20. The official account is now concluded. Jehoiada leaves **watchmen** to guard the temple, while the boy king is escorted under heavy guard to the palace. There he assumes the **throne** amid rejoicing of the people. Then Athaliah is killed.

11:21-12:21. *Jehoash's Reign in Judah.* Jehoash rules for **forty years.** The D editor judges him a good king but notes that he did not remove the local shrines.

12:4-8. Most of the account of Jehoash's reign deals with his attempt to **repair** the Jerusalem temple. By this time it had fallen into a sad state. A royal edict orders both the temple tax and the freewill offerings be used solely for this purpose. But the greed of the priests frustrates the pious wishes of the king, and so he takes the matter out of their hands and directs affairs personally. The term **accquaintance** in verses 5 and 7 makes little sense. Possibly some official receiver of tithes is meant.

12:9-16. To avert misappropriation of funds a **chest** is made with a **hole in the lid** where worshipers can deposit their funds directly. Periodically Jehoiada and the king's personal representative empty the chest and weigh out **money** for the repairs. A careful record is kept of the accounts. Verse 16 notes that the priests did not really suffer, since they still received their usual income from **guilt** and **sin offerings.**

12:17-18. One disastrous event during the reign of Jehoash is an invasion by the Syrians. They are able to penetrate to **Gath,** a Philistine city to the southwest, and then turn toward Jerusalem. Jehoash is able to buy off the Syrians only by ransacking the temple and the royal **treasuries,** leaving them empty.

12:19-21. Like Jehoram (see above on 8:16-24) the name Jehoash is shortened and becomes **Joash.** Though this king is assassinated, there is no change of dynasty, as in the northern kingdom. **His son** succeeds to the throne. On **Millo** see comment on I Kings 9:15-23. **Silla** is unknown.

13:1-9. *Jehoahaz' Reign in Israel.* Jehu is succeeded by his son Jehoahaz. Israel is now almost completely subject to the Syrians. The cavalry is almost totally wiped out. The **ten chariots** left to the army contrast sharply with the two thousand attributed to Ahab forty years earlier in Shalmaneser's inscription. It is usually suggested that verses 4-6 are a later addition contradicting the context in verses 3 and 7. Possibly **savior** is a misplaced reference to 14:27.

13:10-25. *Jehoash's Reign in Israel.* On the discrepancy between the figures for Jehoash's reign and those of his father (verse 1) see Chronology in Introduction to I Kings. Jehoash's premature obituary (verses 12-13) reappears in its proper place in 14:15-16. Two stories from the Elisha cycle are inserted in the account of his reign.

13:14-19. The first story concerns the visit of **Joash** (shortened form of Jehoash; see above on 12:19-21) to the aged prophet's deathbed. On Joash's cry in verse 14 see above on 2:9-12*b*. By an act of sympathetic magic Elisha insures victory over Syria. The king is told to **shoot an arrow.** This insures similar victories three times. Indeed the king should have struck more often!

13:20-21. The second legend concerns Elisha's corpse. When a sudden raid by Moabites interrupts a funeral, the deceased is hastily thrown into the tomb of the prophet. Touching the holy **bones** revives the man.

13:22-25. In fulfillment of Elisha's last prediction Jehoash now defeats Syria **three times.** Thereby he recovers some of the territory lost to the Syrians. Verse 23 shows the attitude of the D editor. External sources show that Damascus was weakened during this period by Adad-nirari III of Assyria, who besieged and looted Damascus in 805. **Ben-hadad** II's declining power is also demonstrated by an inscription of Zakir, king of Hamath and Laash.

14:1-22. *Amaziah's Reign in Judah.* Amaziah is said to have **reigned twenty-nine years.** But apparently during about ten years of this time he was a captive (verses 13, 17), and his son Azariah ruled instead (see Chronology in Introduction to I Kings).

14:5-6. Amaziah executes his father's **murderers** (cf. 12:20-21) but spares their **children.** This clemency was so unusual in this time that it is entered in the record. The D editor's comment on it quotes from Deuteronomy 24:16.

14:7. An isolated event early in Amaziah's reign is a successful invasion of Edom. The places mentioned are unknown. Some have placed the **Valley of Salt** near Beer-sheba, but an area near the southern end of the Dead Sea would seem more appropriate (cf. II Samuel 8:13). **Sela** is often identified with the acropolis overlooking Petra—a romantic identification for which there is no proof.

14:8-14. Amaziah's success leads him foolishly to challenge **Jehoash** of Israel to battle. Jehoash replies with a contemptuous parable, but Amaziah persists. The king of Israel invades Judah toward the west. At Beth-shemesh, on the Philistine frontier twenty-four miles west of Jerusalem, the armies meet. Judah is disastrously defeated. Amaziah is captured and presumably taken as a prisoner to Samaria. Jerusalem is taken. Part of its walls are demolished and its treasures are pillaged.

14:15-22. When Jehoash dies **Jeroboam** II apparently releases the captive Amaziah, who lives another **fifteen years** before he is assassinated. **Lachish** was about thirty miles southwest of Jerusalem. When **Azariah** is elected at the age of sixteen, it is evidently on the occasion of Amaziah's capture, not his death. The antecedent of **He** in verse 22 is not certain. In the present context it must be Azariah. But in view of verse 7 the sentence is often thought of as originally applying to Amaziah. **Elath** (or Eloth) was located on the Gulf of Aquaba, in Edom.

14:23-29. *Jeroboam II's Reign in Israel.* Apparently Jeroboam was co-regent with his father, Jehoash, for about twelve years. **In the fifteenth year of Amaziah** he began his sole reign (see Chronology in Introduction to I Kings).

14:25-27. Politically the reign of Jeroboam was one of expansion. From Amos 6:13 it appears that Transjordan was again won for Israel. The old northern **border** at the **entrance of Hamath**—probably the end of the Lebanon and the Anti-lebanon mountains—is **restored.** Israel is extended south to the **Sea**

of the Arabah—that is, the Dead Sea. Verses 26-27 must originally have been the content of the oracle referred to in verse 25. **Jonah** is the prophet about whom the book of Jonah was written. **Gath-hepher** was about three miles northeast of Nazareth.

14:28-29. This obituary notice contains a difficulty. **Damascus and Hamath** never belonged to Israel. The Hebrew says literally "recovered Damascus and Hamath for Judah in Israel," which is absurd. Possibly the author meant that Jeroboam conquered these cities, but the reference to **Judah** remains a puzzle.

15:1-7. *Azariah's Reign in Judah.* Azariah is the throne name for the king known also by his popular name Uzziah (cf. Isaiah 1:1). On his age of **sixteen** see above on 14:15-22. On the other data of verses 1-2 see Chronology in Introduction to I Kings. During the latter part of his long life Azariah becomes a **leper**, and his son **Jotham** governs as a co-regent. For a fuller account of Azariah's reign see II Chronicles 26.

15:8-12. *Zechariah of Israel.* Here begins the account of civil war in the north. After only **six months** Zechariah is murdered by **Shallum** and the dynasty of **Jehu** comes to an end. Ibleam was about fifteen miles northeast of Samaria. On verse 12 cf. 10:30.

15:13-16. *Shallum's Brief Reign in Israel.* After a reign of only **one month** Shallum is in turn assassinated by **Menahem,** who savagely puts down all opposition. On **Tirzah,** the former capital, see comment on I Kings 14:17-18. **Tappuah,** evidently the center of Shallum's support, lay about thirteen miles south of Samaria.

15:17-22. *Menahem's Reign in Israel.* The outstanding event recorded of Menahem's ten-year reign is the western march of Tiglath-pileser III (745-727) and his extraction of a huge tribute. The Assyrian king is here given his Babylonian name, **Pul** (or "Pulu"). His annals give independent confirmation of Menahem's tribute along with that of Syrian states. In order to pay the tribute Menahem assesses the **wealthy men** a heavy tax. A talent equaled three thousand shekels; thus sixty thousand men are forced to contribute.

15:23-26. *Pekahiah's Reign in Israel.* Pekahiah follows his
father peaceably. After **two years** he is assassinated by **Pekah,**
who led a small band of **Gileadites.**

15:27-31. *Pekah's Reign in Israel.* Pekah's reign of **twenty
years,** beginning **in the fifty-second year of Azariah**—that is, at
the time of Pekahiah's assassination—is impossible. This figure
dates the beginning of his reign back by twelve years. The
synchronisms in verse 32 and 16:1 seem to indicate that Pekah's
reigning years were numbered on this basis during his lifetime.
Pekah may well have made such a claim as a way of denying the
legitimacy of the Menahem dynasty and thus justifying his
murder of Pekahiah. Or possibly he may have dated his reign
from the death of Zechariah and claimed to be the rightful
successor of the house of Jehu (see Chronology in Introduction
to I Kings).

On the other hand it has been suggested that Pekah may have
been a partisan of Shallum, who held control over part of the
country as a rival to Menahem. Possible suport for this theory
may be found in verse 32. If this is contemporary, it would
indicate early Judean recognition of such a regime. But a
problem is the identification of Pekah as Pekahiah's **captain** in
verse 25. The records of this period of civil war are so
fragmentary that any explanation of Pekah's claimed overlap-
ping reign can be only conjecture.

15:29-31. The outstanding event during Pekah's reign was the
war of Syria and Israel against Assyria and its disastrous effects
on Israel. The Assyrians came west in 734 and put down the
revolt. They captured the areas of **Galilee** and **Gilead** and
limited Israel to the province of Samaria itself. Shortly
thereafter Pekah was in turn assassinated by **Hoshea.** In his
annals **Tiglath-pileser** states that the Israelites overthrew their
king, Pekah, and that he "places Hoshea as king over them."
Hoshea was to be the last northern king.

15:32-38. *Jotham's Reign in Judah.* The beginning of Jotham's
reign is dated at his taking over the government because of his
father's leprosy (verse 5). On its length see Chronology in
Introduction to I Kings. Two historical notes are given on his

reign. He rebuilt the **upper gate** of the temple—also called the Benjamin Gate (Jeremiah 20:2), probably because it faced north. His reign also saw the beginning of the Syrian-Israelite coalition against judah, an offensive ascribed to Yahweh.

16:1-20. *Ahaz' Reign in Judah.* On the dating and length of this reign see Chronology in Introduction to I Kings. Ahaz was king of Judah at the time of the destruction of the northern kingdom. The D editor condemns him more severely than any other ruler except Manasseh. Nor does he name the queen mother, as is otherwise done for Judean rulers.

16:3-4. The phrase **burned his son as an offering** is literally "made his son to pass through the fire." Some scholars maintain that this refers to an ordeal by fire, but it has generally been interpreted as meaning child sacrifice. It has been suggested that the attack on Jerusalem (verse 5) may have driven Ahaz, like Mesha (3:27), to sacrifice his son, but this is not certain.

16:5-9. Rezin of Syria and **Pekah** of Israel unite to revolt against Assyria and try to force Judah to join. When Judah refuses they besiege Jerusalem, intending to kill Ahaz and install a puppet ruler. Ahaz appeals to **Assyria** for help. He sweetens the appeal with as large a bribe as he can muster. The Assyrians respond by capturing **Damascus** and executing Rezin (in 732) and by capturing most of Israel (see above on 15:29-31). Interrupting the account is the record of the loss of **Elath**, which had been captured by Amaziah (or Azariah, 14:22). The **Edomites** retake it and eject Judeans from that area.

16:10-16. On Ahaz' visit to **Tiglath-pileser** in **Damascus** he sees an Assyrian **altar** which strikes his fancy. He orders it copied for the Jerusalem temple, and it is built by **Uriah.** The old **bronze altar** (cf. I Kings 8:64) is relegated **to the north side** of the new altar and is to be reserved for the king's divinatory rites. The new altar is to serve for the various sacrifices detailed in verse 15. The dedicatory rites of the altar are performed by the king himself—a practice legitimate before the Babylonian exile. The D editor makes no condemnatory statement on these innovations. The passage as a whole must be largely contemporary.

16:17-20. Ahaz has purchased survival from the Assyrians at great cost. To pay the necessary tribute all the bronze accessories of the temple furniture (cf. 7:23-39) are melted down and sent off to Assyria. What is meant by the **covered way for the sabbath** and the **outer entrance for the king** is not known. **Palace** is literally "house" and probably means the temple rather than the king's house.

17:1-6. *Hoshea, the Last King of Israel.* On the erroneous synchronism in verse 1 see Chronology in Introduction to I Kings. The usual absolute judgment of **evil** is strangely mitigated by the D editor. Tiglath-pileser has been succeeded by his son **Shalmaneser V** (727-722). Hoshea conspires against him with **So** (Sibu), **king of Egypt.** Shalmaneser comes west, imprisons Hoshea, and lays siege to Samaria for **three years.** At length it is **captured.**

His successor, Sargon II (722-705), in an inscription claims the victory over Samaria as an achievement of his own reign. However, many scholars believe the city fell some months before his accession. Sargon's account amplifies the biblical record: "I led away as prisoners 27,290 inhabitants, and 50 chariots I collected for my royal force. I rebuilt the city and made it more populous by settling there peoples from lands I had conquered. I set up one of my officers as their governor and imposed taxes customary to Assyrian citizenry." The Israelite captives are taken to northern Mesopotamia and to Media far to the east. There they quickly lose their identity.

17:7-23. *An Editorial Sermon.* The D editor's attitude toward the northern kingdom is expressed here at length. The **people of Israel** separated themselves from the worship at the central sanctuary at Jerusalem. This in turn meant worship at various **high places,** or shrines of the Canaanite type. There they **served idols** and practiced **divination and sorcery. Which the kings of Israel had introduced** is literally "of the kings of Israel that they made"—that is, kings set up by the people rather than by Yahweh. On **Asherim** and **Asherah** see comment on I Kings 14:15b-16. On the **two calves** see comment on I Kings 12:25-31. The **host of heaven** refers to astral deities. On **Baal** see comment on I Kings 16:32-33. On **burned their sons and daughters as offerings** see above on 16:3-4.

17:19. The application to **Judah also** obviously comes from after the Babylonian exile. Probably the whole sermon dates from this period, though scholars who believe the principal D editor worked during the reign of Josiah naturally regard this verse as an addition (see Introduction to I Kings).

17:21-23. All of Israel's **sin** is rooted in the **sins of Jeroboam.** Now the logical consequence has come about. The people are broken up and **exiled to Assyria.**

17:24-41. *The Mixed People of the North.* The ravaged country is forcibly repopulated by settlers from other areas conquered by the Assyrians. **Cuthah** was a town north of **Babylon,** and **Hamath** was in Syria. **Avva** and **Sepharvaim** were probably also Syrian cities. When the countryside is overrun by **lions,** the new settlers attribute it to failure to propitiate the **god of the land.** They petition for the return of some exiled native **priests** to teach them the proper cult. This is granted, and a priest returns to **Bethel** to teach.

17:29-41. Nonetheless the worship in the northern country becomes a peculiar mixture of ancestral and local cult. The immigrants continue to worship their own gods as well as Yahweh. The Babylonians worship **Succoth-benoth**—possibly two deities, **Sakkuth** (Saturn) and Benoth (probably Sarpanitu, the wife of Marduk, Babylon's chief god). **Nergal** was the well-known god of the underworld in Cuthah. **Ashima** was a Syrian goddess. **Tartak** is a corruption of the famous goddess Atargatis, worshiped throughout Syria. The name **Nibhaz** has not been identified with certainty, though a corruption of the altar god Madbacha has been suggested.

The **gods of Sepharvaim** have been identified as Adad-me-lekh and Anu-melekh respectively. On Adad (Hadad) see comment on I Kings 18:20-40. Anu was the chief Babylonian sky god. Both were apparently worshiped under Melekh (or "Molech") rites which included human sacrifice. In verse 29 the people are for the first time called **Samaritans.** Inserted into this account of their religion is a diatribe against these people (verses

34*b*-40). It is composed of D phrases and is of later origin. Probably it was intended to condemn the later Samaritans as idolatrous from the beginning.

IV. JUDAH AFTER THE FALL OF ISRAEL (18:1–25:30)

A. THE THREAT FROM ASSYRIA (18:1–21:26)

18:1-8. *Evaluation of Hezekiah's Reign*. The information in verse 1 seems to be based on incorrect data for Hezekiah, who began his reign around 716, some years after the fall of Samaria (see Chronology in Introduction to I Kings). His great religious reforms are briefly listed in verse 4. Removal of the **high places** seems to imply an early attempt at centralizing all public cult in Jerusalem (cf. 23:4-25). The **bronze serpent** was an old fetish which tradition attributed to **Moses** (cf. Numbers 21:4-9). The Judeans venerated it by acts of worship. The name **Nehushtan** is a word play since it means either "serpent" or "bronze object."

Hezekiah and Josiah (22:2; 23:25) are the D editor's two great Judean heroes. Hezekiah is extravagantly eulogized in verses 5-7*a*. His religious reforms go hand in hand with his nationalism. Politically he **rebelled against the king of Assyria** by attacking Philistine territory, which Sargon of Assyria had captured in 713-711. Hezekiah lived dangerously. But he somehow managed to avoid the full consequences of his rebellion, and for this the D editor shows unbounded admiration.

18:9-12. *Duplication of the Fall of Samaria*. Because of a chronological miscalculation one author thought the fall of Samaria took place during Hezekiah's reign. Thus the data from 17:5-6 are repeated here, together with the D editor's judgment of the reasons for it.

18:13-16. *Tribute Paid to Sennacherib*. This is a short account from contemporary royal and temple annals. Sennacherib's annals give a detailed account of the forty-six cities taken and the large tribute of precious objects and female hostages imposed on Hezekiah—including the **three hundred talents of silver** and thirty talents of gold recorded here. Only abject submission saves Hezekiah from a traitor's death. Submission involves stripping the royal and temple treasuries of precious metals. The only thing left to Hezekiah is his throne and the capital city.

18:17-19:37. *The Assyrian Siege of Jerusalem.* Apparently there are two parallel accounts of the same siege—18:17-19:9*a* and 19:9*b*-37. Both are prophetic stories connected with the Isaiah cycle. The two accounts disagree on certain details, especially on the cause for the lifting of the siege. The stories are further complicated by the mixture of traditions concerning two campaigns—one in 701 and the other toward the end of Sennacherib's life. Later tradition does not distinguish between them. The stories here have combined the events into a single dramatic episode of miraculous deliverance of the holy city.

That two different campaigns are actually involved is clear from the reference in 19:9*a* to Tirhakah, who did not become king of Egypt and Ethiopia until around 689. The second campaign must have taken place in 688 or even somewhat later. The annals of Sennacherib are incomplete for the latter years, and since the outcome of the second campaign was inglorious for him it was not recorded. Unfortunately the biblical stories are prophetic legends and mix fictional elements with already confused facts.

18:17-19:9*a*. *First Account of the Siege.* In this first story the Assyrian army makes loudmouthed demands for immediate surrender. Verse 17 introduces us to three Assyrian officers. The exact distinctions are not clear. In the subsequent story only the **Rabshakeh** acts as spokesman for the besiegers. Apparently the scene takes place outside the walls near the end of Hezekiah's tunnel. Why such an unlikely spot should be chosen is not clear (cf. Isaiah 7:3, from which this geographical note may have been borrowed). Three representatives of Hezekiah speak for the besieged.

18:19-25. This speech seems to be more applicable to the later campaign in view of its references to **Egypt.** However, Egyptian involvement in the earlier campaign makes it difficult to unscramble the actual state of affairs. The fourfold argument of the Assyrian spokesman is most persuasive:

(1) Egyptian promises are untrustworthy as always (verse 21).
(2) Trust in Yahweh is hardly wise in the light of Hezekiah's cultic reforms (verse 22). To the speaker, and perhaps to the original author, these seem to interfere with accustomed worship.
(3) Judean weakness in cavalry makes opposition ludicrous (verses 23-24).
(4) Yahweh has actually ordered Assyria to destroy Jerusalem.

18:26-37. Since **Aramaic** was the common language of the day, it could be understood by Judean and Assyrian alike. That the Assyrian could speak Hebrew is most unlikely. The offensive description in verse 27 refers to the privations of the coming siege. The address to the people in verses 29-35 is largely dependent on 19:10-13. The direct challenge to Yahweh's power to **deliver** out of Assyrian hands is of course the point of the story. The reference to the failure of heathen gods to deliver **Samaria** is further condemnation of the Samaritans (cf. 17:24-41).

19:1-9a. When Hezekiah hears the demands of the Assyrians, he engages in a communal rite of lament. In **sackcloth,** a garb denoting great distress, Hezekiah goes to the temple and seeks the advice of **Isaiah** the prophet. An oracle is sent to the king counseling courage. Yahweh will deliver Jerusalem by creating a **rumor** among the Assyrians which will send them hurrying back to Assyria. There their king will be assassinated. The original conclusion to this oracle must have been verses 36-37. But its fulfillment here is interpreted as news concerning the advance of **Tirhakah king of Ethiopia** and of Egypt. On **Libnah** see above on 8:20-24.

19:9b-37. *A Second Account of the Siege.* This account is tied to the preceding one as a second message from the Assyrians to Hezekiah. Actually it is a parallel to the first popular account. The message arrogantly states the superior strength of the Assyrian king to that of Yahweh. Subject peoples listed are

Gozan near the Euphrates, **Haran** (cf. Genesis 11:31), **Rezeph** northeast of Palmyra, and the children of **Eden** (Beth-eden) south of Haran near the Euphrates. **Tel-assar** is unknown. Verse 13 is the source of 18:34.

19:14-19. Hezekiah responds by presenting the problem to Yahweh. He goes to the temple and offers a complaint prayer. The prayer is directly applicable to the taunting message. Its form indicates it was composed after the exile.

19:20-28. The reply spoken by **Isaiah** is a taunt song against Assyria. With this poem cf. Isaiah 10:5-11. Assyria is proud of its prowess in warfare and arrogantly attributes its conquests to its own strength. By this it has **mocked** Israel's God, who **long ago . . . planned** that Assyria should be the rod of God's anger. Now for its proud insolence God will **turn** Assyria **back.**

19:29-34. Isaiah also gives two prose oracles. God will give a **sign** to demonstrate the promise of the song. This sign will be the abundance of natural growth—that is, of things which are not sown—for two years. Not until the third year will normal seed and harvest occur. So decimated, Judah will repopulate and **bear fruit.** As for the present siege, the arrogant Assyrian will not take the **city,** for God is fighting for Jerusalem.

19:35-37. The outcome is that an **angel** of destruction kills off 185,000 Assyrians that night. A parallel account by the Greek historian Herodotus tells of a plague of mice attacking Sennacherib's army. What really happened cannot be reconstructed. The Assyrians withdraw, and some years later Sennacherib is killed by **Adrammelech and Sharezer,** two of his **sons.** Another son, **Esarhaddon** (681-669), then governor of Babylon, succeeds him. **Nisroch** is probably a corruption of Marduk, the Babylonian god. The **land of Ararat** is the kingdom of Urartu referred to in Assyrian inscription, which was centered around Lake Van in modern Turkey.

20:1-11. *Hezekiah's Sickness.* Hezekiah falls ill, and Isaiah comes with a divine oracle advising him to prepare for death. Hezekiah pleads his cause before Yahweh successfully and receives an extension of **fifteen years.** The prophet then prepares a poultice of figs to bring about the recovery. To this account has been added a miracle story from the Isaiah legends concerning the **sign** of the **shadow** receding on the sundial.

20:12-21. *The Embassy from Babylon.* A long-time foe of Assyria, **Merodach-baladan** (Babylonian Marduk-abal-idinna), has seized the throne of Babylon. The embassy is sent undoubtedly to foment a western coalition against Sennacherib. Hezekiah shows his sympathy by his demonstrating the extent of support he could give in the rebellious venture. The reference in verse 12 to this embassy congratulating Hezekiah on his recovery is editorial; verses 12-19 do not necessarily follow the event of verses 1-11 at all. The date of the embassy must have been shortly after Sennacherib became king of Assyria.

20:16-19. Isaiah's rebuke is in line with his isolationist attitude. The fall of Jerusalem in 586 seems best fitted to the occasion which the D editor has in mind in his reference to a Babylonian exile. Verse 19 apparently gives two responses by Hezekiah. The second is better rendered: "Is it not the case that there will, however, be peace and security in my days?" This is a commentary on the word **good.**

20:20-21. The final obituary and succession notice specifically refers to the building of the famous **conduit**—the water tunnel from the Virgin Spring to the Pool of Siloam.

21:1-18. *Manasseh's Reign.* Manasseh must have ruled as co-regent with his father for about 10 years. Thus he was an adult when he became sole ruler on the death of Hezekiah, around 687 (see Chronology in Introduction to I Kings). His long reign is condemned as completely **evil.** In fact the account deals only with the evil practices which Manasseh reintroduces into the Judean cult.

This is the period of Assyrian strength, and Manasseh holds onto his position by a thoroughgoing Assyrianization of cult practice in Jerusalem. He rebuilds the **high places** and **altars for Baal** (see comment on I Kings 16:32-33). He places an **Asherah** image in the temple (see comment on I Kings 14:15*b*-16), and worships the **host of heaven** (the astral deities) there. The D editor, responsible for the entire account, also mentions human sacrifice, divination practices of various kinds, familiar spirits, and **wizards.** The reference to **two courts** in verse 5 is puzzling. Probably the outer court was the building complex referred to as the "middle court" in 20:4, the area between palace and temple.

21:7-15. To the D editor the evil reign of Manasseh is the explanation for the Babylonian exile in 586. Yahweh promised to David a perpetual dynasty in Jerusalem (II Samuel 7), but this was conditional on its good behavior. Time and again evil kings occupied the throne, but for the sake of David Yahweh did not bring the dynasty to an end. But Manasseh is far worse. The cup of iniquity is now full, and the prophetic word now makes an exile certain (verses 10-15). **Jerusalem** will be completely destroyed.

21:16. To this indictment is added the statement that the evil king also slew many of the faithful. This verse may be the source for the late but unhistorical tradition that Isaiah the prophet was martyred by Manasseh.

21:19-26. *Amon's Reign.* Amon reigns only **two years.** His reign is also condemned by the editor as wholly **evil.** He is assassinated by some underlings in the palace, who are in turn killed by the populace. It is also the **people of the land** who place Amon's son **Josiah** on the throne as his successor. The accuracy of Amon's age of **twenty-two years** at accession may well be questioned, since two years later he has a son eight years old (cf. 22:1).

B. THE D REFORM (22:1-23:30)

22:1-2. *Introduction to Josiah's Reign.* Josiah is—along with Hezekiah—the hero to the D editor. His rule is completely approved (cf. 23:25). His age at accession is given as **eight years.** The accuracy of this statement may well be questioned.

22:3-20. *The Law Code Found.* In 622 Josiah orders temple repairs in terms similar to the reforms commanded by Jehoash (12:9-16), from which the D editor probably borrowed the account. In any event it simply serves to introduce the real point of the story—the finding of the **book of the law** in the temple by **Hilkiah the priest** (not **high priest** as in verses 4 and 8). When it is read to the king, it is said that he **rent his clothes,** a sign of national calamity. He appoints a committe of five to seek divine direction. They go to a cult **prophetess** who lives in the area directly north of the palace and temple complex. **Huldah** gives them an oracle repeating the divine intention expressed in 21:10-15. This prophecy is largely the D editor's interpretation of the later exile, though the statement that Josiah shall die **in peace** in verse 20 is a slip. On the other hand it may preserve an oracle from Josiah's own day.

The book of the law found in the temple has generally been recognized as the original core of Deuteronomy, especially chapters 5; 12–26, and 28. Chapter 5 probably was the original introducton to the actual laws of chapters 12-26. Chapter 28 contains the curses on those who disobey the law—curses which prompted Josiah to such a display of penitence and sorrow. The reforms described in the next chapter all find their basis in Deuteronomy and in no other book of the law in the Old Testament.

The book had probably been in existence at least since the early days of Manasseh. However, the reign of that king was obviously not the time to propose its social and cultic reforms, and it was deposited in the temple and lost. Now the time was ripe. Assyrian power had been broken, and nationalist actions in subject states were again possible. Nationalism and true piety went hand in hand.

23:1-3. *The Covenant with Yahweh.* The first stage of the reform is the public ceremony of covenant renewal. Josiah convokes an assembly of all Judeans and has the **book of the covenant** read to them. The king and the people then solemnly reconsecrate themselves to complete obedience to all the demands found in the book.

23:4-14. *The Reforms of the Cult.* The reform naturally begins in the temple itself. The heathen paraphernalia introduced by Manasseh (cf. 21:3-7) are removed and burned in the valley of the **Kidron,** just outside the city walls. Appropriately, though rather absurdly, the **ashes** are carried to **Bethel**—an editorial note probably based on verses 15-16. Priests engaged in illegitimate cult practices in the **high places** are now out of work (and unemployable). **Constellations** actually means the "signs of the zodiac."

One characteristic of the cultic reform throughout is that heathen cult objects are **defiled,** taken forever out of the sphere of the holy. Thus the **Asherah** image is powdered and scattered on **graves.** Heathen cult **places** are filled with **bones.** Cultic prostitution has its home in the temple area. Here women weave robes (not **hangings**) for the Asherah—that is, ritual garments to be used in the fertility cult.

23:8-14. Verses 8*a* and 9 seem, with verse 5, out of place in the list of defilings. Nonetheless they are central to the reform. All shrines except **Jerusalem** are to be illegal. The priests of the shrines are now to live in Jerusalem and eat priestly rations. But they can hardly take part in the Jerusalem cult (verse 9)—there were too many of them! The reference to **gates** in verse 8*b* makes no sense. Most scholars translate this as "satyrs," i.e. evil spirits or demons. The locations of the **gate of Joshua,** the **chamber of Nathan-melech the chamberlain** and the **precincts,** and the **upper chamber of Ahaz** are all unknown.

The **mount of corruption** is the Mount of Olives, "corruption" being a Hebrew pun on "olives." **Topheth** was a heathen cult place in the southern end of the **Hinnom Valley,** near the Pool of Siloam, dedicated to the cult of **Molech** (see above on I Kings 11:1-8). The idea that the sun god drove winged **chariots** with horses across the sky was widespread. Just how horses were used in the solar cult is, however, not clear. The **altars on the roof** were used for astral worship (possibly of Venus the morning star?). On the altars of **Manasseh** cf. 21:4-5. The heathen high places built by **Solomon** for his foreign wives (I Kings 11:1-8) still exist on the southern end of the Mount of Olives. They too are destroyed.

23:15-20. *The Reform Beyond Judah.* The altar at Bethel particularly has to be profaned since it epitomizes to the D editor the sin of the northern kingdom in breaking away from the cult at Jerusalem. So that it may be **defiled** effectually it is turned into a garbage dump for **bones.** Only the bones of the two prophets involved in the story of I Kings 13 escape desecration. According to the D editor, all this is to fulfill the ancient prophecy uttered on that occasion. The second prophet, however, was not from **Samaria** but from Bethel. The same reform is carried out throughout the north, i.e. **the cities of Samaria.**

23:21-23. *The Passover Celebration.* In accordance with Deuteronomy 16:1-8 what was essentially a domestic feast is now celebrated at the temple at **Jerusalem.** This is a complete innovation, and one which was to fall into disuse quickly. This is the climax of the great reform.

23:24-27. *Summary and Editorial Judgment.* Josiah makes a complete reform based on the book of the law—that is, Deuteronomy. The eulogy of verse 25 flatly contradicts that concerning Hezekiah in 18:5. Appropriately the judgment is put in actual D terms (cf. Deuteronomy 6:5). Some have considered this verse, minus the final clause, to be the ending of an assumed first edition of Kings completed during Josiah's lifetime (see Introduction to I Kings). On verses 26-27 cf. 21:10-15.

23:28-30. *Josiah's Death.* Though Assyria was now in a state of collapse, the Neo-Babylonian Empire was quickly taking its place. Meanwhile **Egypt,** to keep a balance of power, joined a weakened Assyria against the Babylonians. For some misguided nationalistic reason Josiah tries to oppose the Egyptian army at **Megiddo** and loses his life. His son **Jehoahaz** is democratically made **king** to succeed him.

C. The Last Days of Judah (23:31–25:30)

23:31-35. *Jehoahaz' Reign.* The great reform of Josiah dies with him. All his successors are judged to have done **evil** in the sight of Yahweh. After only **three months** as king Jehoahaz is imprisoned by **Neco** of Egypt at his Syrian headquarters. He is then taken to Egypt, where he dies. **Riblah** was strategically located on the Oronte River just at the pass above the Lebanon Mountains. Judah now becomes an Egyptian province. Neco places Jehoahaz' older brother on the throne with the throne name of **Jehoiakim** and imposes a heavy tribute on the country.

23:36–24:7. *Jehoiakim's Reign.* In 605 Neco was severely defeated and Egyptian hopes for Asiatic power were completely deflated. Judah now becomes a Babylonian province. Jehoiakim is a puppet prince under **Nebuchadnezzar** (more accurately spelled Nebuchadrezzar in Jeremiah and Ezekial) **king of Babylon.** The incursion of the Babylonians into Judah is undated, and may have been as late as 601. Jehoiakim foolishly rebels after **three years** but loses his life apparently at the hands of roving tribes. The D editor interprets this all in line with the earlier condemnation of Manasseh in 21:10-15 (cf. 23:26-27). No reference is made to his burial in the obituary notice (cf. Jeremiah 22:18-19).

24:8-17. *Jehoiachin's Reign.* The young king has ruled only **three months** when the Babylonian army lays siege to the city. Jehoiachin quickly surrenders. He, his court, his harem, and his military and social leaders are exiled to Babylon. The city fell on March 16, 597, as is now known from the Babylonian Chronicle. Verse 15 originally followed verse 12, the intervening verses being later additions more appropriate to the final sack of the city eleven years later. Nebuchadnezzar places a third son of Josiah on the puppet throne with the throne name **Zedekiah.** On the number of deportees cf. Jeremiah 52:28. Here only round numbers are given.

24:18–25:7. *Zedekiah's Reign.* Zedekiah is destined to be the last Judean king (597-586). As long as Judah remains loyal to the Babylonians, life can continue. But eventually the pro-Egyptian party wins and Zedekiah rebels—that is, withholds the tribute. On 24:20 cf. 21:10-15. For a fuller account of the final days of Jerusalem cf. Jeremiah 37–39.

25:1-7. The final **siege** begins January 15, 588, and thirty months later, July 19, 586, the walls are breached. The city is deserted by its leaders. The **king's garden** was probably near the Pool of Siloam. The escape route lay at the lower end of the

Valley of Hinnom. The **two walls** (or "double wall") has not been
certainly located, but it must have been at the southern tip of the
city. 'The **Arabah** refers to the deep valley of the Jordan River
and the Dead Sea. The king is captured near **Jericho** and
brought captive to **Riblah** (see above on 23:31-35). Apparently
Nebuchadnezzar himself has remained there (but cf. verse 1).

25:8-21. *The City Destroyed.* The following month (August
15) Jerusalem is razed. The palace, the temple, and **every great
house** in the city are **burned**. The **walls** are broken by the army,
thereby making any future resistance impossible. Many **people**
are exiled to **Babylon** and only peasants are left.

25:13-17. Large **bronze** furnishings of the temple are broken
up, smaller metal vessels are left intact, and all are carried off as
loot. Verses 16-17 are simply the D editor's summary of I Kings
7:15-39.

25:18-21. The Babylonian commander, **Nebuzaradan**, arrests
seventy-two ringleaders in the revolt and brings them to
military headquarters at Riblah. There they are executed by
royal decree. These include five temple personnel, as well as
seven military officials.

25:22-26. *Gedaliah as Governor.* For a fuller account cf.
Jeremiah 40:7–43:7. Nebuchadnezzar appoints a Judean noble
as his viceroy. On Gedaliah's father, **Ahikam**, cf. 22:12 and
Jeremiah 26:24. Gedaliah is treacherously slain by a few
hotheaded nationalists, who also brutally kill the inhabitants of
the new provincial capital, **Mizpah** (see above on I Kings
15:16-22).

25:27-30. *A Final Note of Hope.* Nebuchadnezzar finally dies
in 562 and is succeeded by his son **Evil-merodach** (Babylonian
"Amil-marduk"). He releases the captive **Jehoiachin** after
thirty-seven years of imprisonment on March 21, 561. The
ex-king is given an increased living **allowance** and a great deal of
preferment. Was Amil-marduk about to restore him to his
rightful place as subject ruler in Judah? This will never be
known. A year later he was assassinated by Nergal-sharezer,
who thereby dashed Jewish hopes for immediate restoration.

THE FIRST BOOK OF
THE CHRONICLES

Charles T. Fritsch

INTRODUCTION

Name

In the Hebrew Bible the Chronicles form a single volume.
They are called "the things [or "events"] of the days [i.e.
history]." The Septuagint divided the book into two parts. Here
it has the title "the things which have been passed over,"
referring to those events which were omitted in the former
history books of Samuel and Kings. The name "Chronicles,"
found in German and English Bibles, comes from Jerome's
statement that these books are a "chronicle of the whole of
sacred history."

Place in the Canon

I and II Chronicles, which originally formed one book, were
part of a larger work that included Ezra and Nehemiah. One
proof of this is found in the fact that the conclusion of II
Chronicles 36 and the beginning of Ezra 1 are the same. An even
stronger proof is the common linguistic and stylistic features of
the books and the fact that Ezra-Nehemiah complete the
material which has been lost at the end of II Chronicles. In the

Hebrew Bible these books are found in the Writings, the third division of the Jewish canon. There Ezra and Nehemiah precede I and II Chronicles, which close the canon. In the Septuagint, however, the chronological order is preserved—I and II Chronicles, Ezra, Nehemiah—the order followed in the English Bible.

Content and Purpose

These four books trace the history of the kingdom of Judah from the beginning of the world (Adam) to the restoration of Judaism under Ezra and Nehemiah. According to the Chronicler the rule of God on earth was most perfectly realized in the Davidic monarchy and in the cultic community after the Babylonian exile. The genealogies which introduce the history set the stage for the appearance of David and his dynasty. These records legitimatize the Jews as the lineal descendants of God's chosen people. They also indicate that the Jews have been in the center of God's redemptive plan for the world since the beginning of time.

The brevity of the genealogical tables in I Chronicles 1, especially verses 1-4 and 24-27, shows that the Chronicler takes for granted his readers' acquaintance with these lists in Genesis. He likewise passes over the accounts of Israel's early history because he is interested mainly in the theocracy—that is, God's rule through chosen leaders. For him this begins, not with Abraham, or even Moses, but with David. The special concern for David is reflected in these introductory chapters. Judah and his descendants, including David, come first in the genealogical history of the sons of Israel (Jacob) (I Chronicles 2:3–4:23; cf. 5:1-2). Also, more space is given to Judah and Levi (I Chronicles 6) in these tables than to all the other sons of Israel combined.

After a brief account of Saul's ignominious death the history of the true Israel begins with the glorious reign of David, the ideal ruler of God's people (I Chronicles 11–29). According to the Chronicler, the true Israel—meaning the worshiping community—was founded by David in Jerusalem, not by Moses in the desert. David was the spiritual founder of the temple. He made the detailed preparations for its construction and gave to Solomon the money, building materials, and model for its erection. He was also the organizer of the elaborate temple service and the numerous offices among the temple personnel.

In Chronicles the political and social history of Israel gives way to the history of the cultic community. For the first time the annals of a nation are scored to the accompaniment of musical instruments and singing choirs—with the result that these books sound more like and opera than history. Note especially II Chronicles 13:14 and 20:18-28, where trumpets and choirs win the victories for Abijah and Jehoshaphat.

Solomon's reign was more magnificent than his father's (II Chronicles 1–9). He was extremely powerful, wealthy, and wise. But his main claim to fame in the Chronicler's view was the fact that he built the temple in Jerusalem and organized its affairs. In the accounts of both these rulers the Chronicler has omitted the more sordid details of their reigns which are recorded in Samuel and Kings. He portrays them as the ideal kings of God's people.

After Solomon's reign the history of the southern kingdom of Judah is traced from Rehoboam to the fall of Jerusalem in 586 B.C. (II Chronicles 10–36). Because of the sin of Jeroboam I the northern kingdom became apostate and thus was contemptuously ignored by the Chronicler. The records of Jehoshaphat, Hezekiah, and Josiah are greatly expanded beyond those of the older history because of their interest in religious reforms. Yet the sins of rulers like Ahaz, Manasseh, and Zedekiah far outweighed the pious efforts of these religious heroes. They brought God's wrath on the nation "till there was no remedy" (II Chronicles 36:15-16). With the fall of Jerusalem, God's plans for the redemption of the world appear to be shattered.

The book concludes, however, on a hopeful note (II Chronicles 36:22-23). All is not lost. God's eternal purposes will not be thwarted. The day will come when God's people will return from captivity to Jerusalem. The temple will be rebuilt, and songs of praise will once again resound from the holy hill of Zion.

Date

The Chronicler's work continues through Ezra-Nehemiah (see above under "Place in the Canon"). He tells of the return from captivity and rebuilding of the temple under Zerubbabel late in the sixth century. He ends with a further return and renewal of strict observance of the law under Nehemiah and Ezra a century later. In view of the content and purpose of the total work it is natural to conclude that the author has brought it down to his own day. On this basis the writing is to be dated during the lifetime of Ezra or a short time thereafter—that is, in the last decades of the fifth century or the early part of the fourth. In fact the Chronicler may well have been Ezra himself or one of his close disciples. This dating is supported by the fact that both the Davidic genealogy of I Chronicles 3:19-24 (see comment) and the list of priests in Nehemiah 12 come down to abouth 400 B.C.

There has been serious disagreement among scholars about the date of Chronicles. Many have placed it in the Greek period, after the overthrow of the Persian Empire by Alexander the Great in 333. The chief reasons for the later date are:

(1) The Aramaic in Ezra 4:8–6:18; 7:12-26, an integral part of the Chronicler's work, has been thought to be late.

(2) In the Septuagint and other versions the genealogy of David in I Chronicles 3:19-24 is continued to the eleventh generation after Zerubbabel.

(3) The evident historical order of the careers of Nehemiah and Ezra have been reversed. This suggests a time when the events of the period had been blurred by distance.

The first of these reasons has been largely broken down by recent comparative study of extrabiblical sources. These show that the Aramaic of Ezra fits into the latter part of the Persian period and that certain unusual words assumed to be derived from the Greek are rather of Persian origin. Further, both the extended Davidic genealogy in some versions and the confusion about Nehemiah and Ezra may be attributed to later revision. Other considerations often mentioned in the discussion of the date—for example, the author's anti-Samaritan bias and his emphasis on the place of the Levites in the organization of the community—are applicable to either period. Therefore an increasing number of scholars now favor an earlier date for Chronicles. They place it in the late Persian period if not specifically around 400 B.C.

Sources

The data in the genealogies (I Chronicles 1–9) come from the Pentateuch for the most part. For the history of David and Solomon the Chronicler depends almost entirely on Samuel and Kings. Any differences or additions may be attributed to the Chronicler himself. In II Chronicles 10–36, however, he seems to have used an expanded version of Kings—perhaps the "Commentary on the Book of the Kings" mentioned in 24:27. Citations from prophetic books are found in II Chronicles 16:9 (Zechariah 4:10) and 20:20 (Isaiah 7:9). The Psalter is quoted in I Chronicles 16:8-36 (Psalms 105:1-15; 96; 106:1, 47-48) and II Chronicles 6:41-42 (Psalm 132:8-9).

I. GENEALOGIES FROM ADAM TO DAVID (1:1–9:43)

Genealogies are the backbone of history. In biblical history they are particularly important because they show how God's redemptive purpose has been carried on from one generation to another. For the Chronicler the genealogical tables of the first nine chapters are not just prelude or introduction. They are an integral part of the divine plan of redemption which has been gradually unfolding since the beginning of human history. It reaches its climax in the glory of the Solomonic temple, where God is rightfully worshipped.

The genealogical lists include the descendants of Adam (1:1-3) and Noah and his sons (1:4-26). Abraham and his descendants are traced through Ishmael and Keturah (1:27-33) and through Isaac and his sons Esau (1:34-54) and Israel (2:1-2). Then follow the genealogies of the individual tribes of Israel (2:3–8:40). There is special emphasis on Judah and the line of David

(2:3–4:23), Levi (chapter 6), and Benjamin (chapter 8). The section closes with a list of the postexilic inhabitants of Jerusalem (9:1-16), of temple personnel (9:17-34), and the genealogy of Saul (9:35-44).

A. PATRIARCHAL GENEALOGIES (1:1-54)

1:1-4. *From Adam to Noah and His Sons.* Cf. Genesis 5. Relationship is not mentioned in this list. The godless line of Cain has been purposely omitted. Verses 24-27 carry the line from Shem to Abraham (cf. Genesis 11:10-26). The mere citation of names in these two lists (verses 1-4 and 24-27) indicates that the Chronicler takes for granted that his readers know the sources.

1:5-23. *Descendants of the Sons of Noah.* Cf. Genesis 10. Verse 6 probably should read "Riphath" instead of **Diphath**. The explanation of the name **Peleg** in verse 19 is not clear.

1:28-34. *Sons of Abraham.* This list consists of Isaac and Ishmael and their offspring (cf. Genesis 25:13-16) and the sons of Keturah, the **concubine** of Abraham (cf. Genesis 25:1-4, where she is called his **wife**).

1:35-42. *Sons of Esau and Seir.* Cf. Genesis 36. Esau, who became identified with Edom (Genesis 25:30), is the ancestor of the Edomites.

1:43-54. *Kings of Edom.* Cf. Genesis 36. Verse 43*b* reads literally "before there reigned a king of the children of Israel [over Edom?]."

The Chronicler has added verse 51*a*, which is not in Genesis 36:39-40. He makes it clear that the kings of Edom are replaced by the **chiefs**, who are listed in verses 51*b*-54.

B. GENEALOGIES OF THE SONS OF JACOB (2:1–8:40)

2:1-2. *Sons of Israel (Jacob).* Cf. Genesis 35:23-26. In the Chronicler's list **Dan** is placed before the sons of Rachel, **Joseph** and **Benjamin**.

2:3—4:23. *Genealogies of Judah.* The sons of Judah come first in accordance with the Chronicler's interest in the southern kingdom and the ideal rule of David (cf. 5:1-2). He devotes a hundred verses to this genealogy, which is longer than any of the others. The royal line of David springs from the union of Judah and **Tamar,** a Canaanite woman, Judah's daughter-in-law (cf. Genesis 38; 46:12; Leviticus 18:15). Her name appears in the genealogy of Jesus (Matthew 1:3). **Achar, the troubler of Israel,** is also found in the line of David (cf. Joshua 7, where the name is given as Achan), as well as **Ethan, Heman, Calcol, and Dara** (or Darda), famous for their wisdom (cf. I Kings 4:31).

2:9-55. *Descendants of Hezron.* This, according to the Chronicler, is the most important clan of Judah. From Hezron springs the royal family of **David** (verses 9-17). His descendants include also the important clans of Caleb (**Chelubai,** verse 9) and **Jerahmeel.** According to the Chronicler, David is the **seventh** son of **Jesse.** In I Samuel 16:10-11 and 17:12 Jesse has eight sons, of whom David is the youngest.

3:1-9. *Descendants of David.* Those born to David in **Hebron** are listed in verses 1-4 (cf. II Samuel 3:2-5). **Daniel,** the **second** son, is called Chileab in II Samuel 3:3. The length of David's reign in Hebron and in **Jerusalem** (verse 4; contrast 29:27) is taken from II Samuel 5:5. Those born to David in Jerusalem are listed in verses 5-9 (cf. II Samuel 5:14-16). **Bathshua** should be read Bathsheba.

3:10-16. *Kings of Judah.* Athaliah, who was not of the line of David (cf. II Kings 8:26), is not mentioned. **Johanan the first-born** of Josiah is mentioned nowhere else. **Jeconiah,** the son of **Jehoiakim,** was known also as Coniah (Jeremiah 22:24) and Jehoiachin (II Kings 24:6). **Zedekiah** was the uncle of Jehoiachin, whom he succeeded. **Son** here is a conventional term signifying blood relationship.

3:17-24. *The Davidic Line After the Exile.* This is the only place where **Zerubbabel** is the son of **Pedaiah** and nephew of **Shealtiel.** Elsewhere he is called the son of Shealtiel (cf. Ezra 3:2; Nehemiah 12:1). Perhaps he may have been the real son of Pedaiah and the legal adopted son of Shealtiel. For **sons of**

Pedaiah in verse 19 the Septuagint reads "sons of Shealtiel."
Shenazzar, a brother of Pedaiah, is probably to be identified
with Sheshbazzar, who was put in charge of restoring the temple
(Ezra 1:7-11). The difficult Hebrew text of verse 21 seems to list
six **sons of Hananiah.** But the Septuagint and other versions
make each the son of the preceding, thus adding five
generations (see Introduction).

4:1-23. *Additional Genealogies of Judah.* In verse 1 for **Carmi**
read Caleb (cf. 2:18-19, 50-51). A popular etymology of the name
Jabez is found in verse 9. In the following verse Jabez prays
away the curse of his name. **Mered** (cf. 2:34-35) must have been
a man of distinction to marry the **daughter of Pharaoh.**

4:24-43. *Sons of Simeon.* Geographically and historically
Simeon is closely connected with Judah (cf. Joshua 19:9 and
Judges 1:3). The names of Simeon's offspring (cf. Numbers
26:12-14) and their places of dwelling (cf. Joshua 19:2-8) are
followed by a list of princes from the time of **Hezekiah.** These
lead their people in a search for more grazing ground into the
peaceful **valley** of **Gedor,** somewhere in the territory of
Philistia. They also enter the territory of Edom, where they
smite the **Amalekites** who have survived attacks by Saul and
David (cf. I Samuel 14:48 and II Samuel 8:12). **Meunim,** name of
an Arabian tribe living east of Edom, is here probably a scribal
error for "their dwellings."

5:1-26. *Sons of Reuben, Gad, and Manasseh.* The Chronicler
states why he began the genealogies of the tribes of Israel with
Judah. Then the **sons of Reuben** are given (cf. Genesis 46:9).
Reuben lost his **birthright,** i.e. the status of **first-born,** because
he defiled his father's bed (cf. Genesis 35:22*a*; 49:4).

In Genesis 48:8-22 it was not the birthright but a "blessing"
that Jacob gave to the **sons of Joseph,** Ephraim and Manasseh.
Nevertheless **Judah** achieved preeminence and produced a
prince—David (cf. Psalm 78:67-68, where Judah is chosen
above Joseph).

5:4-10. The captivity of **Beerah** is not recorded elsewhere.
Tilgath-pilneser is the Chronicler's misspelling for Tiglath-

pileser III, who in 734/33 overran Transjordan and Galilee and exiled many of the people (cf. verse 26; II Kings 15:29).

The Reubenites are said to live east of the Jordan in **Gilead** and have spread south to the Moabite cities named in verse 8. The **Hagrites** (cf. verses 19-20 and Psalm 83:6) were bedouin living in northern Arabia.

5:11-17. The **sons of Gad** live in **Gilead** and in **Bashan** to the north (but cf. Joshua 13:25-27). They have spread east to **Salecah** in the desert.

5:18-22. This is a more detailed account of the war on the **Hagrites** (see above on verses 4-10). On **Jetur** and **Naphish** cf. 1:31. The **exile** in verse 22 is that of verse 6.

5:23-24. The **half-tribe of Manasseh** is the portion of the tribe living east of the Jordan. It is a prolific group, occupying land to the north of Gad, as far as the Lebanon mountain range.

5:25-26. Because of apostasy Reuben, Gad, and the half-tribe of Manasseh are taken into captivity by **Tilgath-pilneser** (see above on verses 4-10). **Pul,** a usurper, assumed the throne name Tiglath-pileser; only one king is referred to. On the cities of exile cf. II Kings 17:6 and 18:11.

6:1-81. *Sons of Levi.* The list of preexilic high priests from **Aaron** to **Jehozadak,** who was taken into captivity by **Nebuchadnezzar** is given (verses 3b-15). This is preceded by a genealogical record of descendants from Levi to Aaron. Abiathar, of the line of Eli, is not mentioned with **Zadok** as a priest under David, since he supported another aspirant to the throne rather than Solomon (I Kings 1:7; 2:26-27).

6:16-30. In verses 16-19a the sons and grandsons of Levi are named. Then the descendants of the sons are listed: **Gershom** (verses 20-21), **Kohath** (verses 22-24), and **Merari** (verses 29-30). The descendants of **Elkanah,** of the line of Kohath, are given (verses 25-28; cf. verses 33b-38). This is done in order to show that **Samuel** came from the line of Levi, though according to I Samuel 1:1 he was an Ephraimite. Cf. 9:22 and 11:3 for the Chronicler's high opinion of Samuel.

6:31-48. These verses contain the genealogies of the chief singers of David: **Heman** (verses 33b-38), **Asaph** (verses 39-43), and **Ethan** (verses 44-47). According to verse 33 **Samuel** was the grandfather of Heman, one of David's chief musicians (cf. 16:41-42).

6:49-53. The duties of the priests are described, as **Moses . . . commanded.** Then an additional genealogy of the sons of Aaron is given (cf. verses 4-8). Though the Chronicler begins his history with the reign of David, he recognizes the important role that Moses played in Israel's earlier cultic and legal history.

6:54-81. The names of these Levitical cities are taken from Joshua 21. There are many corruptions in the spellings and a few inadvertent omissions.

7:1-5. *Sons of Issachar.* Cf. Numbers 26:23-25.

7:6-12a. *An Uncertain Genealogy.* A list of Benjamin's descendants is also found in chapter 8. There is no genealogy for Zebulun, which according to 2:1 should follow Issachar. In the Hebrew **The sons of** is missing from verse 6. This would read the same as the opening letters of **Benjamin**—suggesting a copyist's error in writing "Benjamin" for "The sons of Zebulun." On the other hand this list does not match other genealogies of Zebulun (Genesis 46:14; Numbers 26:26). It is possible that the genealogy for this tribe has been lost in the transmission of the text. In verse 12a read "Shupham and Hupham" (cf. Numbers 26:39).

7:12b. *The Son of Dan.* On the basis of Genesis 46:23 and the Septuagint this fragment should read: "The sons of Dan, Hushim his son, one."

7:13. *Sons of Naphtali.* Cf. Genesis 46:24-25.

7:14-19. *Sons of Manasseh.* According to Genesis 50:23 **Machir** and his sons were born in Egypt. Here they are associated with an **Aramaean** background. The genealogy is based on Numbers 26:29-33. Parts of the tribe living both east and west of the Jordan are included in this genealogy (cf. 5:23-24).

7:20-29. *Sons of Ephraim.* Cf. Numbers 26:35. Included in this genealogy are the forebears of Joshua (verses 25-27). A disastrous **raid** of Ephraimites into Philistine territory is also

248

recounted. A list of cities belonging to Ephraim and Manasseh has been added.

7:30-40. *Sons of Asher.* Cf. Genesis 46:17 and Numbers 26:44-46. The source from which many of the names recorded here are taken is not known.

8:1-40. *Genealogy of Benjamin.* Cf. Genesis 46:21. Benjaminites in **Geba,** in **Moab** and **Ono and Lod,** in **Aijalon** and **Jerusalem,** and in **Gibeon** are noted. The genealogy of the house of **Saul** is found in verses 33-40 (cf. I Samuel 14:49). **Eshbaal** in verse 33 should be Ishbaal (see comments on I Samuel 14:49-51 and II Samuel 2:8-11). On **Meribbaal** see comment on II Samuel 4:4.

C. The Postexilic Families of Jerusalem (9:1-18a)

After two introductory verses, the postexilic residents of Jerusalem are given in the following order:

(1) Israelites—that is, lay persons of the tribes of **Judah** and **Benjamin** (verses 4-9);
(2) **priests** (verses 10-13);
(3) **Levites** (verses 14-16);
(4) **gatekeepers** (verses 17-18a).

A similar list is found in Nehemiah 11:3-19. The **Book of the Kings of Israel** is not canonical Kings (see Introduction). The **exile** refers to the captivity of the Jews after the fall of Jerusalem in 586 to Nebuchadnezzar. Though Ephraimites and Manassites are mentioned as citizens of postexilic Jerusalem, they are not included in the lists of this chapter.

D. Temple Personnel (9:18b-34)

The **gatekeepers** (verses 18b-32) are of special interest to the author. Their office goes back to the time of Moses and was sanctioned by Samuel and David. They are reckoned among the Levites. Other duties are ascribed them besides keeping the gates. The **singers** in the temple (verse 33) are **on duty day and night**.

E. THE GENEALOGY OF SAUL (9:35-44)

This is an introduction to the opening verses of chapter 10, which describe Saul's tragic end. It is repeated from 8:29-38.

II. THE REIGN OF DAVID (10:1–29:30)

For the Chronicler, David and his rule is the all-important subject in his history of the Hebrew nation. The whole period of the judges and events of Saul's life up to his death are omitted. David's life is idealized. There is no mention of his exile from the court of Saul, his reign in Hebron, and the Bathsheba incident. The Chronicler ignores even the history of the northern kingdom except where it impinges in the affairs of Judah. In his view Saul's attempt to found a kingdom ended in failure. God's redemptive purpose was realized in the history of the southern kingdom, which was founded by David, the Lord's anointed.

A. THE DEATH OF SAUL (10:1-14)

The reason for beginning the history of David with the death of Saul is given in verses 13-14. With this chapter cf. I Samuel 31. As far as the Chronicler is concerned, Saul's whole **house** perished with him. He tells nothing of David's later dealings with Ishbaal (Ishbosheth, II Samuel 2:8–4:12), Meribaal (Mephibosheth, II Samuel 9; 19:24-30), and others of Saul's family (II Samuel 21:1-14).

Because of religious scruples he avoids any references to Ashtaroth (I Samuel 31:10), the hanging of the bodies of Saul and his sons on the walls of Bethshan (I Samuel 31:10), and the burning of the bodies by the men of Jabesh (I Samuel 3:12). As he sums it up, Saul's miserable failure as king of Israel was due to disobedience to the Lord's commandments (cf. I Samuel 15:17-35) and his dealings with a **medium** (cf. I Samuel 28:8-14). This dark picture of Saul is in sharp contrast with the glorious reigns of David and Solomon.

B. ESTABLISHMENT OF THE DAVIDIC KINGDOM (11:1–22:1)

11:1-9. *David's Anointing.* David becomes king of all Israel and captures Jerusalem. On verses 1-3, which describe the anointing of David as king over **all Israel,** cf. II Samuel 5:1-3. David's seven-and-a-half-year rule over Judah at **Hebron** and his long warfare with the house of Saul are passed over (cf. II Samuel 1–4). On verses 4-9, which describe the capture of **Jerusalem,** cf. II Samuel 5:6-10.

11:10-47. *David's Mighty Men.* II Samuel 23:8-39 has been expanded here by the addition of verses 41*b*-47. These mighty men, by their bravery and loyalty, help David establish his kingdom in accordance with the divine purpose.

12:1-22. *David's Supporters Against Saul.* The sources for this material are not known. Men from Benjamin (verses 1-6, 16-18), Gad (verses 8-15), and Manasseh (verses 19-22) join David at different times during this period.

12:23-40. *David's Army at Hebron.* Large numbers of fighting men from every tribe join David at Hebron to make him king. All Israel joins in the coronation festivities, which seem to have messianic overtones.

13:1-14. *An Attempt to Return the Ark.* Cf. II Samuel 6:1-11. The Chronicler places this narrative immediately after the capture of Jerusalem (11:4-9) to show David's concern for the worship of God. Note the different order of events in II Samuel 5:6–6:10. In Chronicles the **priests and Levites** join in the procession which accompanies the **ark,** but they do not appear in the II Samuel narrative. Verses 1-5 introduces the story of the unsuccessful attempt to bring the ark to Jerusalem.

14:1-17. *Miscellaneous Matters.* This chapter concerns

David's dealings with **Hiram king of Tyre,** additions to the royal household, and wars with the Philistines. These events are described in II Samuel 5:11-25, before the removal of the ark from Kiriath-jearim. The Chronicler places them after the removal of the ark, during the three months it is resting in the house of Obed-edom. In verse 12 David has the idol **gods** of the Philistines **burned.** In II Samuel 5:21 they are simply carried away by David and his men.

15:1–16:3. *The Ark Brought to Jerusalem.* The parallel story in II Samuel 6:12-19 is greatly expanded here. The additional material includes elaborate plans for bringing the ark to Jerusalem. The Chronicler is especially interested in the **Levites.** Here they play the dominant role. They **carry the ark.** Bands of Levitical **singers** and musicians accompany the procession. The Levites sacrifice **seven bullocks and seven rams,** whereas in II Samuel 6:13 David sacrifices only "an ox and a fatling." God looks with favor on these preparations. The ark is successfully transferred to Jerusalem and into the **tent which David had pitched for it.**

16:4-43. *The Service of Joy Before the Ark.* None of this material is found in II Samuel except the last verse (cf. II Samuel 6:19b-20a). The Levites have carried the ark up to Jerusalem. They are now **appointed** by David to minister **before the ark** with praise and thanksgiving. By tracing this appointment back to David the Chronicler asures the Levites a legitimate place among the temple personnel in Jerusalem (cf. II Chronicles 5).

16:8-36. The psalm of praise is composed of several elements from the Psalter:

verses 8-22 = Psalm 105:1-15;
verses 23-33 = Psalm 96:1-13;
verses 34-36 = Psalm 106:1, 47-48.

16:37-43. Two holy places are mentioned here. One is at Jerusalem, where **Asaph and his brethren** minister **before the ark.** The other is at **Gibeon** (cf. I Kings 3-4), where **Zadok the priest** and his Levitical assistants offer the sacrifices in the **tabernacle** (cf. 21:29; II Chronicles 1:3-4).

17:1-27. *David's Desire to Build a Temple.* This passage is

taken with slight variations from II Samuel 7. David desires to
build a temple for God, and **Nathan the prophet** agrees. But
God tells Nathan in a dream that this plan is not approved.
Instead God promises to **build** David a **house**—that is, a
dynasty—through the house of God which his son will build
(verses 7-15). "When he [David's son] commits iniquity I will
chastise him with the rod of men, with the stripes of the sons of
men" (II Samuel 7:14*b*) is omitted in the Chronicler's account in
verse 13. This does not fit in with his ideal view of David's
successor. Also "your [David's] house and your kingdom" (II
Samuel 7:16) becomes **my** [God's] **house and . . . my kingdom**
in verse 14. This shows the Chronicler's idea that David is ruler
over God's kingdom. David's prayer of thanksgiving is given in
verses 16-27.

18:1—20:8. *David's Military Victories.* These accounts follow
closely the older sources:

Chapter 18 = II Samuel 8.

19:1—20:3 = II Samuel 10:1–11:1; 12:26-31.

20:4-8 = II Samuel 21:18-22.

David's successful encounters with the **Philistines** (18:1), the
Moabites (18:2), the kingdom of **Zobah** (18:3-4), **Damascus**
(18:5-10), **Edom** (18:12-13), the **Ammonites** and the **Syrians**
(19:1—20:3), and the Philistine **giants** (20:4-8) are related. His
administrative officers are listed in 18:14-17.

The story of David's kindness to Meribaal (Mephibosheth; cf.
II Samuel 9) is omitted here—probably because the Chronicler
has stated in 10:6 that all of Saul's house perished with him at
Gilboa. Also omitted are the odious story of David and
Bathsheba (cf. II Samuel 11:1–12:25) and the accounts of family
intrigues and revolts against David (cf. II Samuel 13:1–21:14).
Again, these do not fit the Chronicler's idealized figure of
David.

20:5. Here **Elhanan** slays **Lahmi the brother of Goliath the
Gittite.** According to II Samuel 21:19 "Elhanan . . . , the
Bethlehemite, slew Goliath the Gittite." In I Samuel 17 David
kills the giant. The Chronicler's account of this episode is
probably an attempt to reconcile the two narratives in Samuel.

21:1–22:1. *David's Census and the Plague.* This passage derives from II Samuel 24, with some important variations:

(1) **Satan,** a supernatural evil emissary, is said to have **incited David to number Israel.** In II Samuel 24:1 God does the inciting. The Chronicler avoids the idea that a holy God can perpetrate a sinful act.

(2) **Levi and Benjamin** are not included in the census. On Levi cf. Numbers 1:49. Benjamin may have been omitted because Jerusalem lay in Benjaminite territory.

(3) There are more frequent references to the **angel**—nine times as compared with three times in Samuel. This reflects the Chronicler's belief in a transcendent God who deals with humans more and more through intermediaries. The divine nature of this angelic emissary is indicated by the fact that he stands **between earth and heaven.**

(4) David pays **six hundred shekels of gold by weight** (i.e. in a balance; see below on 29:1-22a) for the **site of the threshing floor.** In Samuel he pays only fifty shekels of silver for it. By exaggerating the cost the Chronicler emphasizes the great value of the temple site.

(5) The burning of the offering by **fire from heaven** indicates divine approval of the site for the future temple.

(6) The authenticity of the site is further emphasized by the words of 22:1, which have a polemical ring. Jerusalem is the true center of worship as opposed to **Gibeon,** but perhaps even more as opposed to any Samaritan holy place. Because of this, David cannot sacrifice any more at the high place of Gibeon, where the **tabernacle** has been (21:28–22:1; but cf. II Chronicles 1:1-6).

C. Preparations for the Temple and the Cult (22:2–29:30)

There are no parallels for this section in either Samuel or Kings. The Chronicler would like to make David builder of the temple. Since history stands in his way, he stresses David's preparations so strongly that the temple ideally appears to be his work.

22:2-19. *David's Preparation for the Temple.* The Chronicler describes some of the building **materials** which David provides for the temple—stone, metal, and wood.

22:6-16. David charges his son **Solomon** to build the temple. Cf. the prophecy of Nathan (17:1-15) to which David refers. In I Kings 2:1-9 David gives his last instructions to Solomon without mentioning the temple. Note the astronomically high figures in verse 14 to describe the amounts of **gold** and **silver** which David sets aside for building the temple.

22:17-19. David also exhorts the **leaders of Israel** to help Solomon in this important task of building a **sanctuary** for the **ark** of the Lord.

23:1-32. *Organization of the Levites.* After the Levites are counted they are organized into three divisions according to the **sons of Levi:** Gershonites, Kohathites, and Merarites.

23:24-32. The Levites are no longer required to **carry the tabernacle** and its equipment since there is now a central sanctuary. This appears to be the reason the age limit for Levites is increased ten years (verses 24, 27; cf. verse 3). The main work of the Levites is to **assist** the Aaronic priests in the temple services.

24:1-19. *Divisions of the Aaronic Priesthood.* The **sons of Aaron,** through **Eleazar and Ithamar,** are divided into twenty-four classes. Their duties are determined **by lot.**

24:20-31. *An Additional List of Levites.* The relation to 23:6-24 is not clear. The Gershonites are omitted and some new names are added.

25:1-31. *Divisions of the Temple Singers.* The leaders of the musical guilds come from the Levitical families of **Asaph,** of **Heman,** and of **Jeduthun.** That these singers **prophesy with lyres, with harps, and with cymbals** seems to indicate that they are closely related to prophetic circles. In verse 5 Heman is called **the king's seer,** whereas in II Chronicles 29:30 Asaph is called "the seer" and in II Chronicles 35:15 Jeduthun is called "the king's seer." In II Chronicles 20:14 "the Spirit of the LORD" comes upon "a Levite of the sons of Asaph," who then gives a message to King Jehoshaphat in the same manner as the prophets of old. And in II Chronicles 34:30 "Levites" is substituted for "prophets" in the parallel passage in II Kings 23:2. All this seems to indicate that in the days of the Chronicler prophetic inspiration had been transferred to the Levitical singers. The subdivisions, with their order of succession in the service, are given in verses 9-31.

26:1-32. *Further Levitical Offices.* The doorkeepers are descended from three families. Their duties are assigned by **lots.** The financial officials listed in verses 20-28 are responsible for the **treasuries of the house of God** and the **gifts** dedicated to the temple, including spoils of war. Officials are chosen as **officers and judges** in the areas both east and west of the Jordan (verses 29-32).

27:1-34. *Military and Civil Administration.* The army (verses 1-15) is organized with twelve officers, each with **twenty-four thousand** men. They are appointed for military duty, one for each **month.** The names of the officers are taken from 11:11-12.

27:16-24. David appoints leaders **over the tribes of Israel.** For some reason Gad and Asher are omitted. **Zadok,** who is said to come from Aaron, represents all the people.

27:25-34. The officials in charge of David's personal affairs oversee his **treasuries,** fields, and flocks. They also serve as his personal counselors.

28:1–29:30. *David's Last Words and Acts.* David announces to the assembled officials of Israel that Solomon is to be his successor, according to God's own choosing. The palace intrigues, violence, and murder associated with Solomon's accession in I Kings 1–2 are not mentioned by the Chronicler.

28:11-21. David has received the **plan of the . . . temple** from God (cf. Exodus 25:9, where the plan of the tabernacle is given to Moses by God). This is given over to Solomon with parental words of encouragement.

29:1-22a. David asks the assembled people to give freely toward the construction of the temple, as he has done. The response is overwhelming, and David pours out his heart in prayer and praise to God. **Darics** were Persian gold coins used in the Chronicler's day. They were of course an anachronism for the time of David, when precious metal used for money had to be tallied by weight (cf. 21:25). A talent was sixty-two and a half pounds.

29:22*b*-30. Solomon is made king **the second time** (cf. 23:1). The book closes with a résumé of David's rule.

THE SECOND BOOK OF
THE CHRONICLES

Charles T. Fritsch

Introduction

See the Introduction to I Chronicles. The outline of the
contents indicated by the headings continues that in I
Chronicles.

III. The Reign of Solomon (1:1–9:31)

The purpose of the Chronicler's history is clearly revealed in
his description of Solomon's reign. He idealizes Solomon by
omitting certain unfavorable events recorded in I Kings: the
troubles connected with his accession (I Kings 1–2), his marriage
to Pharaoh's daughter (I Kings 3:1), his worship of foreign
deities, his love for foreign women, the political and military
troubles at the end of his reign (I Kings 11). Instead he
emphasizes the building of the temple and the organization of its
affairs.

A. The Establishment of Solomon's Kingdom (1:1-17)

1:1-13. *Solomon at Gibeon.* The story of Solomon's prayer for
wisdom is based on I Kings 3:4-14. Gibeon is said to be the place

where the Mosaic tabernacle and the **bronze altar** are at this time (cf. I Chronicles 16:39 and 21:29). David has **brought up the ark** to Jerusalem, but no provision has been made for sacrificial offerings there.

1:14-17. *Solomon's Wealth and Power.* Cf. I Kings 10:26-29. The **horses,** which come from Asia Minor, bring less money than the **chariots** from **Egypt.**

B. THE BUILDING AND DEDICATION OF THE TEMPLE (2:1–7:11)

2:1-18. *Preparations for the Temple.* This account is based on I Kings 5. Solomon receives building materials and **skilled** labor for the temple from **Huram** (Hiram) **the king of Tyre.** He conscripts the laborers from the **aliens** in Israel (cf. I Kings 5:13, 15, where Israelites are conscripted). On **Huram-abi** cf. I Kings 7:13-14.

3:1-17. *The Construction.* Cf. the longer account in I Kings 6–7. The site of the temple is said to be **Mount Moriah,** where God appeared to David (cf. I Chronicles 21), and where Abraham offered up Isaac (Genesis 22:2). **A hundred and twenty cubits** for the **height** of the **vestibule** should probably read "twenty cubits," since the temple itself is only thirty cubits high (cf. I Kings 6:2). On the **cherubim** see the comment on I Kings 6:23-28. The two bronze **pillars,** named **Jachin** and **Boaz,** were symbolic, free-standing columns which stood outside the inner chamber (see comment on I Kings 7:15-22).

4:1-22. *The Furniture and Vessels.* Cf. I Kings 7:23-51.

5:1–7:11. *The Dedication.* The **gold** and **silver** and all the **vessels** which belonged to David are brought into the temple treasury. Then the **ark of the covenant** is carried from the tent which David pitched for it in the Jebusite stronghold of **Zion** to its permanent resting place in the **inner sanctuary** of the temple (cf. I Kings 8:1-11). According to the Chronicler the **Levites** carry the ark; in I Kings 8:3 it is the priests. Only the priests, however, may place it in the sanctuary.

5:11-14. The Levites were appointed by David to be the chief musicians of the temple (I Chronicles 16:4). Now they sing joyful songs of **praise and thanksgiving** to the accompaniment of **musical instruments.** The climax of this outburst of praise is reached when the **glory of the LORD filled the house of God.**

6:1-42. This chapter is taken almost word for word from I Kings 8:12-50. It contains Solomon's words to the people and the prayer of dedication. There are few significant differences in the Chronicler's account. Here the **covenant** is **with the people of Israel** rather than "with our fathers, when he brought them out of the land of Egypt" (I Kings 8:21). This illustrates the Chronicler's view that the covenant relationship with Israel did not begin at Sinai but existed from the very beginning of Israel's history. The **bronze platform** on which Solomon kneels in prayer before the congregation is not mentioned in Kings.

6:40-42. The conclusion of the prayer is strikingly different from that in I Kings 8:50*b*-53. A quotation from Psalm 132:8-10, eulogizing **David** and the temple tradition fittingly concludes the dedicatory prayer according to the Chronicler's view. Here Solomon asks that God be **attentive** to the prayers offered in (or toward) **this place** because of the love for David, God's **servant.** In the older account God is to give ear because of the love for Moses, who led Israel out of Egypt. The bringing of the ark into the temple is the climax of the service of dedication for the Chronicler. God now dwells in the holy place in the temple, where priest and Levite minister before God's presence and the people worship in holy array.

7:1-11. Divine approval of the new temple is shown. Fire **came down from heaven and consumed** the sacrifices and **glory filled** the **house.** The great **feast** concludes with sacrifices offered by king and people, and with great thanksgiving.

C. The Remainder of Solomon's Reign (7:12–9:31)

7:12-22. *Solomon's Dream.* Following the dedication ceremonies Solomon has a dream one **night.** God appears and assures him that his prayer will be answered. The divine blessing will be his if he keeps God's **statutes.** If he does not, the people will be uprooted from the **land,** and the magnificent temple will be deserted (cf. I Kings 9:2-9).

8:1-18. *Solomon's Activities.* Cf. I Kings 9:10-28. Cities are built, and laborers are conscripted from the alien peoples living in Canaan. The religious **feasts** are duly observed. The journey of Solomon's navy to **Ophir** for **gold** is noted. The Chronicler speaks of **cities** being **given** to Solomon by **Huram** (Hiram), reversing the historical record of I Kings 9:11-14 that Solomon sold "twenty cities in Galilee" to Hiram for 120 talents of gold.

Tadmor, an oasis 120 miles northeast of Damascus and later known as Palmyra, is defended by some scholars as a place where Solomon would establish protection for his trading operations. But it is more likely that the Chronicler confused the reference in I Kings 9:18 to Tamar, south of the Dead Sea.

8:11. The Chronicler's great respect for the ark is shown in Solomon's statement that his foreign-born wife must not dwell **in the house of David king of Israel, for the places to which the ark of the LORD has come are holy.** Cf. I Kings 9:24, where this religious note is not found.

9:1-12. *The Queen of Sheba's Visit.* This story is taken from I Kings 10:1-13 with little change. The theocratic viewpoint of the Chronicler is strikingly brought out in verse 8, however. **Set you on his** [God's] **throne as king for the LORD your God** contrasts with the parallel in I Kings 10:9, which simply has "set you on the throne of Israel."

9:13-28. *Solomon's Wealth.* Cf. I Kings 10:14-28.

9:29-31. *Solomon's Death.* Cf. I Kings 11:41-42. In accordance with his idealization of Solomon the Chronicler omits any mention of his love for foreign women, his idolatries, and his military and political problems described in I Kings 11.

IV. The Kings of Judah (10:1–36:21)

This portion of the Chronicler's history deals with the kings of the southern kingdom. He ignores the history of the northern kingdom except where it impinges on the affairs of Judah. The reason for doing this is found in 13:5-11. New material, not in Kings, is introduced into his accounts of Judah's rulers. Special attention is given to the activities of prophets and priests in the life of the nation.

A. Rehoboam (10:1–12:16)

10:1-19. This chapter is an almost exact duplication of I Kings 12:1-19. However, the crowning of Jeroboam (I Kings 12:20) is not mentioned by the Chronicler.

11:1-23. New material in this chapter includes Rehoboam's building activity, especially the fortification of **cities** in the southern part of Judah. This was evidently to be a protection against Egypt. The immigration of **priests** and **Levites** to Judah and a record of the members of Rehoboam's family have also been added.

12:1-12. The invasion of **Shishak king of Egypt** is described with the addition of theological comments (cf. I Kings 14:25-28). The chapter concludes with some general remarks concerning Rehoboam's rule and the notice of his death (cf. I Kings 14:29-31).

B. Abijah (13:1-22)

I Kings 15:7 simply states that "there was war between Abijam [Abijah] and Jeroboam." On this basis the Chronicler proceeds to give a detailed account of one of the battles between the two kings. There is no mountain known as **Zemaraim.** However, there was a town of this name in the territory of Benjamin, probably about five miles northeast of Bethel.

13:4b-12. In Abijah's speech the northern kingdom is condemned because it has broken away from the Davidic dynasty and the legitimate cult. Judah, on the other hand, has the true God on its side and the **priests with their battle trumpets** at the head of its army. Therefore it is assured of victory (cf. 20:22, where another battle is won by songs of praise and musical instruments). The **covenant of salt** probably refers to the eternal duration of God's covenant with David. Salt is a preservative and thus a symbol of what abides. The Davidic covenant is a favorite theme with the Chronicler (cf. 21:7).

13:13-22. In spite of the overwhelming number of the enemy's forces and Jeroboam's military tactics, Abijah wins the battle. The report of Jeroboam's death is premature, since according to I Kings 15:8-9 he outlived Abijah. In contrast with Jeroboam's humiliating defeat Abijah increases in strength.

C. ASA (14:1–16:14)

The basis of this section is I Kings 15:9-24, which has been greatly expanded. Asa's piety (14:2) and zeal for cultic reform (14:3-5; 15:1-19) are the reasons for the peace which prevails during most of his reign (cf. I Kings 15:16)

14:9-15. Asa's military power is tested by **Zerah the Ethiopian**—literally "Cushite." The term here may refer instead to the Sabean tribe of southwest Arabia, since the name Zerah is philologically related to a Sabean princely title. God routs the enemy in response to the king's fervent prayer. There is no parallel account of this battle in the older history.

16:1-12. The generally peaceful reign of Asa is shattered at the end by a battle with **Baasha king of Israel** (cf. I Kings 15:17-22). His successful rule ends in disgrace as the prophet **Hanani** (perhaps the father of the prophet Jehu; see below on 18:1–19:3) rebukes him for relying on the king of Syria in fighting Baasha rather than on God. Asa puts the prophet in jail for his condemnation. This, in the Chronicler's mind, is the reason for Asa's fatal disease **in his feet.**

16:13-14. In spite of his apostasy Asa receives a magnificent burial at which precious **spices** are burned in his honor.

D. JEHOSHAPHAT (17:1–20:37)

The Chronicler's account of this glorious reign is based on I Kings 22. There are several important additions. In chapter 17 Jehoshaphat's piety and his military power are noted. Of special interest is his appointment of five lay **princes,** nine **Levites,** and two **priests** (17:7-9) to go throughout Judah and teach the people the law of God.

18:1–19:3. *Alliance with Israel.* This is the only extensive reference to the history of the northern kingdom in Chronicles. It is taken with few changes from I Kings 22:1-35*a.* The two kingdoms are brought close together through the **marriage** of Jehoram the son of Jehoshaphat to Athaliah the daughter of Ahab (18:1; cf. 21:6). This alliance led to the introduction of idolatry into Judah and the near extinction of the royal family (cf. 22:10-12). Jehoshaphat is severely rebuked by a prophet for making this alliance, but is promised that divine retribution will be averted because of his inherent goodness (19:2-3). According to I Kings 16:1 **Jehu the son of Hanani** was a prophet of the northern kingdom in the time of Baasha, some 35 years earlier (see above on 16:1-12).

19:4-11. *Civil Reforms.* Courts are set up throughout the land. Judges of impeccable character are appointed to preside over them. In Jerusalem a higher court of appeal is established to deal with both religious and secular matters.

20:1-30. *Jehoshaphat's Victories.* News comes that a vast army of **Moabites and Ammonites** is invading Judah from Edom. Jehoshaphat prays for deliverance. God answers through **Jahaziel,** a Levite, who is moved by the **Spirit** to prophesy **victory** in the ensuing battle (see comment on I Chronicles 25:1-31). With words of assurance (verse 20) and songs of **praise** the army of Judah marches out into the **wilderness of Tekoa** to meet the enemy, whom they find already destroyed because of internal dissension. In verse 1 **Meunites** is a guess, based on 26:7, at correcting a corruption in the text. It may refer to the **inhabitants of Mount Seir,** the mountain range of Edom, attacked by their allies (verse 23). **Hazazon-tamar** in verse 2 should probably be identified, not with **Engedi** on the western shore of the Dead Sea, but with Tamar farther south.

20:31–21:1. *The Conclusion of Jehoshaphat's Reign.* Of special interest here is the account of the king's naval activities. His alliance with the wicked king **Ahaziah** of Israel is given as the cause of the wrecking of his fleet at **Ezion-geber** on the Gulf of Aqaba. The prophet **Eliezer** is not mentioned elsewhere. Cf. a different account of this episode in I Kings 22:48-49.

E. JEHORAM (21:1-20)

Cf. II Kings 8:17-22. The new material emphasizes the wickedness of Jehoram.

21:2-4. Jehoram has six **brothers,** all of whom he kills. The duplication of **Azariah** is probably an error in copying one of the names. **Princes** means, not members of the royal family, but men in positions of authority. For **Judah** the Hebrew text reads "Israel." Some scholars, taking this as correct, suggest that it reflects an authentic record that certain northern officials were stationed in Judah during this period.

21:7. Here the Chronicler sounds a favorite note. He revises II Kings 8:19 to declare that, in spite of Jehoram's great wickedness, God will **not destroy the house of David, because of the covenant which he had made with David.** The **lamp** which God gave to David and his sons is a figure of life which has messianic overtones (cf. I Kings 11:36; 15:4; II Kings 8:19; Psalm 132:17).

21:11-20. Jehoram's introduction of pagan rites into Judah, as well as his murders, will bring disasters on the nation, his family, and himself. This is prophesied in a **letter** purportedly written by **Elijah**—who actually was no longer alive at this time (cf. II Kings 3:11-12). In fulfillment God sends the **Philistines** and **Arabs** against Judah. Jehoram suffers heavy personal losses, which leave him only one son. In the Hebrew **Jehoahaz** is a transposition of the letters composing the name Ahaziah (cf.

22:1; on **youngest son** see below on 22:1-9). Finally, as predicted in the letter, Jehoram dies of a dreadful **disease** and is buried in dishonor.

F. Ahaziah (22:1-9)

Cf. II Kings 8:26-29. **Forty-two years old** would make Ahaziah two years older than his father (cf. 21:20) and is no doubt a copyist's error. II Kings 8:26 in the Hebrew has twenty-two, in the Septuagint twenty—a somewhat more credible age for Jehoram's **youngest son.** His brief but wicked reign is under the domination of the queen mother **Athaliah,** the daughter of **Ahab.** The alliance between the two kingdoms involves Ahaziah in the revolt of **Jehu** and brings about his death (cf. II Kings 9).

G. Athaliah (22:10–23:21)

Athaliah is the daughter of Ahab and wife of Jehoram. On hearing of the death of her son Azariah, she destroys the **royal family of . . . Judah** (cf. II Kings 11:1-3). Only one escapes, the infant **Joash** (a shortened form of Jehoash). He is hidden by his aunt, **Jeho-shabeath** (Jehosheba in Kings)—the Chronicler adds that she is the **wife of Jehoiada the priest.** Chapter 23 tells how, after seven years, the boy is brought forth from hiding and anointed king. Athaliah is assassinated (cf. II Kings 11:4-20). The Chronicler's account emphasizes the role of the **Levites** in the plot, as well as the reorganization of the temple services. Note that David's organization of the Levites was based on Mosaic legislation (23:18).

H. Joash (24:1-27)

The reign of Joash may be divided into two parts. In his earlier years he **did what was right** under the influence of **Jehoiada** (cf.

II Kings 12:4-16), restoring the temple with the help of a **chest** for contributions. After the death of Jehoiada, Joash turns to evil ways. He orders the death of **Zechariah the son of Jehoiada,** who has proclaimed judgment on Judah. As a result he is defeated by a small force of **Syrians** (cf. II Kings 12:17-18). Note that when God is not with Israel's forces, the enemy with few men can defeat a very large army. On the other hand, but a small army with God's help can defeat a much larger enemy force (cf. 13:3, 13-19). Bedridden because of wounds received in battle, Joash is assassinated by **his servants.** The Chronicler adds that he was not buried in the **tombs of the kings**—a further sign of his degradation (cf. II Kings 12:19-21).

I. AMAZIAH (25:1-28)

This account is based on II Kings 14. The description of the battle with **Edom** has been expanded. Two unnamed prophets with words of warning are introduced by the Chronicler (verses 7-8 and 15-16).

J. UZZIAH (26:1-23)

Uzziah's prosperous reign was one of the longest in Judah's history. The short account of it in II Kings 15:1-7, where he is called Azariah, is expanded by the Chronicler. Uzziah's military victories, building activities, and great interest in husbandry and agriculture are graphically described in verses 6-15. The **Meunites** were probably a desert tribe living east of Edom. According to the Chronicler, Uzziah is stricken with **leprosy** because he burns **incense on the altar** in the temple in defiance of the **priests.**

K. JOTHAM (27:1-9)

Jotham, having ruled as co-regent during his father's affliction (26:21), becomes king at Uzziah's death (cf. II Kings 15:32-38).

The Chronicler expands the earlier account of Jotham's reign by noting his building activities and his defeat of the **Ammonites.** He, like his father, **did what was right in the eyes of the LORD.** A cor was five bushels.

L. AHAZ (28:1-27)

This chapter is based on II Kings 16, with many alterations. Ahaz' apostacies bring on attacks by the Syrians and by the Israelites. In II Kings the **king of Syria** and **Pekah** invade Judah together. Verses 9-15 then give the curious account of the release of the Judean prisoners by the Israelites at the instigation of **Obed** the **prophet.** Ahaz asks the Assyrian king, **Tilgath-pilneser** (see comment on I Chronicles 5:1-26), to intervene against the invading **Edomites** and **Philistines.** In II Kings he asks for help against the coalition of Syria and Israel. The king of Assyria comes—but as an oppressor rather than a deliverer. The iniquitous reign of Ahaz comes to an end with the introduction of Syrian deities into Judah and the closing of the temple at Jerusalem (but cf. II Kings 16:10-18).

M. HEZEKIAH (29:1–32:33)

Because Hezekiah was a God-fearing man and great reformer, the Chronicler found his reign of special interest. The account of it in II Kings 18–20 deals mainly with political events. The Chronicler emphasizes its religious reforms, expanding one verse (II Kings 18:4) into 3 chapters (29–31).

29:3-19. At the very beginning of Hezekiah's reign the **doors** of the temple are **opened** and the sanctuary is **cleansed.** Notice the prominent place given to the **Levites,** in accordance with the Chronicler's religious outlook.

29:20-36. A happy day of rededication follows, with sacrifices, songs of praise led by the Levites, and personal consecration of the people. When the people bring more offerings than the priests can handle, the Levites help them. The Levites are noted as having been **more upright in heart . . . in sanctifying themselves**—that is, in preparing themselves ritually for such service.

30:1-27. After the temple is in order, Hezekiah orders a national observance of the **passover at Jerusalem.** The subjugated Israelites of the northern kingdom are invited. Those in the territory occupied by the Samaritans in the Chronicler's day scorn the invitation, but those farther north accept. The observance is held in the **second month** of the year rather than the first. Many **priests** remain unsanctified and the people—especially those from the north—have to have more time to come to Jerusalem. The postponement is allowed by law. The enthusiasm is such that the feast is prolonged **another seven days.** Cf. another great passover festival in Josiah's time described by the Chronicler (35:1-19).

31:1-21. Hezekiah's religious zeal is shown further in his destruction of pagan cultic centers in both northern and southern kingdoms, his reorganization of the temple personnel, and his efforts to get adequate support for the maintenance of the clergy.

32:1-33. The Chronicler's account of Sennacherib's invasion is abbreviated from II Kings 18:13–20:21. Verses 2-8, which describe the king's frantic efforts to build up the defenses of **Jerusalem,** are taken from an independent source.

N. MANASSEH (33:1-20)

Verses 1-9, describing Manasseh's idolatrous practices, parallel II Kings 21:1-9. The Chronicler then adds new material describing Manasseh's captivity, repentance, and return to purify Jerusalem (verses 10-19). Assyria had much trouble within and without its vast empire during the last part of Ashurbanipal's reign. Thus there may be some historical basis for the Chronicler's statement that Manasseh was brought to **Babylon** in chains and later released, though no mention of this incident is found either in Kings or in the Assyrian records. But Manasseh's repentance and his reforms in Jerusalem, seem contrary to the evidence. The pagan practices which he introduced into Israel's religion were still prevalent in the days of Josiah. The **prayer** mentioned in verse 19 is purportedly preserved in the Prayer of Manasseh in the Apocrypha.

O. AMON (33:21-25)

Amon follows in his father's **evil** ways and is assassinated in the palace (cf. II Kings 21:19-24).

P. JOSIAH (34:1–35:27)

This section parallels quite closely II Kings 22–23, with some abridgment and addition.

34:3-33. According to the Chronicler, Josiah's reforms start **in the twelfth year** of his reign (cf. II Kings 23:4-20). In Kings the reforms are not undertaken until after the discovery of the **book of the law** (cf. II Kings 22:3–23:3). The Chronicler emphasizes the role of the **Levites** in **repairing** the temple and in its services (cf. II Kings 22:3-7).

35:1-19. The Chronicler describes in great detail the celebration of the **passover,** which is simply mentioned in II Kings 23:21-23. Notice again the prominent part played by the Levites in the passover rites.

35:20-27. The tragic death of Josiah is treated in more detail by the Chronicler than in the earlier history (cf. II Kings 23:29-30). In 609 B.C. Pharaoh **Neco** set out with his Egyptian army to **Carchemish** on the upper Euphrates. There he planned to join Assyrian remnants attempting to hold out against the Babylonian mop-up of the overthrown Assyrian Empire. The Chronicler is probably correct in saying that Josiah opposed Neco at the pass of **Megiddo** and was mortally **wounded** in the battle. The unhappy defeat and death of this ideal young king was difficult to justify according to the orthodox dogma of retribution. The Chronicler attempts to do it by stating that Josiah sinned. He wrongfully ignored a divine oracle given to him by Neco himself which forbade him to oppose the pharaoh in battle.

Q. JEHOAHAZ (36:1-4)

Cf. II Kings 23:31-35. A younger son of Josiah named Shallum is crowned by the **people of the land** and takes the throne name Jehoahaz. He reigns only **three months** before he is deposed by Neco and deported to Egypt. In his place Neco sets up his brother **Eliakim** under the throne name **Jehoiakim** and demands a large **tribute.**

R. JEHOIAKIM (36:5-8)

Cf. II Kings 23:34–24:7. In 605 **Nebuchadnezzar** (better Nebuchadrezzar, as in Jeremiah and Ezekiel) defeated Neco at Carchemish (see above on 35:20-27). Neco was driven back to Egypt. Soon after this Nebuchadnezzar succeeded to the Babylonian throne and began demanding tribute from the little western states, including Judah. Possibly at this time he came to Jerusalem and **bound** Jehoiakim **in fetters** and despoiled the temple. However, there is no hint of such an attack elsewhere in the Old Testament or in Nebuchadnezzar's own chronicle. In about 601 an apparent Babylonian attempt to invade Egypt failed. This event may have encouraged Jehoiakim to withhold his tribute to Babylonia (cf. II Kings 24:1-2). As a result Nebuchadnezzar besieged Jerusalem in 598. During the course of the siege Jehoiakim died, probably by assassination (cf. Jeremiah 22:18-19 and 36:30).

S. JEHOIACHIN (36:9-10)

Cf. II Kings 24:8-17 and 25:27-30. Jehoiachin was the throne name of Jeconiah (cf. I Chronicles 3:16-17). That he was more than **eight years old** is indicated by his having wives (cf. II Kings 24:15) and children (cf. Jeremiah 22:28). Perhaps the word **ten** was somehow displaced from his age and came to be added to the **three months** of his reign (cf. II Kings 24:8). **In the spring of the year**—March 16, 597, according to Nebuchadnezzar's chronicle—Jehoiachin capitulated to the siege started before his father's death. He and his family and the leading citizens of Judah were taken to Babylon in the first deportation of exiles. According to II Kings 24:17 and Jeremiah 27:1 **Zedekiah** was not Jehoiachin's **brother** but his uncle, another son of Josiah (cf. I Chronicles 3:15-16).

T. ZEDEKIAH (36:11-21)

Cf. II Kings 25:1-21 and Jeremiah 52:1-27. Like his brothers and nephew, Zedekiah behaves wickedly. Further, he refuses to heed the words of **Jeremiah the prophet.** The **leading priests and the people** join him in scorn of the **prophets,** and as a result **the wrath of the LORD rose against his people, till there was no remedy.** Jerusalem is captured by the Babylonians after a long siege, and the temple is destroyed. The survivors are taken into exile to Babylon—though Jeremiah 52:16, 29 states that the Babylonians left the "poorest of the land" and took only 832 persons. The exile is to last for a **sabbath** consisting of **seventy years.** Apparently it was considered as ending, not with the overthrow of the Babylonian Empire by **Persia** in 539 and the return to Jerusalem, but with the completion of the second temple over twenty years later.

U. THE DECREE OF CYRUS (36:22-23)

This repetition of Ezra 1:1-3a (see comment) may have been added to show that at one time Ezra followed II Chronicles (see Introduction to I Chronicles). More likely, however, its purpose is to bring the book, and the Hebrew Bible, to a hopeful conclusion (cf. the similar hopeful ending in II Kings 25:27-30).

THE BOOK OF EZRA

Charles T. Fritsch

INTRODUCTION

Contents and Sources

The history of Judaism after the Babylonian exile is related in these two books. Centering around certain leaders, the events are as follows:

(1) The return of exiles to Jerusalem in 538 under Shesh-bazzar with the permission of Cyrus (Ezra 1–2). The list of returning exiles in chapter 2, repeated with minor variations in Nehemiah 7:6-73a, actually refers to those returning with Zerubbabel (cf. 2:2).

(2) The rebuilding of the temple under Zerubbabel, beginning in 520, the second year of Darius I (Ezra 3–6). The confusion between Shesh-bazzar and Zerubbabel persists. It is stated that the latter began the building in 538. But because of opposition—including correspondence with Artaxerxes actually pertaining to the later rebuilding of the walls (4:7-22)—he had to postpone it till 520, when rediscovery of the decree of Cyrus cleared the way for its completion.

(3) A return and reforms under Ezra (Ezra 7–10) and the reading of the law by Ezra and its acceptance by the people (Nehemiah 7:73b–10:39)—a misplaced excerpt belonging with

Ezra 7–10). There is uncertainty about the date of Ezra's activity.

(4) The rebuilding of the walls of Jerusalem under Nehemiah. This begins in 445, the twentieth year of Artaxerxes I, under whose authority Nehemiah acts (Nehemiah 1:1–7:73a; 11–13).

The reader of these books is impressed by the number of sources the Chronicler has used. The most important of these are:

(a) Temple records: "the book of the genealogy" (Nehemiah 7:5) and "the Book of the Chronicles" (Nehemiah 12:23), which is not the biblical work of the same name.

(b) The decree of Cyrus, in Hebrew (Ezra 1:1-4) and in Aramaic (6:3-5).

(c) Aramaic sources: mostly correspondence between the enemies of the Jews and the Persian court (Ezra 4:7-22; 5:6-17; 6:2-12) and the letter given to Ezra by Artaxerxes (7:12-26).

(d) Nehemiah's "memoirs" (Nehemiah 1:1–7:73a and portions of chapters 11–13). These passages are written in the first person, in a style distinct from other parts of the books, and universally recognized as the authentic composition of Nehemiah himself.

(e) Ezra's narrative (Ezra 7–10; Nehemiah 7:73b–10:39), part of which is written in the first person and has the appearance of being autobiographical (Ezra 7:27–8:34; 9:1-15).

The Chronicler's interest in records of all kinds, especially genealogies, is shown by the various lists found in the two books:

Ezra 2:2-69; 7:1-5; 8:1-14; 10:18-43;

Nehemiah 7:7-22; 10:1-26; 11:4–12:26.

Place in the Canon

Ezra and Nehemiah were originally part of a larger work that included I and II Chronicles (see Introduction to I Chronicles). In the Hebrew Bible Ezra and Nehemiah precede I and II Chronicles. Together they make up the last four books of the Writings—that section of the Hebrew scriptures that did not fall under "law" or "prophets." It is clear for several reasons that Ezra and Nehemiah were originally attached to the end of the

Chronicler's history, in the correct chronological order. This original order is preserved in the Greek Septuagint as well as in English Bibles.

The separation of Ezra and Nehemiah in our English Bibles rightly emphasizes the importance of the two title personages in the restoration period of Jewish history. However, it obscures the original unity of the writing. This is indicated by the subject matter and by the usage in the Hebrew manuscripts, where the two are found as a single book up until 1448.

That they remained one book in the Septuagint at first is shown by their being in this form in the fourth century manuscript Codex Vaticanus. But Origen, who died in A.D. 254, already knew of their separation in Greek. In the Latin Vulgate Ezra is called "Esdras I" and Nehemiah "Esdras II." Under the influence of the Vulgate the Christian practice has been to treat them as two books.

Date and Authorship

One of the most puzzling problems in these books is the historical order of the two men Ezra and Nehemiah and the relation between their work in establishing the Jewish community after the exile. From the order of the books in the Bible it is natural to assume that Ezra appeared in Jerusalem before Nehemiah. The dates given in the text—for Ezra the seventh year of Artaxerxes (7:7) and for Nehemiah the twentieth year of Artaxerxes (Nehemiah 2:1)—seem to corroborate this view. But this apparently simple chronology raises a number of problems.

If Ezra preceded Nehemiah, it is strange that Nehemiah nowhere mentions Ezra's work in his memoirs. In all of Nehemiah's reforms there is no indication that he is enforcing the law introduced by Ezra and accepted by the people. If Ezra came first, then we must conclude that his reforms were a miserable failure and that Nehemiah had to come just a few years later to reinstitute them. On the other hand, if Nehemiah used his political authority as governor to enforce certain provisions of the Mosaic law, it is understandable that Ezra,

275

coming later, should call for acceptance of this law in its entirety, including more stringent measures about intermarriage with non-Jews.

Eliashib, the high priest when Nehemiah arrives (Nehemiah 3:1), is said to be the father (Ezra 10:6) or grandfather (Nehemiah 12:10-11, 22) of Jehohanan, who is apparently the high priest in the time of Ezra (10:6). In the light of these and other evidences many scholars are convinced that Nehemiah must have preceded Ezra. They have attempted to solve the chronological problems on this basis. Besides the dates mentioned above, these problems include references which appear to make the two men contemporaries (Nehemiah 8:9; 10:1; 12:26, 36). To allow for an overlap in their careers some scholars have conjectured that there may be a textual error in the date of 7:7. They suggest that Ezra came to Jerusalem later in the reign of Artaxerxes, probably in his twenty-seventh or thirty-seventh year.

A much more widely accepted view is that Nehemiah 2:1 means the twentieth year of Artaxerxes I (445) and Ezra 7:7 refers to the seventh year, not of this king (458), but of Artaxerxes II (397). According to this view Nehemiah and Ezra were not contemporaries at all. The references indicating that they were must be considered erroneous.

The confusion about the order of Nehemiah and Ezra has been one of the factors leading many scholars to date the Chronicler at a later time when the sequence of the two leaders was forgotten. But the reversal is not necessarily evidence that the Chronicler was ignorant of their correct order. Rather it is probable that he wanted to include Nehemiah's important role in his overall plan. Therefore he simply appended the memoirs at the conclusion of his own work.

Later copyists are no doubt responsible for several dislocations—most noticeably the placing of part of the Ezra narrative within the Nehemiah memoirs (Nehemiah 7:73b-10:39). They were also responsible for inserting the references associating Ezra and Nehemiah. An increasing number of scholars now recognize that the most natural date for the Chronicler's writing is soon after the last event he describes—that is, the first decades of the fourth century (see Introduction to I Chronicles). Assuming such a date, it is not unlikely that the Chronicler was a disciple of Ezra—or possibly even Ezra himself. The portion of Ezra's narrative in the first person (7:27–8:34; 9:1-15) displays to some extent the Chronicler's characteristic style.

These two books form the conclusion and climax of the Chronicler's work. In them he proclaims with unshakable assurance the saving acts of God in the days since the exile whereby the Jewish community, delivered from bondage, was brought again into the Land of Promise.

I. THE RETURN UNDER SHESHBAZZAR (1:1–2:70)

1:1-4. *The Decree of Cyrus.* Verses 1-3*a* are repeated in II Chronicles 36:22-23. In fulfillment of the prophecy of **Jeremiah** (cf. Jeremiah 29:10) God **stirred up the spirit of Cyrus** to proclaim an edict of deliverance for the Jewish people. The **first year** refers to Cyrus' first regnal year (538) as ruler of the former Babylonian Empire. He had been **king of Persia** about twenty years before capturing Babylon in 539.

1:2-4. The decree not only orders the rebuilding of the temple but also permits **whoever is among you of all his people** to go to Jerusalem. **All** here fits in with the Chronicler's idea that northern Israelites who had been in preexilic Jerusalem were also among those who returned. Jews remaining in Babylon are invited to assist the venture with their contributions. Another version of this decree in Aramaic is found in 6:3-5. There is no reason to doubt the essential authenticity of either account. The Hebrew document may represent the oral **proclamation** made throughout the empire to all Jews. The Aramaic text is in the form of a written memorandum of a king or other public official.

1:5-11. *The Return.* Those who return are the family heads of the tribes of **Judah and Benjamin,** who according to the Chonicler constitute the postexilic community. Also returning are the **priests** and **Levites,** who are the religious personnel needed for the temple services. In accordance with the decree the returning exiles are given gifts of money and **goods** by their neighbors who remain behind.

As a royal gesture of good will Cyrus returns the precious **vessels** taken by **Nebuchadnezzar** when he detroyed the temple. They are put into the hands of **Shesh-bazzar,** who is probably to be identified with Shenazzar, a younger son of Jehoiachin, the king of Judah taken into exile by Nebuchadnezzar in 597. Some of the Hebrew terms for the vessels in verses 9-11 are not clear, and the figures in the Hebrew text are hopelessly confused. Those in the Revised Standard Version are taken from I Esdras.

2:1-70. *The List of Returning Jews.* The text assumes that this list refers to those who returned to Jerusalem under Shesh-bazzar in the days of Cyrus. The list itself, however, does not include his name. Actually a careful study of the document indicates that it is a composite census list, made up of data drawn from different sources. It is repeated with minor variations in Nehemiah 7:6-73*a.* In its present form it may come from Nehemiah's day.

2:2*a. A List of Leaders.* Eleven names are given here without any genealogy, indicating perhaps that they are well-known people. There are twelve persons listed in Nehemiah 7:7. **Zerubbabel** is the grandson of Jehoiachin and nephew of Shesh-bazzar (see above on 1:5-11). **Jeshua** is called "Joshua the high priest" in Haggai and Zechariah. Both are known to have been leaders of the postexilic Jewish community in the time of Darius I during the rebuilding of the temple. Their position at the head of this list may indicate that they led a group of returning exiles shortly before the rebuilding. Or it may be that at one time they were leaders of the returned exiles, since possibly the eleven men named were not contemporary but successive. However, it is evident that the Chronicler assumed one of two things:

(1) Zerubbabel and Jeshua accompanied Shesh-bazzar in 538 and took over the leadership from him on arriving in Jerusalem.

(2) More probably, Shesh-bazzar and Zerubbabel were alternate names for the same man.

2:2b-35. *A List of Laymen.* These are classified by families (verses 3-20) and by cities (verses 21-35). The numbers often differ from those in the Nehemiah list (for example, cf. verses 5-6 with Nehemiah 7:10-11). **Sons of** should be understood as "descendants of," since the list refers to rather remote ancestors. There are various types of personal names included in this list. Some are of Babylonian and Persian derivation. **Gibbar** (verse 20) is given in Nehemiah 7:25 as Gibeon. As a place name this should not appear before verse 25 in a list which works north. It may be the personal name Gaber.

2:21-35. The cities mentioned here fall into three major groups:

(1) those in the mountainous area from **Bethlehem** north to **Harim** (verses 21-32);

(2) those to the west in the coastal area (verse 33);

(3) those to the east in the Jordan Valley (verses 34-35).

The other Elam in verse 31 is in contrast with the Elam in verse 7.

2:36-58. *Lists of Temple Personnel.* First the **priests** are mentioned. They belong to four families. **Jeshua** is probably to be identified with the high priest who was a contemporary of Zerubbabel (cf. verse 2; 10:18). The number of priests (4,289) is extremely large, almost a tenth of all those returning to Jerusalem.

2:40. In Ezra-Nehemiah, the priests are generally distinguished from the **Levites,** who are here mentioned next. They number only **seventy-four.** Evidently Levites were not inclined to leave Babylonia for Jerusalem, where they would be doing menial tasks in the temple (cf. Ezekiel 44:9-14 and Nehemiah 10:13). Or possibly only a few Levites had been taken into captivity by Nebuchadnezzar.

2:41. Next in order come the **singers,** who are the descendants of **Asaph** (cf. I Chronicles 16:4-6). The singers are identified with the Levites in 3:10, throughout the Chronicles, and in several verses of Nehemiah 11-12. In this passage and in several others the Levites are carefully distinguished from the singers.

2:42. The **gatekeepers** follow next in order. Their duties are described in I Chronicles 9:17-32, where they are identified with the Levites. In this passage, as well as in others, they are distinguished from the Levites.

2:43-54. After the gatekeepers the **temple servants** are listed. According to 8:20 they were "set apart" (i.e. given) by David and his officials to serve the Levites. The large number of foreign names in the list probably indicates that most of this group were captives of war. Their special place of residence was on the Ophel mount, opposite the Water Gate, which probably led out to the spring of Gihon (Nehemiah 3:26). In I Chronicles 9:2, as well as here, they are distinguished from the Levites. But like the singers and gatekeepers they were eventually incorporated into the Levitical order (cf. I Chronicles 23:28).

2:55-58. The last list of temple personnel identifies the **sons of Solomon's servants.** The origin and duties of this special class of people are somewhat obscure. They may have been descended from the laborers who Solomon drafted for the building of the temple (cf. I Kings 5:13-18). They are included in the total in verse 58 and also among the temple servants in Nehemiah 10:28.

2:59-63. *Persons Lacking Genealogies.* The presence of this brief list reveals the keen interest of the people in racial and religious purity. The uncertainty of the priests' genealogies posed a special problem since they might contaminate the holiness of the temple. **Governor** here is a Persian title, *tirshatha*. It is applied specifically to Nehemiah in Nehemiah 8:9; 10:1. No doubt it was applicable also to Shesh-bazzar and Zerubbabel, who had similar authority from Persian rulers. The persons designated here depends on the date of this part of the list. The **Urim and Thummim** refer to the sacred lot (see comment on I Samuel 14:36-46). There is no other clear evidence that this method of ascertaining the divine will was in use in postexilic times.

2:64-67. *Numerical Summaries.* The total number of return-ees—42,360—is found also in Nehemiah 7:66 and I Esdras 5:41. However, the preceding figures in the three lists disagree at various points and in no case add up to the total. The **male and female singers** were professional entertainers employed at banquets, feasts, and funerals. They are not to be confused with the temple singers in verse 41.

2:68-70. *Summaries of Gifts.* These **offerings** are given by the people for the purpose of rebuilding the temple. The parallel passage in Nehemiah 7:70-73a differs markedly in details and the stated amounts of the gifts. **When they came to the house of the LORD** must refer to the **site** of the temple, which now lies in ruins. **Darics** were Persian coins first issued by Darius I. They were probably not in use during the early years of his reign when the temple was being built. A mina equaled one and a quarter pounds. Verse 70 describes ideally the restored condition of the land.

II. THE RECONSTRUCTION OF THE TEMPLE UNDER ZERUBBABEL (3:1–6:22)

3:1-6a. *Reestablishment of Altar and Sacrifices.* The restoration begins with the resumption of the cult. The rebuilding of the altar of **burnt offerings** being the first step. In David's time there was an altar in Jerusalem before the temple was built (II Samuel 24:25). After the destruction of the temple sacrifices were still offered there (Jeremiah 41:5). Now it is of utmost importance that an altar be set up in Jerusalem before the temple is rebuilt.

3:1-2a. In what year the **seventh month** falls is not clear. The Chronicler apparently has in mind the first year of Cyrus (cf. 1:1; 3:8a). But since **Jeshua** and **Zerubbabel** are said to have built the altar, his source probably meant a year in the time of Darius I. Once again the Chronicler has telescoped the work of Zerubbabel with that of his uncle, Shesh-bazzar (see above on 2:2a). Here Jeshua precedes Zerubbabel, probably because this passage deals with cultic matters and Jeshua is the high priest of the restored community. On **son of Shealtiel** see comment on I Chronicles 3:17-24.

3:2b-3. The altar is built **as it is written in the law of Moses the man of God** (the Mosaic regulation is in Exodus 20:25). The reason for the hasty erection of the altar is said to be **the fear which was upon them because of the peoples of the lands.** With the altar set up, the returnees will be assured of God's help against their foes.

3:4-6a. The regulations for the sacrifices and set feasts are reinstated before work is started on rebuilding the temple. This is in line with the Chronicler's special interest in cultic matters. The sacrifices for the **feast of booths,** or tabernacles, are described in Numbers 29:12-38. On the **continual burnt offerings** cf. Exodus 29:38-42 and Numbers 28:3-8. On the sacrifices connected with the celebration of the **new moon** cf. Numbers 28:11-15. On the **appointed feasts** cf. Leviticus 23:2-37 and II Chronicles 8:13. The **freewill offering** could be offered by individuals on great feast days or on any other occasion.

3:6b-13. *The Laying of the Foundation.* This account is strongly reminiscent of the building of Solomon's temple (I Kings 5–6; II Chronicles 2–3). The **grant . . . from Cyrus** probably refers simply to Cyrus' permission to rebuild the temple and his promise of help. Here Zerubbabel and Jeshua are said to have begun the work by laying the foundation, though in 5:16 this is ascribed to Shesh-bazzar (see above on 2:2a; 3:1-2a for an explanation of this apparent confusion). The Chronicler's special interest in the **Levites** is shown by the important role they play in the work—in spite of the small number that have returned from Babylonia (cf. 2:40). On the minimum age limit of the Levites cf. I Chronicles 23:24, 27.

3:10-13. The people rejoice when the **foundation** is laid. **Priests and Levites** lead the service of praise and thanksgiving instituted by David (cf. I Chronicles 15:16). The refrain, from Psalm 136:1, is used frequently by the Chronicler (I Chronicles 16:34; II Chronicles 5:13; 7:3; and 20:21). Intermingled with the

joyful shout is the **sound of . . . weeping,** for many of the people remember the magnificence of the old temple destroyed by Nebuchadnezzar.

4:1-5. *Samaritan Opposition.* The **adversaries of Judah and Benjamin** are the descendants of the mixed population of the province of Samaria, formerly the northern kingdom of Israel. When the Assyrians took this area in 722, they deported many Israelites and resettled the land with foreigners (cf. II Kings 17:24). **Esarhaddon** (681-669) evidently followed the same policy, since the present adversaries claim to have been in the land since his time. These Samaritans offer assistance in building the temple. They claim to worship the same God as the Jews. Zerubbabel and Jeshua refuse their offer on the technicality that Cyrus has given permission only to the Jews to rebuild the temple. This exclusiveness of the Jews arouses the hostility of the **people of the land,** who oppose them **all the days of Cyrus . . . , even until the reign of Darius.**

4:6-24. *Later Samaritan Interference.* Chapters 5 and 6 deal with the building of the temple in the reign of Darius I. This section, which describes further Samaritan opposition in the days of Darius' son **Ahasuerus** (Xerxes I, 486-465) and grandson **Artaxerxes** I (465-424), is therefore chronologically out of order. The correspondence with Artaxerxes about the rebuilding of Jerusalem must have occurred only a short time before Nehemiah came to the city in 445. The Chronicler has placed this material about seventy years too early. This was to reinforce his idea that the Samaritans were wholly responsible for the delay in completing the rebuilding of the temple.

4:7-16. A **letter** to **Artaxerxes** accusing the Jews is described and quoted in full in the **Aramaic** language, which begins in verse 8 and continues through 6:18. It appears from verses 7-8 that there may originally have been two letters which have been combined by the Chronicler. Because of the **rebellious** nature of the Jewish people the king is advised to halt the **rebuilding** of Jerusalem. When restored, the city would pose a threat to the Persian overlords. This concern with the **city** and its **walls** of course does not fit the Chronicler's context, which has to do with opposition to rebuilding the temple. **Bishlam** is probably not a man's name. It may be a greeting, "in peace," as in the Septuagint. **Osnapper** is probably a corruption of Ashurbanipal, an Assyrian king (around 669-629). **Beyond the River** refers to the country west of the Euphrates River.

4:17-24. In his **answer** Artaxerxes reports that the records confirm that Jerusalem has been rebellious throughout its history. Therefore he decrees that all work on the rebuilding of the city must stop. **Plainly** in verse 18 means "in translation." In verse 24 the Chronicler attempts to tie all this into his account. He declares that as a result of the letters, work on the temple is halted **until the second year of the reign of Darius** (cf. verse 5).

5:1–6:22. *The Completion of the Temple.* The temple narrative, interrupted after 4:5, now continues. The **Jews** were discouraged by the Samaritans in their first attempt to rebuild the temple (4:4). Now they are spurred on to resume their work by **Haggai and Zechariah.** The exhortations of these prophets are recorded in the books bearing their names. According to Zechariah 1:1 Zechariah was not the **son** but the grandson of **Iddo.**

5:3-5. When the people start to work, a new difficulty immediately develops. Officials of the Persian government, **Tattenai** and **Shethar-bozenai,** come to investigate. They want to know who has given permission to rebuild the temple. On receiving a reply—which is not reported till verses 11-16—they let the work proceed pending consultation with the king.

5:6-17. Tattenai writes a **letter** to Darius about the situation. He notes his own concern and reports the answer the Jewish **elders** gave him when questioned about their building activity. In a remarkable confession of guilt they have admitted that God **gave them into the hand of Nebuchadnezzar** because of their unfaithfulness. They claim that **Cyrus** issued a **decree** authorizing **Shesh-bazzar** to rebuild the temple. On the basis of this he **laid the foundations of the house of God** (contrast 3:8-10, where Zerubbabel and Jeshua are said to have begun the work on the temple). The letter closes with the suggestion that the **royal archives** be searched for this decree. The Aramaic word translated **huge** (verse 8) and **great** (6:4) is of uncertain meaning. Discovery of an inscription applying it to small objects has shown that it does not refer to the size of the **stones.**

6:1-12. Darius orders a search for the document, which is discovered in **Ecbatana,** the summer **capital** of Cyrus and his successors. The Aramaic form of the edict, given here, differs slightly from the Hebrew text in 1:2-4. This version seems to be an expansion of the simple permission to return. Cf. the measurements of Solomon's temple (I Kings 6:2; II Chronicles 3:3), which differ from those given here in verse 3 (one dimension is missing). **Three** rows of **stones** (on **great** see above on 5:6-17) and **one** row of **timber** are specified for the walls of the inner court. Darius then issues a new decree that the Persian officials are to support the work with funds. He threatens those who attempt to **alter** this decree with severe punishment.

6:13-22. In accordance with the decree of Darius, and with the cooperation of the Persian officials, the Jews complete the temple on the **third . . . of Adar, in the sixth year . . . of Darius,** i.e. March 12, 515. The joyful **dedication** ceremonies are not to be compared with Solomon's dedicatory service, where thousands of animals were sacrificed (cf. I Kings 8; II Chronicles 5–7). A fitting climax to these ceremonies is the celebration of the two great feasts, **passover** and the **feast of unleavened bread.** Hebrew is resumed in verse 19, following the Aramaic section (4:8–6:18). **King of Assyria** is an anachronism in the Persian period. In the context the phrase would naturally refer to Darius.

III. THE RETURN UNDER EZRA (7:1–8:36)

7:1-28. *Ezra's Commission.* **After this** is literally "after these things." The interval it denotes extends from the completion of the temple in 515 to the coming of Ezra to Jerusalem **in the reign of Artaxerxes**—probably over a century later, in 397 (see Introduction).

7:1-10. The genealogy of Ezra traces his ancestry back to the chief priest **Aaron.** He is not only a priest (cf. verses 11-12, 21) but also a **scribe skilled in the law of Moses.** The scribe was originally an official of the royal court (cf. II Samuel 8:17). The position became associated with the studying and copying of the law. Ezra is the ideal representative of this later type of scribe. His deep devotion to the law throughout his life is shown by his studying, obeying, and teaching it.

7:11-26. In a **letter** in the Aramaic language **King Artaxerxes** authorizes Ezra to go to Jerusalem with a party of compatriots. There they are to investigate the moral and religious conditions of the Jews in the homeland and deliver gifts gathered in **Babylonia** for the support of the temple. The king promises additional funds, if needed, from the royal **treasury.** He orders the provincial **treasures** to provide Ezra with any further funds and supplies he requires. He also exempts the temple personnel from taxes and forced labor. Ezra is directed to **appoint magistrates and judges** with full authority to enforce **the law of your God and the law of the king.** In verse 22 a talent was sixty-two and a half pounds, a cor five bushels, and a bath five gallons.

7:27-28. In this hymn of praise Ezra for the first time appears as the speaker. From here through chapter 9 (except 8:35-36) the so-called Ezra memoirs are in the first person. In chapter 10 and the continuation in Nehemiah 7:73*b*–10:39 the narrative is in the third person.

8:1-36. *Ezra's Journey to Jerusalem.* Just as a list of returnees under Zerubbabel and Jeshua is given in chapter 2, so a list of those who return under Ezra is given here. Unlike the earlier list, this begins with the priests (verse 2), though there is no heading to identify them. The lay families are then named. Many of the names duplicate those in 2:1-15.

8:15-20. Ezra gathers his group at **Ahava,** an unknown site by a **river** in Babylonia, in order to make final preparations for the trip. Then he discovers that there are no Levites in the company. Relatively few joined Zerubbabel's group (2:40). Now **none of the sons of Levi** have volunteered to return to Jerusalem. Through the efforts of **Iddo** from **Casiphia** (both unknown) thirty-eight Levites are recruited for the trip, as well as two hundred and twenty **temple servants** (see above on 2:43-54).

8:21-36. After fasting and prayer to insure a safe journey, Ezra entrusts the precious gifts of **gold** and **silver** to the **priests** for safekeeping during the trip. The exaggerated amounts recall the Chronicler's extravagant figures where the temple is concerned (cf. I Chronicles 21:25; 29:1-9; on **darics** see above on 2:68-70). Ezra and his party set out and arrive at Jerusalem after a four-month journey (7:9). The gifts are handed to the priests and Levites in the temple, and sacrifices are offered in thanksgiving for bringing the group safely to Jerusalem. The king's orders are delivered to the provincial authorities.

IV. RELIGIOUS REFORMS (9:1–10:44)

The reforms attributed to Ezra include the dissolution of mixed marriages narrated here and the reading of the law and its acceptance by the people described in Nehemiah 7:73*b*–10:39. The order in which they belong is uncertain. In I Esdras 8:68–9:55 the account of the mixed marriages is followed by the reading of the law, indicating that Nehemiah 7:73*b*–10:39 belongs after Ezra 10. On the other hand, whereas the assembly about mixed marriages is dated in the ninth month (10:9), the reading of the law is placed in the seventh month (Nehemiah 8:2). The absence of a year date in either case may mean that the seventh year of Artaxerxes, when Ezra arrived in Jerusalem, is still to be understood (cf. 7:7-9; 8:31). On this basis Nehemiah 7:73*b*–8:18, at least, should be inserted before Ezra 9 (see comment on Nehemiah 9:1-5*a*). Historically it seems likely that Ezra would first acquaint the people with the law and win their acceptance of it. After this he could undertake the severe measure of demanding that a considerable number of leading citizens divorce their foreign wives.

9:1-5. *The Problem of Mixed Marriages.* The **officials** of the community inform Ezra that many Jews, including **priests and**

Levites, have been intermarrying with **the peoples of the lands.** These are described as Israel's enemies of old. By these mixed marriages pagan practices are being introduced into the community which corrupt both religion and society. On hearing this news Ezra tears his clothes and pulls out his hair as signs of his deep remorse. After the people have **gathered round** him throughout the day to see this strange spectacle, Ezra falls on his **knees** and lifts his **hands** in prayer.

9:6-15. *Ezra's Prayer.* This prayer of confession and intercession is one of the great prayers of the Bible. Ezra reviews the past sins of his people which brought on their suffering and humiliation under foreign rulers. Even now, when their condition is better because of the beneficent rule of the Persian kings, the people **have** again **forsaken** the **commandments** of God. By intermarrying with the surrounding peoples they have incurred God's wrath. How can this **remnant** stand before a just God in this sinful condition? The Hebrew word rendered **protection** in verse 9 means "wall." It should probably be so translated, since Ezra is listing things which the returnees have actually accomplished. The laws ascribed to the prophets in verses 10-12 are more properly derived from the Deuteronomic tradition (cf. Deuteronomy 7:1-3, 12; 23:6), which of course was deeply influenced by the prophets.

10:1-5. *Public Confession of Guilt.* Ezra's prayer ends on the note of fear that God can no longer do anything for the people. It produces the immediate effect that Ezra has wanted: **the people wept bitterly** because of their sins. Through their representative, **Shecaniah,** they confess their guilt and propose that drastic action be taken. They vow before God that they will **put away** the foreign **wives and their children** in accordance with the regulations set up by Ezra.

10:6-17. *The Public Assembly.* After Ezra has **spent the night** in fasting, a proclamation is sent forth to the **returned exiles** to **assemble at Jerusalem.** Attendance is mandatory under threat of severe punishment. The **chamber of Jehohanan** to which Ezra withdraws for the night probably refers to a temple chamber or cell where Jehohanan, the high priest, has his living quarters. The assembly meets in the **ninth month** (December; see above on 9:1–10:44), the beginning of the rainy season. Ezra simply repeats the recommendation of Shecaniah (cf. verse 3) and the people acquiesce. The procedure of the reform is outlined and carried out with little opposition.

10:18-44. *A List of Offenders.* The list of those who have **married foreign women** includes **priests** (verses 18-22), **Levites** (verse 23), one of the **singers** and three **gatekeepers** (verse 24), and certain lay families of Israel (verses 25-44). All these give up their wives and **children.**

THE BOOK OF NEHEMIAH

Charles T. Fritsch

INTRODUCTION

See the Introduction to Ezra.

I. NEHEMIAH'S COMING TO JERUSALEM (1:1–7:73a)

1:1-11a. Nehemiah's Concern for Jerusalem. From his brother **Hanani** (cf. 7:2) and a group of companions who have just come from **Judah,** Nehemiah receives word that there is **great trouble** in the **province,** i.e. Judah. The **wall of Jerusalem** has been breached and **its gates . . . destroyed by fire.**

1:1b-3. The date is given as **Chislev**—that is, the ninth month (December), **in the twentieth year.** But later events are dated in **Nisan**—that is, the first month (April), in the same year. Some scholars explain this apparent discrepancy as indicating that the author counted from an autumn new year, as was the custom in preexilic Judah, even though the Babylonian calendar beginning in the spring was the standard throughout the Persian Empire. Others assume a copying error in the first date—that it should read "in the nineteenth year of Artaxerxes." In either case the first date is December 446 and the second April 445 (see Introduction to Ezra). **Susa,** the capital of ancient Elam, became

290

the **capital** of the Persian Empire. Whereas Ezra and the Chronicler emphasize returned exiles, Nehemiah views the inhabitants of Judah as those **who escaped exile.** They were the descendants of those left in the land by Nebuchadnezzar.

1:4-11a. Nehemiah is overcome with grief at the news of the shocking conditions in Judah. He prays to the LORD **God of heaven** for his **people.** His prayer, like Ezra's (Ezra 9:6-15), is largely composed of Deuteronomic phrases. It includes a confession of past sins and an appeal to God to **hear the prayer of thy servant.** Some scholars believe the prayer was inserted into Nehemiah's memoirs by the Chronicler. Since **this man**—meaning the king—has not previously been mentioned, it has been suggested that verse 11a, or a part of it, originally followed 2:4.

1:11b–2:10. *Permission to Go to Jerusalem.* As **cupbearer to the king**—and **queen** (verse 6)—Nehemiah holds one of the highest positions in the Persian court. As an intimate servant he was probably a eunuch. According to Deuteronomy 23:1 this would exclude him from the Jewish community, but in postexilic times a more lenient attitude was taken (cf. Isaiah 56:3-5). On the date in verse 1 see above on 1:1b-3. Nehemiah's request to visit Jerusalem is granted by the king. He is given letters of introduction to **governors of the province Beyond the River**—that is, west of the Euphrates. He also gets permission to use **timber** from the **king's forest** in Lebanon for construction work in Jerusalem.

2:9-10. Opposition is immediately encountered. **Sanballat,** a Samaritan leader from Beth-horon in Ephraim, and **Tobiah,** from Ammon in Transjordan, are displeased to hear that **someone had come to seek the welfare of the children of Israel.** Actually they are afraid that their power over Judah will be curtailed with the coming of a royally supported official such as Nehemiah.

2:11-20. *Inspection of the Wall.* Nehemiah, who alone is mounted, secretly sets out at night with a few servants to inspect the battered **walls of Jerusalem.** He will formulate his plans for reconstruction.

2:13-16. Locating the gates is a difficult problem because of uncertainty about the area of Jerusalem in Nehemiah's day. Some scholars believe that the ruined walls surrounded only the eastern hill, with little enlargement from the time of Solomon. Others maintain that the walls had been extended by later kings of Judah across the central valley and around the western hill. If the smaller limit is correct, the **Valley Gate** probably was on the western side of the old City of David, opening into the central valley. If this valley was already within the walls, this gate must have been on the southern or western side of the newer wall opening into the Hinnom Valley.

The **Jackal's Well** (Hebrew "Dragon Well") could be a name for the spring En-rogel (cf. I Kings 1:9). The refuse of the city was carried to the Valley of Hinnom through the **Dung Gate** in the southern part of the wall. The **Fountain Gate** on the southeast led either to En-rogel or to the Gihon Spring. The **King's Pool** was no doubt a reservoir collecting water from Gihon.

2:17-20. Nehemiah informs the Jewish leaders and the people of the city of his plans to build the wall. They enthusiastically respond, **Let us rise up and build.** Added to the opposition noted in verse 10 is **Geshem** from the province of Arabia south of Judah. Probably unaware of Nehemiah's official capacity as an emissary of the king, the three enemies consider this new effort of the Jews as rebellion.

3:1-32. *Workers Rebuilding the Wall.* The reconstruction of the wall and its gates begins at the **Sheep Gate.** This was probably in the northeastern part of the city wall, near the temple, since **Eliashib the high priest . . . with his brethren the priests** works on this gate. The mention of Eliashib as high priest in the days of Nehemiah is important for the dating of Nehemiah and Ezra (see Introduction to Ezra).

3:3-32. The rebuilding of the gates and walls proceeds in the following order:

(1) the **Fish Gate,** on the northern part of the wall (verses 3-5);

(2) the **Old Gate,** or more accurately the "Gate of the Old," presumably on the western side (verses 6-12);

(3) the **Valley Gate,** the **Dung Gate,** and the **Fountain Gate** (verses 13-15; see above on 2:13-16);

(4) the **Water Gate** on the eastern, probably leading to the Gihon Spring (verse 26);

(5) the **Horse Gate** (verse 28) and the **Muster Gate** (verse 31), also on the east, near the temple area.

Finally the **Sheep Gate** is mentioned again (verse 32), a full circuit having been made counterclockwise around the walls of the city. On the problem of locating these and other places mentioned in this chapter see above on 2:13-16. Note that women also take part in the work of restoring the walls (verse 12).

4:1-12. *Opposition of Sanballat and Tobiah.* The opposition noted in 2:10, 19 now takes on more concrete form with the increased activity of the Jewish workers. Nehemiah's reaction to the taunting questions of Sanballat and Tobiah is an imprecatory prayer (verses 4-5). It is reminiscent of certain psalms (cf. Psalms 54 and 64) and prophetic outbursts against the enemy (cf. Jeremiah 18:23 and 20:11-12). Insults soon give way to threats of attack. A lament by **Judah**—that is, the community—shows the inner weakness of the people (verse 10; contrast verse 6). The enemy from without is planning a secret attack. The rumor of attack is confirmed by those coming into Jerusalem from outlying areas (verse 12).

4:13-23. *Nehemiah's Plans for Defense.* But Nehemiah cannot easily be discouraged. In the face of danger he sets up a defense strategy for the workers. He sets armed groups in the **open places** under the cover of the **wall** where they can maneuver more freely if attacked. Armed men also take their places among the workers. The workers themselves labor **with one hand** and hold their weapons in the other. A special alarm system is set up to **rally** the people to any place of attack along the wall. Finally Nehemiah orders whose who live outside the city to come within its protecting walls during this time of danger. As the leader of the people he sets the example of devoted service and hard work for all to follow.

5:1-19. *Relief for the Poor.* The poor cry out to Nehemiah that they desperately need food for their families. They have no **money** to buy the bare necessities of life. They cannot borrow because they have no property to put up as collateral. They refuse to see their families starve while their rich neighbors prosper and refuse to give them aid. Those with some property have mortgaged it **to get grain.** Others have even sold their children into slavery in order to repay the money they have **borrowed** for the **king's tax.**

5:6-13. When Nehemiah hears these protests he becomes **very angry.** He proposes that **interest** no longer be charged on borrowed money and that everything that has been taken on pledges be restored. The people agree to his proposal and the bargain is sealed by an **oath.** Nehemiah's symbolic act in emptying his **lap** (better "sash," which was used like a pocket for carrying money) emphasizes the penalties for breaking the pledge.

5:14-19. Nehemiah's administration as governor lasts **twelve years**—445-433. During that time he claims that he has not taken any money from the people for his own support. Indeed, he has never even taken the money allowed him for his household expenses.

6:1-14. *Plots Against Nehemiah.* On hearing of the progress on the wall **Sanballat** and **Geshem** (cf. 2:19) try to lure Nehemiah out of the city. They propose a meeting in **Ono,** on the plain of Sharon, northwest of Jerusalem. Nehemiah anticipates danger. He refuses the invitation on the basis of the **work** he has to do in Jerusalem.

6:5-9. Sanballat next accuses Nehemiah of planning a rebellion and setting himself up as **king** in Judah. Nehemiah vehemently denies this.

6:10-13. Finally Tobiah and Sanballat hire **Shemaiah,** who is probably a priest. He invites Nehemiah to take shelter **within the temple** to escape being murdered. Nehemiah refuses to do this for two reasons. First, he is no priest and would violate the sanctity of the temple if he entered it. Second, he will not put his own personal safety above that of his fellow Jews.

6:15-19. *Completion of the Wall.* The period of time for the

completion of the wall is given as **fifty-two days.** The success of
the project is a witness to the **nations** of the people's zeal and
God's goodness. **Tobiah** still remains a thorn in the flesh for
Nehemiah, however. His marriage into an eminent Jewish
family gives him contact with many important people in Judah,
who serve his evil ends as spies and propogandists.

7:1-73a. *A List of Returning Jews.* After the city is secured,
Nehemiah decides to take a census—probably to replenish the
population of Jerusalem (verse 4). It is in the course of taking the
census that the list of those who returned to Jerusalem under
Zerubbabel is found, presumably in the temple (verse 5*b*). The
list largely duplicates Ezra 2:1-70 (see comment); the differences are very slight.

II. Further Reforms of Ezra (7:73*b*–10:39)

At this place in the narrative the Nehemiah memoirs break off
and Ezra reappears as the main character. Apparently this
section is a misplaced part of the Ezra narrative (see comment on
Ezra 9:1–10:44 and below on 9:1-5*a*).

7:73*b*–8:12. *The Reading of the Law.* The people gather
before the **Water Gate** to have the law read to them by Ezra **on
the first day of the seventh month.** If this refers to Ezra's first
year in Jerusalem, the time is only two months after his arrival
(cf. Ezra 7:7-9). **The book of the law of Moses** was probably not
the Pentateuch—the first five books of the Bible—as we know it,
but only certain portions of it. Ezra reads the text in Hebrew
(verse 3), and the Levites translate it aloud in Aramaic, the
common speech in postexilic Palestine. From this procedure
developed the Targums, the Aramaic translation of the Old
Testament.

8:9-12. On hearing the law read, the people **weep** because of
their sins and the punishment which is to come upon them.
They are told to rejoice, however, because **this day is holy**—a
day on which they have come to hear again the words of the law.
If, as is probable, Ezra and Nehemiah were not contemporaries

(see Introduction to Ezra) **Nehemiah, who was the governor** must be a later addition.

8:13-18. *Celebration of the Feast of Booths.* A closer reading of the law by the secular and ecclesiastical leaders of the community leads to the discovery that they have not kept the **feast of the seventh month**—which was the feast of booths, or tabernacles—as prescribed by Moses. The observance described here is different in some details from that prescribed in the Mosaic law. That the feast has not been observed since the days of **Jeshua** (Joshua) **the son of Nun** must refer to some special phase of the ritual. The Chronicler has mentioned its observance earlier (II Chronicles 8:13; Ezra 3:4). The **Gate of Ephraim**, from which the road led to Ephraim, was located in the northern section of the city wall.

9:1-5a. *A Time of Mourning.* Some scholars have suggested that this chapter should follow Ezra 9–10. The deep mourning of the people would be more understandable if it were due, not to the reading of the law, but to concern over mixed marriages. **Separated themselves from all foreigners** makes no sense following chapter 8, but it does mean something if it refers to the divorce proceedings described in Ezra 10. The date in verse 1 would then be the **twenty-fourth** day of the first month (Nisan, or April; cf. Ezra 10:17). **A fourth of the day** means three hours.

9:5b-37. *A Confession of Sin.* This penitential psalm is an independent unit introduced here because it seems to reflect generally the attitude of the people. **And Ezra said,** which is not found in the Hebrew text, is supplied from the Septuagint. The recital of God's mighty acts from creation to the conquest of Canaan is followed by confession of sin and the acknowledgment of God's mercy, even in time of punishment. The psalm ends on the note of despair as the writer describes the sad plight in which the people find themselves.

9:38–10:39. *A Renewal Covenant.* **Because of all this,** or better "in spite of all this"—that is, the sorrow and suffering which they are enduring—the people renew their covenant relationship with God. They **set their seal** to the pledge they make.

10:1-39. This list begins with Nehemiah and **Zedekiah,** the secular authorities of the community, and includes **priests** (verses 3-8), **Levites** (verses 9-13), and laymen (verses 14-27). It is incorporated here as naming those connected with the covenant ceremony. However, closer study shows that the list is from a different source. For example, Ezra's name is not found, and the order of the groups in 9:38 is the reverse of that found in the listings themselves.

10:28-39. The covenant obligations of the community are assumed under a **curse** and **oath** formula **to walk in God's law.** The obligations include avoidance of mixed marriages, observance of the **sabbath,** as well as the sabbatical year, and support of the temple and its personnel. Because of the similar topics it has been suggested that the author of this material based it on Nehemiah's account in chapter 13.

III. FURTHER ACTIVITIES OF NEHEMIAH (11:1–13:31)

11:1–12:26. *Various Lists.* Since this material has no relationship with what immediately precedes, it probably is to be connected with 7:73*a* or, more specifically, with 7:4-5*a*. The problem of repopulating Jerusalem would certainly have something to do with Nehemiah's desire to take a census. It is proposed that a tenth of the population live in the **holy city.** There follow lists of the **chiefs of the provinces who lived in Jerusalem** and of the **villages** and towns settled by Jews outside of Jerusalem. In 11:23 **the king** may refer to a Persian ruler.

12:1-26. This is a list of **the priests and the Levites** serving under the various high priests, whose genealogy is given in verses 10-11. **Jonathan** is a mistake for **Johanan** (cf. verses 22-23) or Jehohanan, the high priest in Ezra's time (Ezra 10:6; see Introduction to Ezra). **Darius the Persian** may refer to either Darius II (423-404) or Darius III (336-331). According to the Jewish historian Josephus, **Jaddua** was the high priest when Palestine was taken by Alexander the Great (333). Therefore, Darius III may be meant. This reference has been cited as evidence that the Chronicler wrote during the Greek period (see Introduction to I Chronicles), but it may be a later addition to his text. The **Book of the Chronicles** in verse 23 is not the biblical book but one of the Chronicler's postexilic sources. Verse 26*b* is probably an interpolation, since Nehemiah and Ezra do not fit into a list dated **in the days of** respective high priests.

12:27-43. *Dedication of the Wall.* After the **Levites** and **singers** are gathered together in Jerusalem from the surrounding areas, the ceremony of purifying the wall takes place. Though the specific rites of this ceremony are not mentioned, it may be surmised that sacrifices are offered and probably blood or holy water is sprinkled on the wall.

12:31-43. Next two groups, moving **in procession** in opposite directions, walk around the top of the wall to the accompaniment of **musical instruments** and singing choirs. Apparently starting at the Valley Gate, the first group marches around the south of the city and the second around the north till they come near the temple on the northeast (on the places named see above on 2:13-16; 3:1-32; 8:13-18). According to the present text **Ezra** leads the first company and Nehemiah accompanies the second. But if Ezra and Nehemiah were not contemporaries, as seems likely (see Introduction to Ezra), the clause about Ezra must be a later addition. The two groups converge in the temple court, where **sacrifices** are offered and all **rejoice with great joy.**

12:44–13:3. *The Ideal Community.* The **contributions** for the temple personnel fill the storehouses, since the people are pleased with the service that the **priests** and **Levites** are rendering. The ideal cult, founded by **David,** has continued throughout the postexilic period from **Zerubbabel** to **Nehemiah.**

13:1-3. During a reading of the **book of Moses**—that is, some portion of the Pentateuch (cf. 8:1)—a passage is noted stating that an **Ammonite or Moabite** is to be excluded from the **assembly of God** (cf. Deuteronomy 23:3-5). On the basis of this Mosaic law the people exclude **all those of foreign descent,**

either from the temple services or possibly from the entire community.

13:4-9. *Expulsion of Tobiah.* In opposing the rebuilding of the wall Tobiah gave Nehemiah particular trouble (6:17-19). Now Nehemiah returns to Persia after an administration of twelve years (445-433, verse 6; cf. 5:14). Tobiah proceeds to move into the temple quarters with the permission of **Eliashib the priest,** one of those with whom he is **connected.** Many interpreters have taken this to mean the high priest who helped Nehemiah in rebuilding the wall, but the description suggests rather a priest of lower rank.

After some time—perhaps on hearing of such irregularities—Nehemiah asks the **king** for permission to go back to Jerusalem. The date and length of his second sojourn there are not known. Discovering Tobiah's trespass on his arrival, Nehemiah is **very angry,** and ejects him and his belongings from the temple quarters. As an Ammonite (cf. 2:10) Tobiah must be excluded from the temple (verses 1-3). More seriously, as an enemy of Nehemiah he cannot be allowed to live in the heart of the city.

13:10-14. *Restoration of Tithes.* In contradiction to the claim of 12:47 the people are failing to support the temple personnel by giving their tithes. As a result the **Levites** have had to leave their duties in the temple to work in the fields. Nehemiah organizes a group of **officials** to oversee the **storehouses** and **distribute** the food to the temple personnel.

13:15-22. *Sabbath Reforms.* The observance of the sabbath was one of the distinctive features of Jewish religion. Because it set the Jews apart from their Gentile neighbors, it was a cause of constant friction. The desecration of the sabbath both by Jews and by Gentile traders in Nehemiah's day brings drastic action to keep the day **holy.** The **gates** of Jerusalem are to be closed on the sabbath and guarded by the Levites. Verse 18 probably refers to a passage like Jeremiah 17:21-27.

13:23-29. *Mixed Marriage Reforms.* Nehemiah's violent reaction against his countrymen who have married **foreign women** is in sharp contrast with Ezra's actions when faced with the same problem (Ezra 9:1-5). An appeal is made to the example of **Solomon,** who sinned in taking foreign wives (cf. I Kings 3:1; 11:1-8). Nehemiah makes the people **take oath** that they will not indulge in this practice any more. One offender is singled out for special notice in verse 28—apparently because he is related to **Sanballat,** Nehemiah's enemy (cf. 2:10; 4:1-2, 7-8; 6:1-14). He is **chased**—that is, banished from the city.

13:30-31. *Conclusion.* The book closes with a brief review by Nehemiah of his work and a prayer for God's remembrance of him **for good.**

THE BOOK OF ESTHER

H. Neil Richardson

INTRODUCTION

Esther is a brief historical novel written to explain the origin of the Jewish festival Purim. Here the feast is said to commemorate a victory of the Jews of the Persian Empire over their enemies.

In the story Ahasuerus, king of Persia, deposes his queen, Vashti, for disobedience. He selects Esther as her successor without knowing that she is a Jewess. Esther's cousin and guardian, Mordecai, disobeys the prime minister, Haman. In consequence, the angry Haman secures the king's consent to a decree that all Jews in the empire are to be killed on an appointed day.

At Mordecai's urging Esther invites the king and the prime minister to a dinner, at which she pleads for her people and accuses Haman. The outcome is that Haman is executed. Then Mordecai is permitted to issue a second decree authorizing the Jews to defend themselves and kill their attackers on the appointed day. At the conclusion of the slaughter Esther and Mordecai order an annual observance, henceforth to be known as Purim. The book is the work of a skilled literary artist. This writer keeps the reader in suspense as he unfolds the successive stages of the plot and brings it to an effective climax with Esther's accusation of Haman.

Authorship and Date

The statement that "Mordecai recorded these things" (9:20) has been taken by some in ancient times and even today as indicating that Mordecai wrote the book. The reference, however, seems to be merely to the document sent out to urge annual commemoration. Thus the work should be viewed as anonymous. In any case the viewpoint of the storyteller is not that of a contemporary but of one who looks back to the reign of Ahasuerus from a much later time. The king was actually Xerxes I (486-465; see below on 1:1). The author makes no mention of the known historical events of Xerxes' career. Indeed during the time of the Persian invasion of Greece he shows the king in Susa testing candidates for the queenship (see below on 2:12-14).

Various historical and chronological inaccuracies lead to the conclusion that the book is something less than dependable history. It must have been written a long time after the events it describes. This is borne out by the reference to the Jews as "scattered abroad and dispersed among the peoples" (3:8)— which was much more true in later times than under Xerxes.

It is probable that the Septuagint translation of Esther was made before 77/76 B.C. Acquaintance with the book about that time is confirmed by II Maccabees 15:36. However, Jeshua ben Sira, writing around 180, describes a long list of heroes of Israelite history (Ecclesiaticus 44-49) but makes no mention of Esther and Mordecai. Surely he could be expected to include them if he knew about them. Significant also is the fact that as yet no fragment of the book has been found among the Dead Sea scrolls, produced by the Qumran community that existed around 150 B.C.–A.D. 70. Finally, there is no quotation or allusion to it in the New Testament.

The book's attitude of vindictiveness toward Gentiles fits well in the age of the Maccabees and their revolt against their Greek rulers. It particularly fits in the materialistic reign of John Hyrcanus (134-104), who beginning around 128 forcibly converted the peoples of Idumea, Samaria, and Galilee. Such considerations lead many scholars to date Esther somewhere around 125.

On the other hand there is much in the book that suggests that it was written in Persia. There is a high degree of accuracy in the details of Persian court life. A considerable number of words borrowed from the Persian language are scattered throughout. Some scholars explain the former by saying the author had traveled in Persia or had read a great deal about the country and its people. But such explanations fail to come adequately to grips with the problem of word borrowings.

Thus there seems a strong possibility that the book was written by a Jew living in geographical proximity to the setting of his story even though at some chronological distance. For example, he may have lived in or near Susa (see below on 1:2-8) in the latter days of the Persian Empire, around 350. This supposition would explain the book's combination of accuracy and inaccuracy. It would also account for the general unfamiliarity with it in Palestine until its sudden popularity in the first century A.D.

Purpose and Significance

It has been argued that the festival of Purim began simply as a literary invention of the author of Esther and came to be celebrated because of the popularity of the story. However, most scholars agree that celebration of the festival came first and that the book was written to justify it. Justification was needed since such a festival is not mentioned in the other books of the Bible. Like other holy days of Judaism it is here given a setting in a historical event—one in which Jews were delivered from virtual annihilation.

In all likelihood Purim was originally a non-Jewish celebration. A group of Jews no doubt adopted it from their neighbors, presumably in some part of the Persian Empire. They made it their own by interpreting it as the commemoration of a victory over persecutors. Whether some historical incident underlies this connection is uncertain. There is a striking though superficial resemblance of the names Mordecai and Esther to those of Babylonian deities Marduk and Ishtar. This had led some scholars to assume a mythological basis for the book. A similar possible connection of Vashti and Haman with names of Elamite gods has suggested to them a myth of rivalry between the two sets of national deities, with the Babylonian gods coming out victorious.

However, a text has been discovered which mentions a high official at Susa during the early years of Xerxes' reign named Marduka. This, along with the fact that Esther is a credible Persian feminine name meaning "star," seems to indicate that the characters of the story are intended to represent historical persons rather than deities. It is possible that a local conflict occurred in connection with celebration of the festival. This was remembered on later anniversaries and, as the celebration spread, was magnified to involve the whole Persian Empire.

Purim is still observed on the 14th-15th of Adar (cf. 9:21)—that is, about March 1. It is a wholly secular holiday. Its only religious aspect is the reading of Esther in the synagogue. Even this is in a nonreligious atmosphere, being accompanied by considerable noise-making. Otherwise Purim is a time of merrymaking, feasting, visiting, and giving gifts (cf. 9:22).

Aside from its purpose of explaining Purim the book may be seen as a protest against persecution of minority groups, whether religious or ethnic. Haman has become the prototype of one motivated by prejudice and blind hatred against persons of another faith, race, or nationality. In this sense the book has an important religious significance.

It is true that in a specific sense the book makes no mention of religion. The word "God" never appears. Nothing is said of prayer—though fasting is practiced at one time of crisis. Indeed the book expresses a vindictive spirit at odds with the ethical teaching of both Old and New Testaments. On the other hand it does reveal God's will by showing the terrible consequences of hatred. An attitude which brings about the denial of justice to other human beings and the massacre of God's children must be wrong.

Unity

Most scholars regard 9:20–10:3 as a later addition, on the basis
of both differences in language and inconsistencies in thought.
The arguments are not decisive, however. The entire book
might well be viewed as the work of one author. On the other
hand there is little question that the several sections which make
the Septuagint version about a third longer than that in the
Hebrew Bible are insertions by other hands. These are mostly
intended to make up for the religious deficiencies. Jerome
placed these passages in an appendix in the Latin Vulgate. They
were included in the Protestant Apocrypha under the title "The
Additions to the Book of Esther."

Place in the Bible

In the Hebrew Scriptures Esther is included among the
Writings, the third and latest division. The book is the last of the
five scrolls—Song of Solomon, Ruth, Lamentations, Ecclesiastes, Esther—read in the synagogue on the respective feast
and fast days. Neither Jews nor Christians, however, have been
happy with the presence of the book in the canon of holy
scripture. Its status was hotly debated by the rabbis all through
the first two centuries A.D., and they obviously accepted it only
because of the demand of the masses. Among Christians also
there was question about its status. Martin Luther declared that
he wished it did not exist. It must be admitted that without the
popularity of the festival of Purim the book would have had little
to recommend it for a place in the canon. At the same time,
Esther does have a message, even though stated negatively,
concerning God's will for humanity.

I. THE DEPOSING OF VASHTI (1:1-22)

1:1-8. *Ahasuerus' Banquets.* The author at once gives his
story a setting of grandeur. He relates historically accurate
information about the vast size of the Persian king's empire and
the magnificence of his palace. To this is added a fantastic

exaggeration of the size and length of his feasts—a six-months-long house-party for all the officials of the empire followed by a week-long party for all the common people of the city.

1:1. The name **Ahasuerus** is an English approximation of the Hebrew and Aramaic *Ahashwerosh*. This name has been found in inscriptions as the equivalent of the Persian *Khshayarsha,* known also through classic Greek transcription as Xerxes. Xerxes I (486-465) inherited from his father Darius I an empire which truly extended **from India to Ethiopia.** According to the contemporary Greek historian Herodotus, it was divided into twenty major administrative areas known as satrapies. These in turn may well have been subdivided into **one hundred and twenty-seven provinces.**

1:2-8. The governmental center of the Persian Empire was the city of Persepolis. The phrase translated **Susa the capital** refers rather to the "citadel of Susa," a large acropolis which was formerly the capital of Elam. There Darius built a luxurious palace as a winter residence. Excavation of its court has shown that the description here is based on accurate information about it. The banquets also have some foundation in the reputation of the ancient Persians for lavish entertaining.

1:9-12. *Vashti's Disobedience.* Herodotus states that Xerxes' queen was Amestris, daughter of a Persian general. But the fact that **Vashti** is an Elamite name suggests that it may represent a historical person—possibly a local princess who was added to the royal harem. The author gives no motivation for her refusal to appear at the king's bidding. Early rabbinic interpreters concocted the explanation that she was ordered to appear wearing only the **royal crown.**

1:13-22. *An Example to All Women.* The detail given this episode contrasts with the bare statement preceding. It reveals not only the author's judgment of his ancient readers' sensibilities but also his skill in establishing the idea of the irrevocability of the **laws of the Persians and the Medes.** This will be needed later to explain why the conflict could not be simply called off (cf. 8:8). The same idea is similarly essential to the story of Daniel and the lions' den (Daniel 6:8, 12, 15). Since this idea is contrary to historical evidence, it seems to indicate literary relationship; but which work is dependent on the other is not clear.

1:22. The sending out of the decree in every **language** of the empire is a literary device to emphasize its wide dissemination. Actually the official correspondence of the Persian imperial administration was all in Aramaic, the international language of trade and diplomacy throughout the Near East during this period. The provincial governors would be responsible for translating proclamations into the many local vernaculars.

II. INTRODUCTION OF MORDECAI, ESTHER, AND HAMAN (2:1–3:6)

2:1-18. *The Selection of a New Queen.* The seven counselors shrewdly advise an irrevocable deposition. Thus they go about protecting themselves from the vengeance of a restored queen when the king sobers up and regrets losing her. To distract him his **servants** propose an ancient counterpart of a modern beauty contest to pick Miss Persia—with the significant difference that all the contestants are to be added to the royal **harem** as **concubines.** Early rabbinic commentators viewed Esther's voluntary marriage to a Gentile as unthinkable. They declared **all the beautiful young virgins** of the empire drafted; but the author does not make this point clear.

2:5-6. Jeconiah is the alternate name of Jehoiachin, who was taken to Babylon with the first body of exiles in 597 (II Kings 24:10-16). Some defenders of the author's historical accuracy have taken verse 6 to apply to **Kish,** whom they assume to be Mordecai's great-grandfather. But in normal Hebrew usage it must apply to Mordecai.

The author has telescoped the time between 597 and 483, the third year of Xerxes (1:3). Perhaps he shared the notion of the author of Daniel that Ahasuerus was the father of Darius (Daniel 9:1) and that both preceded Cyrus (Daniel 6:28). Thus, he thought of his story as set during the exile rather than after it.

Shimei (cf. II Samuel 16:5-14) and **Kish** (cf. I Samuel 9:1-2) were prominent early Benjaminites. They probably are named as remote rather than immediate ancestors.

2:7-11. The Hebrew name **Hadassah** means "myrtle." **Esther** is a Persian name meaning "star." Reflected here is a practice which still prevails to some extent among the Jews of giving both a Hebrew and a non-Hebrew name to their children. Esther is Mordecai's young cousin—not his niece as in the Latin versions—whom he has reared. He tells her to keep secret her relationship to him and the fact that she is a Jewess—an important element in the plot. Doing this means she must eat unclean **food** and otherwise ignore the distinctive observances of the Jewish law. Yet, inconsistently, Mordecai himself risks almost certain recognition of the relationship by his solicitude. He does not hesitate to display his own Jewishness (3:4). His access to the vicinity of the harem suggests that he holds some minor official position. This—and the means of maintaining contact without revealing the secret—are details the author has not cared to clarify.

2:12-18. After **twelve months** of **beautifying** herself each girl is permitted to spend a night with the king (verse 14). Earlier it has been implied that the number of virgins assembled is quite large. Evidently, according to the story, the king is in his palace in Susa and this process of selection lasts about three years (cf. 1:3). It ends when he selects Esther in the **tenth month** of his **seventh year,** i.e. January 478. Historically Xerxes spent most of this period in Asia Minor and in Greece, which he attacked unsuccessfully in 480-479. **Granted a remission of taxes** is literally "caused a rest." The idiom is not found elsewhere and its precise meaning is uncertain (see Revised Standard Version footnote).

2:19-23. *Mordecai's Service to the King.* Verse 19a is obscure and probably corrupt. It has been suggested that it may refer to transfer of the **virgins** who have not yet had a turn to the second harem (cf. verse 14). Mordecai's **sitting at the king's gate** seems to imply that he is a minor official of the court (see above on verses 7-11). **Hanged on the gallows** refers not to strangulation by a rope, but probably to impalement on a sharp stake and slow death by starvation. This was a Persian mode of execution from which the Romans got the idea of crucifixion. The **Book of the Chronicles** is of course not the biblical book but the royal annals of the Persian court.

3:1-6. *The Origin of Haman's Hatred.* The villain of the story is now introduced. **Agagite** is probably intended to identify him as a descendant of the king of the Amalekites who was the occasion of Saul's losing the kingdom (cf. I Samuel 15). This would heighten the conflict between him and Mordecai, who is a descendant of the family of Saul (see above on 2:5-6).

The reason for Mordecai's refusal to pay homage to the new prime minister is not given. In the Septuagint he states that he will not bow to anyone but God, and rabbinic interpreters explained that Haman wore an idol on his robe. Perhaps the Hebrew text implies that Haman sees Mordecai's attitude as arising from religious views shared by other Jews. Accordingly he wants to **destroy all the Jews.**

III. The Danger to the Jews (3:7–5:14)

3:7-15. *The Edict of Extermination.* Haman casts a **lot** to discover the most propitious day for his planned annihilation of the Jews. Evidently "till the thirteenth day" has accidentally been dropped following **day after day** in verse 7 (cf. verse 13). The idea is that the lot is first cast to determine the day of the month and then again to determine the month. **Pur** is a Persian word borrowed from the Akkadian. Thus it must be explained by the Hebrew word for "lot."

3:8-11. The Jews have always observed **laws**—dietary and otherwise—which have prevented their assimilation with their neighbors. It is to these laws rather than civil laws that Haman refers. The bribe he offers with his petition is a tremendous sum (10,000 talents of silver would be 625,000 pounds). The king's apparently casual reply in verse 11 is probably to be understood as accepting it. **As it seems good to you** is no doubt the ancient

Near Eastern courtly equivalent of "if you please." The **signet ring** was used to impress a distinctive design into the seal of a document. Thus it served as the king's signature.

3:12-15. The **edict** is issued in the king's **name** and sent out in every **language** (see above on 1:22). The **couriers** are an authentic reference to the empire-wide postal system established by Cyrus around 535. The ordering of the massacre eleven months in advance (cf. verses 12*a*, 13*b*) is clearly a literary device to give Mordecai and Esther an opportunity to come to the aid of their people.

4:1-17. *Mordecai's Appeal to Esther.* Torn **clothes,** a rough **sackcloth** garment, **ashes** scattered over the head, and **wailing** were common mourning customs of the ancient Near East. Mordecai's behavior at the palace **gate** and his refusal to put off his sackcloth are obviously designed to impress on Esther the seriousness of the situation and motivate her to take action. On the other hand the **mourning among the Jews,** which includes **fasting,** surely would involve a plea for divine pity and deliverance. Therefore it would include prayer and other religious practices of Judaism. The author's failure to mention these is quite noticeable (see below on verses 15-17).

4:5-9. Through an intermediary Mordicai reports to Esther all the details of the **decree** and its issuance. He even gives the **exact** amount of the bribe, which he has no doubt learned from court gossip. He urges Esther to appeal to the king on behalf of her people.

4:10-12. The frequency of political assassinations in ancient times gave reason for strict security precautions surrounding all monarchs. Anyone suspiciously aggressive in approaching a king would put his life in danger. But there are accounts of persons who initiated audiences with Persian kings given by Herodotus and other ancient historians. These do not mention such extreme restrictions as Esther here describes.

Of course harem rivalries might cause even an official queen to fear making a nuisance of herself at a time when she appears to be out of favor. It is evident, however, that by assuming only one possible way for Esther to speak to the king the author has exaggerated the danger in order to enhance her heroism. An authentic touch is the **golden scepter,** which Persian kings extended to those permitted to approach the throne.

4:13-14. Mordecai's final plea to Esther is very persuasive, though she might well doubt his threat that she would be killed along with **all the other Jews.** The expression **from another quarter** is strange and has been much discussed. Any other book of the Bible would say "God" here. Most ancient interpreters and some today have taken the phrase to mean "God." This would be in line with the practice in rabbinic Judaism of avoiding use of divine names by substituting such terms as "heaven." But the author's apparent deliberate avoidance of religious references elsewhere in the book suggests that here he is referring to human help, perhaps without any particular source in mind. Mordecai's concluding question, **Who knows whether you have not come to the kingdom for such a time as this?** challenges what little courage Esther possesses. It is often quoted to emphasize each individual's responsibility.

4:15-17. The fast which Esther requests of the Jews of the city can aid her approach to the king only as a religious observance soliciting divine help. As such it would naturally be accompanied by verbal expression of the help desired—that is, by prayer. Thus some commentators believe that in referring to fasting the author intends to imply prayer. On the contrary, however, it is evident that he has intentionally avoided any hint of a religious purpose in the fast. To make up for the omission the Septuagint version of the story includes lengthy prayers by Mordecai and Esther following verse 17.

5:1-14. *Esther's First Dinner.* Feeling let down by the author's account of Esther's easy and successful approach to the king, someone composed an expanded version of verses 1-2, found in the Septuagint. In this account Esther sensibly invites him and the prime minister to a **dinner** as the best occasion for presenting the concern. But interpreters have long been troubled to explain why, having arranged a perfect after-dinner setting, she does not come right to the point instead of inviting the two to a second dinner.

The explanation is purely literary—to provide suspense and opportunity for further developments of the plot before the climax. Thus Haman is given a chance to gloat and to deepen the contrast between his own exalted opinion of himself and his ultimate fall. The excessive height—about seventy-five feet—of the **gallows** (see above on 2:19-23) which he orders for Mordecai would serve little practical purpose. But as a literary exaggeration it sounds impressive.

IV. THE TABLES TURNED (6:1–8:2)

6:1-13. *The Glorification of Mordecai.* The sleeplessness of a king is a familiar literary device. Here it affords occasion for the reading of royal records throughout the night in an effort to put him to sleep. The result is a coincidental reminder of his unpaid debt to Mordecai. The question **Who is in the court?** inquires about any high official who at the moment may be available for consultation. Ironically it is Haman coming at dawn to request Mordecai's execution. In his conceit the unsuspecting prime minister plans the honor to be paid the man he is expecting to destroy. As a final stroke he is ordered to carry out his plan in person. That the king commands this honor for a Jew indicates he does not know that the edict of extermination recently issued in his name is directed against the Jews. Authenticity of the **royal crown** on the horse's head is suggested by Assyrian monuments depicting horses wearing crowns with tall plumes.

6:14–7:10. *Esther's Second Dinner.* The story reaches its climax as Esther now states her position. Her explanation is somewhat obscure (7:4). Apparently the **loss to the king** refers to the huge bribe (3:9), which she fears he may be reluctant to forgo. The **wrath** which drives him into the **garden** may be inspired not so much by his prime minister's misdeeds as by the realization that he has been used in a plot without knowing what was going on.

Haman's **falling on the couch** is for the purpose of grasping and perhaps kissing Esther's feet in a common ancient Near

Eastern gesture of petition. The king mistakes Haman's abject groveling for a sexual attack and is stirred to immediate action. Unmoved by her enemy's plea, Esther shows no compunction about bearing false witness by silence. An attendant calls attention to the **gallows** Haman has prepared for Mordecai. The king orders that Haman be executed on it.

8:1-2. *Completion of the Reversal.* In ancient times the execution of a criminal was usually accompanied by confiscation of their property. In this case the king gives Haman's **house**—that is, estate (cf. 7:9)—to Esther. She in turn gives it to Mordecai. To complete the turning of the tables the king also gives Mordecai the **signet ring** (see above on 3:8-11). Thus Mordecai is elevated to Haman's former office of prime minister—a post for which his now-revealed relationship to the queen is apparently considered sufficient qualification.

V. THE REVENGE OF THE JEWS (8:3–9:19)

8:3-8. *The Irrevocable Edict.* At this point all that seems needed to bring the story to a happy ending is withdrawal of the decree for extermination of the Jews. But so simple a solution would not explain the annual celebration of Purim. A conflict and victory in which all the Jews of the empire participate is needed. Therefore the author now makes use of the fiction he has set up at the beginning of the story (see above on 1:13-22). He has stated that under Persian law a royal decree **cannot be revoked.** In response to Esther's renewed plea for her people the king can only tell her and Mordecai to **write as you please.** They are free to send out a new decree circumventing the unrevoked **edict** ordering the Jews' destruction. Despite what has come to light he seems as unconcerned as before over what the result may be for the citizens of his empire (cf. 3:11).

8:9-14. *The Counter Edict.* Following the same procedure as his predecessor (cf. 3:12-15) the new prime minister sends out an edict. This one is designed to counteract that issued by Haman two months and ten days earlier. As before it is

)

distributed in the various languages (see above on 1:22) by means of the imperial postal service (see above on 3:12-15). But this time the author emphasizes its urgency by adding a reference to **swift horses** from the royal stable—mentioned also by other ancient authors.

Some commentators have claimed that Mordecai's decree merely allows the Jews to **defend their lives,** literally "stand for their life." But the following duplication of the wording of the earlier decree (cf. 3:13) clearly gives them the same right as their opponents to take the initiative and to **avenge themselves upon their enemies.**

8:15-17. *Public Acclaim of Mordecai.* The author continues to contrast Mordecai and Haman. Whereas the people of **Susa** were "perplexed" by Haman's issuance of the earlier decree (3:15), they now greet Mordecai with loud cheers as he walks forth in his official regalia. The **Jews** throughout the empire of course rejoice at this turn in their favor. **Declared themselves Jews** has been taken by some to mean that **many** merely pretended to be Jews. But since the Jews themselves would scarcely be deceived by false claims, the reference is more probably to proselytes. Some scholars have taken this to be an allusion to forced conversions to Judaism in the time of John Hyrcanus (see Introduction).

9:1-10. *The Day of Slaughter.* Thus far in the story only Haman has been presented as an enemy of the Jews—though perhaps Mordecai's instruction to Esther to keep her Jewishness a secret (2:10) has hinted at the existence of prejudice. Now it appears that the Jews have large numbers of **enemies** throughout the empire. The identity of these enemies is unclear.

In defiance of the **king's command and edict** issued by Haman, supposedly irrevocable, the **royal officials** change to the side of the Jews (verse 3). The assumption of some interpreters that the attackers are soldiers of the Persian army acting under orders seems unjustified. Rather the enemies of the Jews must be understood as neighboring peoples within the empire who **sought their hurt** because they **hated them.** It is evident that the author is writing at a time when he can expect that his Jewish readers will be accustomed to having enemies and will take them for granted without explanation.

9:11-19. *An Added Day.* Mordecai has received great acclaim from the people of Susa (8:15). Therefore, it is surprising that within the limited area of the **capital,** i.e. citadel (see above on 1:2-8), the Jews have so many enemies that **five hundred** are killed. Undoubtedly the low point in the book comes when Esther, not satisfied with this number, requests a second day of slaughter.

The reason for this additional day, however, is not to increase the statistics by **three hundred** but to explain why the date of Purim varies in different places. As indicated here, Jews in the **villages** observe it on the **fourteenth** of Adar whereas those in **Susa** and presumably other cities have their festival on the **fifteenth.** The hanging of Haman's **ten sons** who have already been killed (verses 7-10) is probably not an inconsistency. It simply confirms that the **gallows** served not only for execution of criminals but also for public display of their bodies (see above on 2:19-23). Remembering that the book is fiction we need not be concerned by the report throughout the empire of **seventy-five thousand** killed—especially since the Septuagint reduces it to fifteen thousand. Nor should we be surprised that there are no Jewish casualties.

VI. ANNUAL OBSERVANCE OF PURIM (9:20–10:3)

9:20-32. *Instructions for the Festival.* Verses 17-19 clearly assume a one-day festival observed on different dates by rural and urban Jews. But this section calls on all Jews to celebrate a two-day festival taking in both dates. Because of this inconsistency and differences in style and vocabulary many scholars believe this section comes from a different author (see Introduction). Its purpose is to emphasize the legality of Purim. The repeated stress on **letters to all the Jews** is to insure that this festival, which has no basis in the Pentateuch, will be

recognized as official in the life of Judaism. It is not enough that
it have its basis in a historical event. It must be legalized by
official documents. This reflects a characteristic view of
postexilic Judaism. The addition here of **gifts to the poor** is a
natural aspect of such an occasion of joyousness and remains a
part of the observance to this day.

9:23-28. Possibly verses 24-25 are intended to summarize part
of what **Mordecai had written to them.** But if so, it probably
does not mean that the whole book is to be understood as a
transcript of Mordecai's letter. In verse 25 the name **Esther** has
been supplied by many translators because the verb **came** is
feminine, and is equivalent to "she came." But probably this is a
scribal error and should read "he came" as in the Septuagint,
referring to Haman. The name **Purim** by which the festival came
to be known is a Hebrew plural form. It is now explained as the
plural of **Pur,** the **lot** used by Haman to select the day for
destroying the Jews (see above on 3:7-15). **All who joined them**
refers to proselytes (see above on 8:15-17).

9:29-32. The legality of Purim is further emphasized by a
command of Queen Esther in a joint letter with Mordecai. The
reference to **fasts** may indicate that this letter was added to
establish the custom of fasting on the day before Purim in
commemoration of Esther's fast (4:16).

10:1-3. *Exaltation of Mordecai.* The wealth and **power** of
Ahasuerus enhance the **honor** of his prime minister, Mordecai.
The reference to the official annals of **Media and Persia** is
patterned after similar statements in I and II Kings and is
intended to authenticate the historicity of the book. Probably
the best thing that can be said for Mordecai—and the best thing
in the book—is that **he sought the welfare of his people and
spoke peace to all his people.** This is a fitting conclusion. But the
Septuagint follows it with an interpretation of the dream of
Mordecai described at the beginning of that version and a
colophon authenticating the Greek translation (see
Introduction).

FOR FURTHER STUDY

JOSHUA

John Bright in *Interpreter's Bible*, 1953; *A History of Israel*, 1959, chapter 3. Martin Noth, *History of Israel*, 2nd ed., 1960, Part 1. E.M. Good in *Interpreter's Dictionary of the Bible*, 1962; J.M. Miller in *Interpreter's Dictionary of the Bible Supplement*, 1976. W.F. Albright, *The Biblical Period from Abraham to Ezra*, 1963, chapter 3.

JUDGES

J.M. Myers in *Interpreter's Bible*, 1953. Martin Noth, *History of Israel*, 2nd ed., 1960, Part 1, Part 2, chapter 1. John Bright, *A History of Israel*, 1959, chapter 4. C. F. Kraft in *Interpreter's Dictionary of the Bible*, 1962. W. F. Albright, *The Biblical Period from Abraham to Ezra*, 1963, chapter 4; M. G. Rogers in *Interpreter's Dictionary of the Bible Supplement*, 1976.

RUTH

Israel Bettan, *The Five Scrolls*, 1950, pp. 49-72. George A. F. Knight *Ruth and Jonah*, 1950. H. H. Rowley, "The Marriage of Ruth," in *The Servant of the Lord*, 1952, pp. 161-86. Samuel Sandmel, *The Hebrew Scriptures*, 1963, pp. 488-93.

I AND II SAMUEL

H. P. Smith, *A Critical and Exegetical Commentary on the Books of Samuel*, 1899. S. R. Driver, *Notes on the Hebrew Text and the Topography of the Books of Samuel*, 1913. A. R. S. Kennedy, *The Book of Samuel*, (no date). G. B. Caird in *Interpreter's Bible*, 1953. Martin Noth, *A History of Israel*, 1958. John Bright, *A History of Israel*, 1959. Stephen Szikszai in *Interpreter's Dictionary of the Bible*, 1962. M. Tsevat in *Interpreter's Dictionary of the Bible Supplement*, 1976.

I AND II KINGS

C. F. Burney, *Notes on the Hebrew Text of the Books of Kings*, 1903. John Skinner, *Kings*, 1904. W. E. Barnes, *The First-Second Book of the Kings*, 1911. J. A. Montgomery and H. S. Gehman, *A Critical and Exegetical Commentary on the Books of Kings*, 1951. N. H. Snaith in *Interpreter's Bible*, 1954. Martin Noth, *History of Israel*, 1958. John Bright, *The History of Israel*, 1959, chapters 5–8. Stephen Szikszai in *Interpreter's Dictionary of the Bible*, 1962. P. R. Ackroyd in *Interpreter's Dictionary of the Bible Supplement*, 1976. E. R. Thiele, *The Mysterious Numbers of the Hebrew Kings*, rev. ed., 1964.

I AND II CHRONICLES

E. L. Curtis and A. A. Madsen, *A Critical and Exegetical Commentary on the Books of Chronicles*, 1910. A. C. Welch, *The Work of the Chronicler*, 1939. I. W. Slotki, *Chronicles*, 1952. C. C. Torrey, *The Chronicler's History of Israel*, 1954. W. A. L. Elmslie in *Interpreter's Bible*, 1954. R. H. Pfeiffer in *Interpreter's Dictionary of the Bible*, 1962. P. R. Ackroyd, in *Interpreter's Dictionary of the Bible Supplement*, 1976.

EZRA AND NEHEMIAH

H. W. Ryle, *The Books of Ezra and Nehemiah*, 1901. C. C. Torrey, *Ezra Studies*, 1910. L. W. Batten, *A Critical and Exegetical Commentary on the Books of Ezra and Nehemiah*, 1913. A. C. Welch, *Postexilic Judaism*, 1935. R. A. Bowman in *Interpreter's Bible*, 1954. R. H. Pfeiffer in *Interpreter's Dictionary of the Bible*, 1962. S. Talmon, in *Interpreter's Dictionary of the Bible Supplement*, 1976.

ESTHER

L. B. Paton, *Esther*, 1908. R. H. Pfeiffer, *Introduction to the Old Testament*, 1949 pp. 732-47. B. W. Anderson in *Interpreter's Bible*, 1954. D. W. Harvey in *Interpreter's Dictionary of the Bible*, 1962. W. L. Humphreys in *Interpreter's Dictionary of the Bible Supplement*, 1976.

ABBREVIATIONS AND EXPLANATIONS

ABBREVIATIONS

D — Deuteronomic; Deuteronomist source

E — Elohist source
Ecclus. — Ecclesiasticus
ed. — edited by, edition, editor
e.g. — *exempli gratia* (for example)
ERV — English Revised Version
esp. — especially

H — Holiness Code

J — Yahwist source
JPSV — Jewish Publication Society Version

L — Lukan source
LXX — Septuagint, the earliest Greek translation of the Old Testament and Apocrypha (250 B.C. and after)

M — Matthean source
Macc. — Maccabees
MS — manuscript

N — north, northern
NEB — New English Bible

P — Priestly source
p. — page
Pet. — Peter
Phil. — Philippian, Philippians
Philem. — Philemon
Prov. — Proverbs
Pss. Sol. — Psalms of Solomon
pt. — part (of a literary work)

Q — "Sayings" source

rev. — revised
RSV — Revised Standard Version

S — south, southern

trans. — translated by, translation, translator

viz. — *videlicet* (namely)
Vulg. — Vulgate, the accepted Latin version, mostly translated A.D. 383-405 by Jerome

W — west, western
Wisd. Sol. — Wisdom of Solomon

Interpreter's Concise Commentary

QUOTATIONS AND REFERENCES

In the direct commentary words and phrases quoted from the RSV of the passage under discussion are printed in boldface type, without quotation marks, to facilitate linking the comments to the exact points of the biblical text. If a quotation from the passage under discussion is not in boldface type, it is to be recognized as an alternate translation, either that of another version if so designated (see abbreviations of versions above) or the commentator's own rendering. On the other hand, quotations from other parts of the Bible in direct commentary, as well as all biblical quotations in the introductions, are to be understood as from the RSV unless otherwise identified.

A passage of the biblical text is identified by book, chapter number, and verse number or numbers, the chapter and verse numbers being separated by a colon (cf. Genesis 1:1). Clauses within a verse may be designated by the letters *a, b, c,* etc. following the verse number (e.g. Genesis 1:2*b*). In poetic text each line as printed in the RSV—not counting runovers necessitated by narrow columns—is accorded a letter. If the book is not named, the book under discussion is to be understood; similarly the chapter number appearing in the boldface reference at the beginning of the paragraph, or in a preceding centered head, is to be understood if no chapter is specified.

A suggestion to note another part of the biblical text is usually introduced by the abbreviation "cf." and specifies the exact verses. To be distinguished from this is a suggestion to consult a comment in this volume, which is introduced by "see above on," "see below on," or "see comment on," and which identifies the boldface reference at the head of the paragraph where the comment is to be found or, in the absence of a boldface reference, the reference in a preceding centered head. The suggestion "see Introduction" refers to the introduction of the book under discussion unless another book is named.

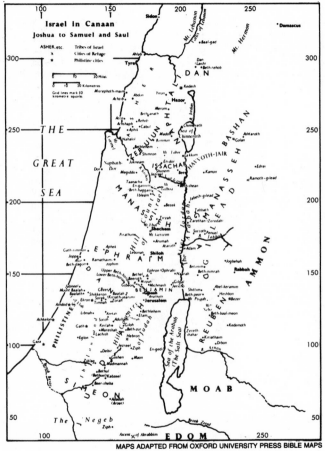

Israel in Canaan
Joshua to Samuel and Saul

ASHER.etc.   Tribes of Israel
       Cities of Refuge
       Philistine cities

Grid lines mark 50
kilometre squares

THE
GREAT
SEA

PHILISTINE

SIMEON

The Negeb

ASHER

ZEBULUN

NAPHTALI

DAN

BASHAN

ISSACHAR

MANASSEH

EPHRAIM

BENJAMIN

GAD (GILEAD)

MANASSEH

REUBEN

AMMON

MOAB

EDOM

Sidon
Tyre
Damascus
Mt. Lebanon
Mt. Hermon
Baal-gad
Dan
Laish
Beth-rehob
Kedesh
Hazor
Sea of Chinnereth
Ashtaroth
Golan
Edrei
Ramoth-gilead
Kamon
Jabesh-gilead
Beth-shean
Succoth
Penuel
Jabbok
Jogbehah
Rabbah
Heshbon
Abel-keramim
Bezer
Kedemoth
Dibon
Arnon
Brook Zered
Ascent of Abrabbim
Jerusalem
Shiloh
Shechem
Bethlehem
Hebron
Gaza
Ashkelon
Ashdod
Ekron
Gath
Lachish
Eglon
Debir
Beer-sheba
Sea of the Arabah (The Salt Sea)
En-gedi

Joshua to Samuel and Saul

MAPS ADAPTED FROM OXFORD UNIVERSITY PRESS BIBLE MAPS

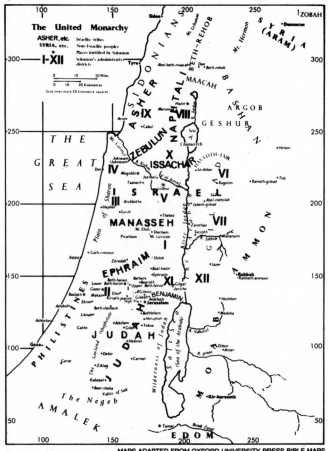

The United Monarchy

ASHER, etc. Israelite tribes
SYRIA, etc. Non-Israelite peoples
       ★   Places fortified by Solomon
   I–XII   Solomon's administrative
             districts

0   10   20 Miles
0   10   20 Kilometers
Grid lines mark 50 kilometre squares

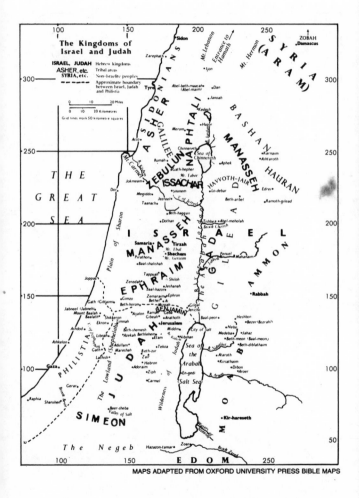

MAPS ADAPTED FROM OXFORD UNIVERSITY PRESS BIBLE MAPS